How to Go On
LIVING
When Someone
You Love
DIES

How to Go On LIVING When Someone You Love DIES

Therese A. Rando, Ph.D.

BANTAM BOOKS
NEW YORK • TORONTO • LONDON • SYDNEY • AUCKLAND

How to Go on Living When Someone You Love Dies
A Bantam Book / published by arrangement with
Lexington Books

PUBLISHING HISTORY
Lexington Books edition published 1988
Bantam edition / August 1991

Certain pieces of this work have been adapted
from the author's previous professional writings,
Grief, Dying, and Death: Clinical Interventions for Caregivers
(Research Press, 1984),
Parental Loss of a Child *(Research Press, 1986),*
and Loss and Anticipatory Grief *(Lexington Books, 1986),*
with the permission of the publishers.

Previously published under the title Grieving.

Library of Congress Cataloging-in-Publication Data
Rando, Therese A.
  [Grieving]
  How to go on living when someone you love dies / Therese
A. Rando.
      p. cm.
  Reprint. Originally published: Grieving. Lexington, Mass.:
Lexington Books, 1988.
  Includes bibliographical references and index.
  ISBN 0-553-35269-5 (pbk.: alk. paper)
  1. Grief. 2. Bereavement—Psychological aspects. I. Title.
[BF575.G7R355 1991]
155.9'37—dc20   91-7380
                                                                CIP

Published simultaneously in the United States and Canada

Bantam Books are published by Bantam Books, a division of
Bantam Doubleday Dell Publishing Group, Inc. Its trademark,
consisting of the words "Bantam Books" and the portrayal of a
rooster, is Registered in U.S. Patent and Trademark Office and in
other countries. Marca Registrada. Bantam Books, 1540 Broad-
way, New York, New York 10036.

PRINTED IN THE UNITED STATES OF AMERICA
30 29 28 27 26

*This book is lovingly dedicated
to the following select group of cherished individuals who,
in very special and idiosyncratic ways,
give meaning to my life:*

*Lawrence C. Grebstein
Marion A. Humphrey
Vanderlyn R. Pine
Rita E. Rando
Barbara A. Vargas*

Contents

PART IV
Resolving Your Grief

PART V
Getting Additional Help

Acknowledgments

Having usually written for professional audiences, I find that the task of writing a book on mourning for the general public has indeed been a mammoth one. However, my conviction that the book needed to be written has been bolstered by the words and actions of several people currently in my life and some who now sadly are gone.

I must acknowledge immediately the wealth of personal and professional support I received from Ann Wendel of Research Press in Champaign, Illinois. What a special person she is to be so interested in one of her author's other works. Her concern for this project went beyond our professional relationship and is part of our personal one. Without a doubt, she was one of my most ardent supporters and convinced me of the value and necessity of this book. I cannot thank her enough for all she did to encourage, facilitate, and validate this endeavor.

Patricia Sammann provided the developmental editing of this book. Without her capable editorial work I could not have gotten through the numerous roadblocks that interfere with an academic author's transition to trade writer. She gave me guidance and support, criticism and support, and direction and support. Mourning a recent loss of her own, Pat has contributed parts of herself to this work. On behalf of myself and all future readers, I only can offer deepest appreciation. Pat has her own dedication for this work: *To my father, Ray, who knew the secrets in people's hearts and who loved them anyway.*

I would be remiss not to mention the professionals at Lexington Books for their contribution to this work. Thanks go to Margaret Zusky, Stephen Dragin, and Dorothy Lohmann.

I cannot ever write a clinical book without mentioning the debt I have to my current and past patients who have taught me so very much about life, death, and grief. They, who are such a part of my own life, keep me in touch with the important issues and remind me of both the strength and the fragility of humankind in the face of major loss. For this I am most grateful.

Again in this book, as in previous works, I publically must acknowledge the profound influence of J. Eugene Knott, Ph.D., on my early professional development in this field.

There were two who were once pivotal supports in my life during times of grief and mourning. Words are inadequate, yet I must acknowledge them. In unique ways, they each helped me to cope; I owe both of them for assisting me with major losses in my life. Their being gone from my life leaves me bereaved, but their having been here makes me so much the better for it. My warmest gratitude goes to Rick P. Gebhart and Philip Maini, Jr. Thank you both for having been in my life at the important times and in the special ways that you were.

To my administrative assistant and dear friend, Barbara A. Vargas, there is much to say in appreciation, but none of it can convey sufficiently the depth of reliance upon and affection for my companion and alter ego for the past seven and a half years. Suffice it to say she had to be one of the people to whom this book is dedicated.

To Beth and Randy goes the reminder "Be good, stay together, remember everything we taught you, and don't forget us."

Ultimately, the most special acknowledgment of all must go to my parents, Thomas A. and Letitia G. Rando, who gave me the strength and belief in myself to survive the indescribable mourning caused by their untimely deaths, and to the person who most helped and continues to help me to do it, my best friend, Anthony.

PART

I

Learning about Grief

1

Knowing More Can Help

APRIL 1ST was a beautiful, sunny day that year. I vividly recall sitting in the dentist's chair in the late afternoon, waiting for my annual examination, and wondering whether there was enough time left in the day for anyone to pull any April Fool's Day tricks on me. I had successfully avoided several at my high school earlier that day. Six and a half hours later, I got the answer to my question. Fate had decided to play the cruelest April Fool's Day trick of all: My father, never sick a day in his life, dropped dead without warning.

Thus began the chain of events that led to my writing this book. They have been solidified since then by many deaths, most notably the unnecessary death 50 weeks after my father's of my mother, who died from negligent medical care following successful open-heart surgery. This death, too, was without warning, and hit me and my younger sister and brother at a time when we had not even gotten back on our feet following the death of our father.

At that time, there were no resources for the general public to help us understand the painful and confusing processes of grief. There was no open discussion of death and grief; few people specialized in its treatment; and no materials were available to help me see I was not going crazy.

Could I have coped better if information had been available to me when I needed it? Could I have been spared additional pain if my expectations for myself and others had been more realistic? Yes! Would this have brought my loved ones back? No, but it would have helped me deal with that fact much better.

Purpose of This Book

I have written this book for you, a griever, in the hopes that the information in it will help you to cope better with the painful, but necessary, process of grieving over the death of someone you love. It is hard work, this grief, but I believe it should not be more difficult for you than it has to be. I believe that people cope better when armed with appropriate information and expectations. Indeed, one of the most important things I do in my work with bereaved individuals is to give them this information to support what they need to do and to help them avoid the unnecessary pain and stress fostered by society, caregivers, and even friends, who give wrong advice and place unrealistic and inappropriate expectations on them.

I have been dissatisfied with other self-help books. Some of them are too trite or oversimplified. Others are too despairing and forget to point out that people *do* survive the death of someone they love. There are some that are too unrealistic: They focus on growth and transformation after the death and do not help you deal with the pain and stress of the grief leading up to that growth.

I have found that most have an insufficient understanding of what is necessary to successfully resolve grief. Many have a too short-term perspective: They fail to be specific in giving you guidance on how to move adaptively into your new life without forgetting your old one. For example, they don't help you develop a new type of relationship with your deceased loved one or talk about how to keep that person "alive" appropriately. While many books profess to look at the multidimensional experience of grief, most in fact look at only a few types of emotional responses and fail to understand that grief is experienced on all levels of the personality. The stereotypical myth of a griever being sad and depressed, sitting in a corner and crying, is too often perpetuated. In fact, grief is much more complicated and diverse.

One of the concerns I have had is that most books, and even more people, caregivers as well as society in general, fail to understand that grief is an intensely personal event. No two people will ever grieve in the same fashion, even when they have lost the same person. For this reason, parents who lose the same child can be as different as if they had no connection whatsoever and each had lost someone different. Your own grief will be unique and unlike any other's, despite the fact that you may share some similarities with other grievers.

Different losses impact upon us in various ways and leave us with diverse needs. The loss of a spouse is not like the loss of a parent; the loss of a friend is not like the loss of a child. Each places its own demands upon you. It is unfair for others to treat you with expectations for one bereavement when you have suffered another. While there are some similarities among loss experiences, there also are major differences that must be taken into account not only by others who are concerned about or caring for you, but by you yourself. It is dangerous not to look at the unique dilemmas posed by specific types of losses. What a bereaved parent needs in order to cope with the death of a child will necessarily differ from the needs of a young father of three children whose wife dies, which again will be different from what an aged widow will need.

"But People Have Been Dying Forever. Why Is Grief So Hard Now?"

A hundred years ago you would not have needed to read this book. As compared with today, the typical American family of that time had strong social and emotional ties. They were close to one another and had deep roots in their community where they had lived for many years. They were available as sources of support and guidance for each other when death occurred. Families lived with relatives and took care of the ill and elderly. Children grew up seeing death as a natural part of existence. They were familiar with death in nature. They saw it in the animals around them and the land on which they lived. More important, they saw family members die and observed how others coped with grief and mourning. When deaths did occur, often there were strong religious beliefs that helped families cope. Rituals and ceremonies provided support and gave the family direction about how to be bereaved. All of this gave the bereaved person some meaning, security, predictability, and control.

Social, technological, and medical changes in the last hundred years have left Americans poorly equipped to deal with death and the social and emotional changes it brings. You and I have fewer people we are close to who can help us cope with our grief. We are less familiar with death, since it happens chiefly to the ill and elderly, whom we tend to put in hospitals or nursing homes. We are less familiar with death in nature because we tend to live in cities. In addition, we have fewer resources to utilize in coping with our bereavement, since there has been a decline in religious beliefs and a move away from funerals and other rituals that had acted as therapeutic outlets for our grief. We have fewer models to observe after the death because we are a more mobile society and tend not to live with our extended families. Because we are a society where the average family moves every few years, we are not as close to our communities as we were then, when we knew everyone in our neighborhood and they would help us in times of stress. Now we tend to deal with our bereavements in a more isolated fashion.

Medical advancements have changed the types and courses of illnesses we die from. No longer do our loved ones develop an illness and then die immediately. Now there are extended illnesses in which those we love can die over a period of months or years, and these kinds of deaths bring their own special problems and stresses. Today there are issues concerning the role of money in medical care and how it is decided who will reap the benefits of such things as artificial hearts, kidney transplants, and other expensive and limited resources. These bring up ethical dilemmas that we never had to contend with previously. Changes in infant mortality mean that there will be fewer bereaved parents of younger children but because of an increase in longevity, more parents will live to see their adult children die. Also, more middle-aged adults will have to deal with the deaths of their parents at the same time they are dealing with their own midlife crises. Previously these parents would have died when their children were younger.

Our increased technology means that we now have to deal with different types of death. For example, in the past when there were no airplanes, we did not have the experience of losing loved ones in airplane crashes. Now there are an increasing number of technological disasters, as well as consequences of other "advancements" in society, such as the major chemical disasters in Bhopal, India, and at Love Canal.

Changes in our society have been paralleled by increased suicide and homicide rates. Traditional relationships have changed as well. For example, there are more socially unsanctioned losses now with the increase in nontraditional relationships such as living together without being married or relationships between gay men or lesbian women. The high rate of remarriage, which blends stepfamilies, also brings difficult issues. For instance, who stands in the receiving line, the new wife or the former wife who had been married to the deceased for twenty years?

As you can see, all of these developments have contributed to changing conditions for you as a griever. As a result, you have more dilemmas to cope with, fewer resources to help you, fewer models to follow, and less experience to fall back on in helping you deal with death as a part of life. This is why grief is so hard now in our society.

Myths About Grief

One of the problems caused by all of these changes is that our difficulties with grief have contributed to many myths and misunderstandings about it.

These are dangerous, because you use your knowledge about grief to:

1. Establish your expectations for it.
2. Serve as standards against which you measure how well you are doing with your grief.
3. Determine the type of help and support you should get from others.

If the information you have about grief is faulty or inaccurate, then you risk developing unrealistic expectations about yourself in grief. Since these expectations then become the standards against which you evaluate yourself, it is important that they are appropriate and realistic—if they are not, you will tend to feel guilt and failure if you do not meet them. Additionally, you will not receive the necessary help and support from others, who may judge you to be inappropriate in your grief, perceive you as "crazy" when in fact you are perfectly normal, or fail to understand what you are undergoing and how best to help you cope with it. You set yourself up for additional pain. For these reasons, you need an accurate understanding of the complex experience of grief and the needs of a griever.

I have found that the myths and unrealistic expectations that society maintains for grievers are some of the worst problems any griever has. Many people fail to allow themselves to do what they have to in their grief because they think that there is something wrong with them. Many feel that they should be "over" their grief long before they ever could be. Many hold expectations for themselves that are outrageously unrealistic and that only cause them to berate themselves unfairly when their expectations cannot be met.

Look at the statements below and decide how many of them you believe.

All losses are the same.

It takes two months to get over your grief.

All bereaved people grieve in the same way.

Grief always declines over time in a steadily decreasing fashion.

When grief is resolved, it never comes up again.

Family members will always help grievers.

Children grieve like adults.

Feeling sorry for yourself is not allowable.

It is better to put painful things out of your mind.

You should not think about your deceased loved one at the holidays because it will make you too sad.

Bereaved individuals only need to express their feelings and they will resolve their grief.

Expressing feelings that are intense is the same as losing control.

There is no reason to be angry at people who tried to do their best for your deceased loved one.

There is no reason to be angry at your deceased loved one.

Only sick individuals have physical problems in grief.

Because you feel crazy, you are going crazy.

You should feel only sadness that your loved one has died.

Infant death shouldn't be too difficult to resolve because you didn't know the child that well.

Children need to be protected from grief and death.

Rituals and funerals are unimportant in helping us deal with life and death in contemporary America.

Being upset and grieving means that you do not believe in God or trust your religion.

You and your family will be the same after the death as before your loved one died.

You will have no relationship with your loved one after the death.

The intensity and length of your grief are testimony to your love for the deceased.

There is something wrong if you do not always feel close to your other family members, since you should be happy that they are still alive.

There is something wrong with you if you think that part of you has died with your loved one.

If someone has lost a spouse, he or she knows what it is like to lose a child.

When in doubt about what to say to a bereaved person, offer a cliché.

It is better to tell bereaved people to "Be brave" and "Keep a stiff upper lip" because then they will not have to experience as much pain.

When you grieve the death of a loved one, you only grieve for the loss of that person and nothing else.

Grief will affect you psychologically, but in no other way.

If you are a widow, you should grieve like other widows.

Losing someone to sudden death is the same as losing someone to an anticipated death.

You will not be affected much if your parent dies when you are an adult.

Parents usually divorce after a child dies.

It is not important for you to have social support in your grief.

Once your loved one has died it is better not to focus on him or her, but to put him or her in the past and go on with your life.

You can find ways to avoid the pain of your grief and still resolve it successfully.

How many of these statements do you believe? Each one of them is a myth. None of them is true. Yet, if you believe that they are true you will expect yourself to act and feel accordingly. If you think that you are wrong, for example, because you are angry at your loss or because you are sad during the holidays, you just will be putting an additional burden on yourself. These feelings are normal. There is nothing wrong with you.

How to Read This Book

I hope it has become clear that knowing more about grief can help you resolve it. It can assist you in doing the best you can after someone you love dies. To get the maximum help from this book, resist the natural temptation to skip to the chapters describing the particular death of your loved one. The information in those chapters is based on the assumption that you already have read the information in the earlier chapters about grief, specifically chapter 2 (What Is Grief?), chapter 3 (How Grief Affects You), chapter 4 (What Factors Influence Your Grief), chapter 5 (What to Expect in Grief), and chapter 6 (Sudden versus Anticipated Death).

These describe the processes that influence your grief, how they will affect you, and what you can expect.

The chapters on resolving grief—chapter 14 (What Is Necessary to "Resolve" Your Grief), chapter 15 (Specific Suggestions for Resolving Your Grief), chapter 16 (Personal Bereavement Rituals and Funerals), chapter 17 (What "Recovery" Will and Will Not Mean), and chapter 18 (Solving Practical Problems)—are general and can be applied to all types of deaths. The specific chapters on cause of death (chapter 7); family reorganization (chapter 8); losses of spouse, parent, sibling, and child (chapters 9–12); and helping children cope with death and mourning (chapter 13) highlight information that has not been covered in the more general chapters. Chapter 19 (Finding Effective Professional and Self-Help Group Assistance) and chapter 20 (Resource Listing) are included for those who are interested in or require further assistance.

You will need to personalize the information given. In the end, it doesn't matter what the research says, how anyone else feels, or whether what I have described is common for others; what is important is what *you* experience. Therefore, take the knowledge and principles in this book and use them to your own best benefit. Look at the self-assessment information to determine where you are on each particular issue. Come back to these at later points to see how much progress you are making.

You may notice that throughout the book I have alternated the use of the masculine and feminine pronouns *he* and *she*. This has been done in acknowledgment of the fact that both men and women are grievers. It would be inappropriate to use just one exclusively.

Personal and clinical experience has taught me that knowing more *can* help you in your grief. It is my fervent hope that this book will do just that and will help you to go on living when someone you love dies.

2

What Is Grief?

I N the best of all possible worlds, love would not bring pain. Yet, in our world the reality is undeniable: When we love someone we inevitably set ourselves up for pain and grief when that love is severed. This can take place through separation, divorce, relocation, falling out of love, or death, among other causes. Each of these losses can rupture a love relationship and bring grief. This book will focus on one type of loss—the death of someone you love. It will examine the many reactions you may experience in response to the death of your loved one.

In order to know how to cope with your grief, it is important to know exactly what grief is and how it affects you. In this way, you will be able to understand the sometimes confusing and frightening experiences you might have when you grieve. You will be able to maintain more realistic expectations for yourself and be better able to appropriately evaluate yourself and your needs. Then, you will know better what you will need to do to cope with your personal grief.

As used in this book, the term *grief* refers to the process of experiencing the psychological, social, and physical reactions to your perception of loss. This definition has five important implications that provide essential information about grief.

1. Grief is experienced in each of three major ways—psychologically (through your feelings, thoughts, and attitudes), socially (through your behavior with others), and physically (through your health and bodily symptoms).

2. Grief is a continuing development, involving many changes over time. It will come and go and appear different at different times.

3. Grief is a natural, expectable reaction. In fact, the absence of it is abnormal in most cases.
4. Grief is the reaction to all kinds of losses, not just death.
5. Grief is based upon your unique, individualistic perception of the loss. It is not necessary for you to have the loss recognized or validated by others for you to experience grief.

Another term that will be used throughout this book is *mourning*. The term refers to the conscious and unconscious processes that (1) gradually undo the psychological ties that had bound you to your loved one, (2) help you to adapt to his loss, and (3) help you to learn how to live healthily in the new world without him. Although there is a clinical distinction between the terms "grief" and "mourning," to conform with widespread social usage, the terms will be used interchangeably in this book.

A third term that we shall use repeatedly is *bereavement*—the state of having suffered a loss. To be bereaved means that you have suffered a loss.

Types of Losses

Losses may be of two kinds. First, they may be physical. This means that they are tangible, something you can touch. Examples of a physical loss include losing your husband through death, having your car stolen, or your house burning down.

Losses also may be symbolic. Symbolic losses are psychosocial in nature —related to the psychological aspects of a person's social interactions. They are abstract and cannot be seen or touched. Examples of a symbolic loss include getting a divorce, losing status because of a job demotion, or losing a friendship after an argument.

A physical loss is easily recognized, but a symbolic loss often is not identified as a loss. As a result, you may not recognize that you must take the time to grieve and deal with your feelings about it. Despite the fact that a symbolic loss frequently is not recognized by yourself or others, it will initiate a process of mourning just as a physical loss will.

When Mary Ann was twenty-one, her brother died suddenly in an automobile accident. All of her friends came to support Mary Ann in the funeral rituals, made sure they continued to be in social contact with her, and repeatedly made attempts to have her talk about her feelings. Despite her intense pain, Mary Ann understood why she was hurting, recognized that her grief had many reactions, and felt supported and cared about by her friends.

Eight years later Mary Ann got a divorce. Among other things, she felt depressed, anxious, confused, and insecure. At this point she felt very lonely and unsupported. Her friends were concerned but did not go out of their way to help. Besides, seeing Mary Ann get a divorce made them anxious, for hers had been a model marriage. There were no "official" rituals like a funeral for them to participate in to acknowledge the death of the marriage. They didn't go out of their way to contact her, nor try to get her to talk about her feelings. Although Mary Ann was grieving the death of her marriage, no one, not even she herself, recognized that she was experiencing a normal, although painful, process of mourning. Everyone thought her reactions indicated that she was having a hard time adjusting.

No matter what, loss always results in a deprivation of some kind. Many losses are clearly perceived as unpleasant deprivations, such as the death of a child or the theft of valued jewelry. However, there are others that are less clearly recognized as losses and that do not necessarily result from negative events. These losses occur in response to human development and to normal change and growth. An example of a developmental loss is the decline in physical abilities as one ages. For instance, a person's eyesight may deteriorate, requiring her to depend on glasses. An example of a loss resulting from normal change and growth is seen following the birth of a child. When a couple has a baby, they automatically lose a relative amount of their independence and freedom from responsibility.

Change in itself always involves a loss. At the very least, it is a loss of the status quo, of the way things were. This is why whether a change is positive or negative there is always some dimension of loss to it, with some measure of grief being warranted even if it is negligible.

Some losses are competency-based. For example, graduating from college, having a child leave home, achieving a long-worked-for goal, or terminating therapy are experiences that result in the loss of striving. Also, they all involve change.

Although these experiences do create deprivations, they tend not to be recognized as losses, especially when associated with positive events. As a result, these losses are not grieved. Such situations often cause the people involved to wonder why they feel sad after experiencing what is supposed to be a happy event. For example, an executive may be surprised to find himself feeling depressed after a long-awaited promotion. Just because an event is positive, or has some happiness associated with it, does not mean that it does not also contain elements of grief over the losses that accompany it.

> Edward loved challenges and very much enjoyed his climb up the corporate ladder. For many years he devoted a good portion of his life to becoming chairman of the board for a Fortune 500 company. When he at last achieved his dream, he experienced what his friends called "a success depression." He was depressed, fatigued, and disillusioned and felt a lack of meaning.
>
> What actually was happening was that Edward was grieving the loss of the dream. The challenges and "thrill of the chase" were gone. He felt he had nothing else to aspire to or hope for. Until he paid sufficient attention to this and completed his grief work, he would not be able to enjoy the position for which he had worked so hard and so long.

If you think about it, you will probably find that your most difficult experiences in life have involved a loss of some kind, whether physical or symbolic. Take a minute now and recall the three most difficult situations you have had to deal with in your life.

Chances are that these situations involved some aspect of a physical and/or symbolic loss. It is important for you to recognize this. Some people erroneously think that they have never grieved before simply because they have never had a loved one die.

In fact, all of us are grievers thousands of times over in our lives. This is because grief is a normal reaction to loss, and loss is a natural part of existence. It is a universal experience repeatedly encountered in every person's life. Children lose baby teeth and childhood naivete; a pet kitten dies; a child graduates from high school; a lover is abandoned; a friend fails to achieve a goal; a brother moves away; a wife dies of cancer; retirement occurs.

If the difficult situations you have undergone in your life (recall the three you thought about above) had been interpreted to you as "symbolic deaths" and identified as losses, you probably would have realized that your intense reactions at the time were part of a grief process. This understanding probably would have enabled you to cope better at the time. This is why, for example, you may have had such difficulty after your divorce, your breakup with one you loved, your rejection by your first college choice, or your move to another city. These are all experiences of loss to which, we know, people have many reactions. The reactions are a form of grief. As a griever, it is important for you to identify your symbolic losses. If you do not recognize these losses, you will not be able to grieve appropriately. You also will not recognize or understand the reactions you are undergoing, and this can cause you to suffer needlessly.

As a griever you also must cope with "secondary losses." These are the physical and/or symbolic losses that develop as a consequence of the death of the person you loved. For example, depending on the roles the deceased fulfilled in your life, after his death you will be a changed person because of his loss. Also, you may have to suffer a change of environment, a loss of status, alteration of relationships with other family members, and many other losses because that person is now gone from your life. At times, these secondary losses can cause more problems for you than the initial loss of the death of your loved one.

> John was twenty when his father died. He was in college studying engineering at the time. After the death, John was forced to abandon his dream of becoming an engineer in order to take over the family grocery store his father had owned and operated. Without this, there would have been insufficient income for John's mother and three siblings.
>
> John not only lost his father; he also lost his vocation, his independence (he had to move back home), his girlfriend (after John's withdrawal from the university she found someone else on campus with whom to enjoy her college life), and his role as a happy-go-lucky young adult (he now assumed his father's role in the family as eldest male and chief provider). Until John could identify and grieve over the secondary losses, his grief could not be resolved. Ironically, he could cope better with the death of his father, for which he had been gradually preparing, than with the other losses that his father's death brought about.

Death is not the only cause of secondary losses. Many other major losses prompt their own secondary losses, too. For instance, it is very common for a physical loss to result in a number of symbolic secondary losses. Take the case of a woman who undergoes a mastectomy necessitated by cancer. The loss of a breast is a physical loss. However, other physical and symbolic secondary losses develop. Just being in a hospital setting entails the loss of the familiar home environment. Being sick and dependent upon others for care also causes a loss of independence and control for the individual, who is now in a patient role. The illness of cancer may bring loss of autonomy, loss of predictability, loss of bodily functions, loss of body parts, loss of productivity, loss of pleasure, loss of identity, loss of intimacy, loss of social contacts, loss of self-esteem, and loss of mobility.

Each secondary loss has an impact upon the person and prompts its own grief reaction of some form. Each will need to be mourned. The loss of the breast is not necessarily perceived by the patient as any more or less of a loss than the loss of social contact. The meaning and extent of any given loss will differ for each person according to her own personality and characteristics.

Over and over you encounter loss in your life. To a greater or lesser extent, the same process of grief occurs in reaction to each of these losses. Obviously, small losses will not cause the same amount of grief as will the death of a loved one, but both processes of grief stem from the reactions you have to the perception of loss. They actually are variations on the same theme. The nature, intensity, and length of your grief process will be influenced by a number of variables (see chapter 4 for more on this). Nevertheless, the very same process of grief that initiates the temporary despondency of the nine-year-old boy whose best friend refuses to play with him, also initiates the full-blown grief response of the man whose wife is killed by a drunk driver.

The Work of Grief

As a griever, you need to appreciate the fact that grief is *work*. It requires the expenditure of both physical and emotional energy. It is no less strenuous a task than digging a ditch or any other physical labor. The term "grief work" was coined by psychiatrist Erich Lindemann in 1944 to describe the tasks and processes that you must complete successfully in order to resolve your grief. The term shows that grief is something you must work at actively if you are to resolve it in a healthy fashion. It demands much more than merely passively experiencing your reactions to loss: you must actively *do* things and undertake specific courses of thought and action to integrate and resolve your grief (see chapter 14 for a full discussion of this).

However, grief is not commonly perceived as work. You probably are not prepared for the intensity of your emotional reactions and do not fully understand the importance of accepting and expressing them. You probably do not expect to have to work so hard to accommodate yourself to your loved one's absence or to build a new identity and world for yourself. Grief can deplete you to such an extent that the slightest tasks become monumental, and what previously was easily achievable now may seem insurmountable.

Since most other people are similarly unaware about grief and how much work it involves, they may not provide you with the social or emotional support you need during your grief. In fact, society's unrealistic expectations and inappropriate responses to your normal grief reactions may make the grief experience much worse than it otherwise would be. For instance, if people did not tell you to "Be brave," "Put this behind you," or that "You shouldn't be feeling that way," along with other unhealthy suggestions, you probably would have fewer conflicts about expressing your grief. You also would have more realistic expectations about the grief process and in general would have fewer problems in recovering naturally from it. This is why it is so crucial that society be given realistic and appropriate information about grief. It is time that other people become a support to grievers, not a hindrance.

Your work of grieving entails mourning not only the actual person you've lost but also the hopes, dreams, wishes, fantasies, unfulfilled expectations, feelings, and needs you had for and with that person. These are significant symbolic secondary losses that you must identify and grieve. They include not only what is lost in the present but also what is now lost to the future as well. The widow must grieve not only for the present loss of her beloved husband, but also for the retirement they will not share, their special dreams that will be unfulfilled, his absence at his grandson's birth, and more. This doesn't mean you must do this all at once. That would be overwhelming. Instead, you need to do this gradually throughout the mourning process so you can let go of what is necessary to give up from the past, healthily experience the present, and prepare for the future.

Sometimes the death of a loved one brings up not only grief for what you lost, but also grief for what you never had and now never will have. For example, if you had a very conflicted relationship with your mother, when she dies you may grieve not only for what you have lost, but also for the fact that you never had a better relationship with her, that she never was the kind of mother you wanted her to be, and that now you will never have even the hope that it could change and you could get what you want. In such a case you grieve for the past, present, and future.

Another issue that can complicate your grief work is the fact that major loss always resurrects old issues and unresolved conflicts. The pain, emptiness, and sorrow caused by your separation from your loved one frequently reawaken your earliest and most repressed feelings of anxiety and helplessness as a child. The terror and power of these reawakened memories can be overwhelming to any of us. Old conflicts about dependency, ambivalence, parent–child relations, and security, to name but a few, are also stirred by your experience of loss. They, too, can interfere with a successful resolution of grief. Finally, this is a time when your other not-so-old but still unresolved (or perhaps resolved, but nevertheless still sensitive) losses can come back to haunt you. These can make you feel even more deprived, more vulnerable, and more powerless and out of control. It is terribly unfortunate, yet past issues often arise at the precise moment when you are struggling to confront a current loss. They add to the burden of the grief process. Therefore, when you are dealing with the death of a loved one, you frequently are contending not only with the present loss but also with old losses and unfinished emotional business as well.

> Tilly's husband died at age sixty, following a two-year battle with cancer. Tilly was left alone in her home, since her three adult children lived out of state. After the death, Tilly was surprised to find herself not only feeling grief over the death of her husband but also preoccupied with memories and feelings about her adolescence when her beloved father had abandoned the family.
>
> Tilly thought about how she had reacted then, and she experienced in the present her earlier feelings of loss, fear, insecurity, and confusion. She felt like the fourteen-year-old girl for whom it seemed as if the earth had been shaken when her father walked out the door. Although she knew better, she felt like she was as helpless now as she was then, when she had few resources to help her cope and the world was so frightening. She wanted her father back again, even though he was long dead. It seemed like she was in shock again now as she was when her father left, even though she had anticipated her husband's death. Her present loss had resurrected the long-buried thoughts and emotions from an earlier loss of a significant person in her life.

The Purpose of Grief and Mourning

Grief responses are natural reactions when you experience loss and separation from those you love. They express three things:

1. Your feelings about the loss.
2. Your protest at the loss and your wish to undo it and have it not be true.
3. The effects you experience from the assault on you caused by the loss.

However, the ultimate goal of grief and mourning is to take you beyond these reactions to the loss. It requires your working actively on adapting to it. If you fail to adapt following a major loss, if you don't accommodate to the change but persist as if the world is the same when it isn't, then you are not responding to reality, and this is quite unhealthy. The therapeutic purpose of grief and mourning is to get you to the point where you can live with the loss healthily, after having made the necessary changes to do so.

What must you do to get to this point? You must:

1. Change your relationship with your loved one—recognizing he now is dead and developing new ways of relating to him.

2. Develop a new sense of yourself to reflect the many changes that occurred when you lost your loved one.

3. Take on healthy new ways of being in the world without your loved one.

4. Find new people, objects, or pursuits in which to put the emotional investment that you once had placed in your relationship with the deceased. (See chapter 14 for a full discussion of these processes and chapter 15 for specific suggestions on how to resolve them.)

The bottom line of this active work of grief and mourning, therefore, is to help you recognize that your loved one is gone and then to make the necessary internal (psychological) and external (social) changes to accommodate this reality.

The Phases of Grief

There have been many descriptions offered of the grief process. These have been used to explain the experiences of dying patients, divorcing spouses, persons coping with amputations, survivors of natural disasters, and individuals who have retired. The theories and descriptions have different names and focus on different topics, but they all involve loss. They all cover the same basic feelings. Only the labels differ.

All of the responses to grief fall into three broad categories, which actually constitute the three major phases of response: *avoidance*, in which there is shock, denial, and disbelief; *confrontation*, a highly charged and emotional state in which you repeatedly learn that your loved one is dead and in which your grief is most intense, with reactions to your loss being felt most acutely; and *accommodation*, in which there is a gradual decline of acute grief and the beginning of an emotional and social reentry into the everyday world in which you learn to live with your loss. All of the descriptions of grief for any group include these three broad phases.

Note that we are using the word *phase* and not the word *stage*. This is because some people have misinterpreted previous work in this field. They felt that when grief was described in stages it implied that grief was an orderly and unvarying process, that all people grieved in the same way: on a static, unalterable course, progressing in only one direction without any fluctuation and without any individual variation. In fact, although people may share many aspects of grief, their responses are quite personal. They are influenced by a variety of individual characteristics and psychological, social, and physical factors (see chapter 4 for more on this).

Remember that the three phases are broad and general categories, divided according to major time periods. They are not rigid stages. You will probably move back and forth among them. Not all grievers will experience all the reactions presented. These are only some of the many possible responses to loss.

The Avoidance Phase

"I can't believe it! John cannot be dead!!"

"You've made a mistake, Officer, this is not my daughter."

"No! No! No! No! No!"

"Oh, my God, help me. I will not survive!"

"I cannot feel anything. This must be a dream."

In the avoidance phase, that period of time in which the news of death is initially received, you desire to avoid the terrible acknowledgment that the person you loved is now lost. The world is shaken; you feel overwhelmed. Just as the human body goes into shock after a large enough physical trauma, so too does the human psyche go into shock when confronted with such an important loss. It is the natural reaction to the impact of such a blow.

During this period you may respond in several ways. You may be confused and dazed, unable to comprehend what has happened. You may feel bewildered and numb. Disorganization is normal. If the death was sudden, your responses may be more intense, since you had no time to prepare for it. The news may seem so overwhelming that you cannot make any sense out of it. Such intense responses may continue even after the initial shock. (See chapter 6 for more on sudden death.)

As recognition of what has happened starts to seep in and shock starts slowly wearing off, denial immediately crops up. It is only natural that you would want or need to deny that such a terrible event has occurred. At this point, denial is therapeutic. It functions as a buffer by allowing you to absorb the reality of the loss a little at a time, rather than being completely overwhelmed by it. It is an emotional anesthesia that serves as a protective mechanism.

At this time, you may feel disbelief and a need to know why the death occurred. You also may experience an outburst of emotion. This could be an explosion of anger, overwhelming sadness, hysteria, tears, rageful protest, or screaming. On the other hand, you may quietly withdraw, act mechanically without feeling, or feel as if you are outside of your own body, looking from a distance at what is happening to you. You probably will continue to feel confused and disorganized.

Some survivors initially appear to accept the death and then start to act responsibly—for example, comforting others or making necessary decisions. In most of these cases, the loss is recognized but the emotions of grief are consciously put aside as the grievers try to be strong for themselves and others. Many times men respond in this fashion. Because of their social conditioning they may try to be stoic and in control. In a smaller number of cases, someone may respond in this fashion in an attempt to totally deny the fact of the death, what it means, and/or his feelings about it. If it goes on for too long, this denial of reality can be quite harmful.

The Confrontation Phase

"I feel like part of me has died with her."

"Nothing means anything to me anymore. Not life, not work, not God—nothing!"

"If only I could have persuaded him to go to the doctor sooner."

"All I want is my baby back. Damn you for not bringing her back to me!"

"Finally, it's over. I couldn't have taken much more of the illness. I feel bad, but I just couldn't have endured any more."

This painful time is when you really, truly learn that your loved one is gone. Each time you expect to see your child step off the school bus, but he is not there; each time you reach across the bed to touch your spouse, but there's only empty space; each time you think about telling your mother about the antics of your children only to remember that you buried her two months ago—each time you are frustrated in your desire to be with your loved one, you "learn" again that that person is dead. Each pang of grief, each stab of pain you feel whenever your expectation or desire or need to be with that person is unfulfilled, "teaches" you again that your loved one is no longer here. You want to resist it. You want the "lesson" not to be true.

Because of this, the confrontation phase is that period of time in which your grief is experienced most intensely and your reactions to the loss are most acute. By this time you have recognized and admitted that the loss has occurred; the shock has worn off to a great degree. Denial and disbelief may occur intermittently; however, you experience many new reactions now that come from your confrontation with the death and what it means to you.

This phase has been described as a painful time of "angry sadness." Extremes of emotion are felt, sometimes within a very short time span. Some grievers allow these feelings to be readily expressed. Others are confused about what to do with them or don't want to express them at all. Still others want to express them but find they cannot.

Many times your emotions and needs in grief are in conflict with one another. So, too, are your thoughts about how you should handle all of this. It is a very overwhelming, confusing, and frightening time.

You may experience a great many varied reactions during the confrontation phase of your grief. These all stem from your responses to having your loved one permanently taken away and from attempting to readjust to a new world without the presence of that person. Many of these reactions are discussed in chapter 3.

The Accommodation Phase

"I surprised myself when I heard myself laughing. It had been such a long time."

"Sometimes I feel guilty if I'm not in pain over my brother's death anymore."

"Let's make a donation in Mom's memory."

"How can I be grieving one day and happy the next?"

"Well, I wouldn't consider dating yet, but I would talk with him on the phone."

In the accommodation phase there is a gradual decline of your grief. Slowly you are beginning emotional and social reentry into the everyday world. The intense symptoms of acute grief are diminishing; you are starting to be a little more like your old self. The loss is not forgotten: You are still mourning, trying to modify the emotional investment and ties that bound you to the deceased when that person was alive. The loss is put in a special place that, while allowing it to be remembered, also will free you to go on to new attachments without being tied unhealthily to old ones.

You know now that you will survive, although you never will be quite the same. In some ways the old adage "Once bereaved, always bereaved" is true, but this does not mean that your life stops. You are changed by the loss, but you are beginning to live with it and to cope with the new life that exists without your loved one. The processes of mourning will take a long time. You will develop a new relationship with the deceased, experience changes in yourself that lead to the formation of a new identity, and, ultimately, reinvest your emotional energy in new relationships, objects, and pursuits. Although your mourning process is continuing, the intense symptoms of grief you had during the confrontation phase are becoming fewer and less frequent.

The accommodation phase is not an all-or-nothing phase. It waxes and wanes during the later part of the confrontation phase and continues slowly thereafter. It never arrives all at once, and for some time it coexists with many of the previous reactions.

Guilt often accompanies the beginning efforts at accommodation as you cope with the fact that you continue to live despite the death of your loved one. You may have to struggle with feelings of betrayal when you recognize you still can enjoy life without him. Sometimes you may get caught between wanting to be happy again and holding on to your grief out of fear of "losing" your loved one again. You may be ambivalent about making progress, as if you keep your loved one close by continuing to grieve. This is a conflict that you must work through in order to find meaning and happiness in your life again. It can be a particularly thorny issue for many people. (See chapters 14 and 17 for more on this issue.)

Now that you know something about what grief is, you need to find out more about how it will affect you. In the next chapter, we'll discuss what you are likely to feel, how your grief may alter your interactions with others, and what physical effects it may have.

3

How Grief Affects You

G RIEF is not just sadness or depression. It is a whole host of emotions ranging from anxiety to anger to guilt to confusion to relief and more. Besides affecting your emotions, it reaches into every part of your life, touching your work, your relationships with others, and your image of yourself. In this chapter we will describe the possible effects grief can have on you and why they occur. You can expect grief to have an effect on you psychologically, socially, and physically.

Psychological Effects

Almost any emotion can be part of grief. What makes these emotions hard to handle, though, is their unusual intensity. You also may experience emotions that are not common for you or that seem strange in the context of your loss. The following descriptions may help you make sense of your feelings and accept them as normal for you.

Fear and Anxiety

You may experience panic or feel generalized anxiety. This can occur intermittently or be present all of the time. It stems partially from the normal apprehension all human beings have whenever they must face the unknown and the unfamiliar. In this case, the unknown and the unfamiliar you are facing is both the new world without your loved one and your own difficulty in dealing with this new world. You are plagued by questions: What will it be like? How will I survive? Can I bear this terrible pain? Who can tell me how to be a "good griever"? When will I ever feel normal again? What am I supposed to do?

By definition, any major loss always brings some insecurity, at least temporarily. This occurs naturally as you undergo the transition from the security of what was (having your loved one alive and present) to the insecurity of what is (being without the person who was such an important element in your life).

The feelings of unreality that often accompany a major loss add to your concern about your emotional state, which can further increase your anxiety and insecurity. Grief is a roller-coaster ride of emotion, with foreign feelings and a confused sense of self. These combine with your natural wish to undo the death and make it seem like a horrible nightmare. You try to fathom the incomprehensible situation: How could the one I love so much have been taken from me? It doesn't make any sense, and that only underscores your feelings of confusion and unreality.

You might find that you have feelings of panic and anxiety when you awaken in the morning and remember that you must face another day without the person who died. Many issues may trouble you and intensify these feelings:

Concerns about going it alone

Panic about being able to deal with the separation pain

Fear about what the absence of your loved one will mean to your life

Upset over the recognition that you are markedly different than before

Worry over how the rest of your family is coping

Fright arising from the sense of vulnerability caused by the loss

Terror at the thought of losing others who are close to you

Distress associated with your memories of earlier losses and separations

Heightened emotional and physical arousal that exacerbates your feelings of tension and uneasiness

Recognizing that you have no power to prevent or undo the death of your loved one can cause you feelings of loss of control over your life and world. When the death is unanticipated, these feelings are intensified. You feel overwhelmed because your expectations of continuing to have a life with the person you loved have been violated by that person's death. Also, the myth of your invulnerability has been shattered. Previously, you may have thought "it only happens to other people." Now you know differently. It can be quite frightening to contend with this insecurity and the relative powerlessness you have over protecting your loved ones, as well as yourself, from all pain and grief in life.

During grief it is not unusual to have many reactions that make you feel that you are much different than normal. This can be especially unsettling and make the grief experience more frightening and painful. For example, if you are usually a concerned and loving individual, you may be shocked to find that you feel indifferent to others. If you usually feel in control of your life, you may be surprised to feel that you have totally lost control of everything and that nothing you can do will allow you to "get it together." If you find yourself obsessively reading the obituary pages or experiencing increased distress on the day of the week and the time when your loved one died, as many people do, you may begin to question yourself and wonder if you will ever have any normalcy again. The perception of new reactions that are so vastly different from your normal feelings and modes of behavior can bring great fear and terrifying anxiety.

The variety and intensity of these feelings may be enough to make you wonder if you are losing your mind. You probably are not used to bombardment by such intense feelings and, since these reactions typically are so different, so uncontrollable, so unexpected, and so severe, you might conclude that you have lost touch with reality and are going crazy. You are not. However, when this is combined with all of the other grief reactions you are experiencing, and added to the unrealistic standards you may hold for yourself in your grief and the unexpected type and intensity of your reactions, you may begin to doubt your ability to recover. You can become afraid that you will be stuck in this pain forever, never to cope competently again.

Another source of your anxiety may be the recognition that your usual coping patterns and problem-solving strategies cannot eliminate your grief. While they can help you cope with it, they cannot *solve* it as if it were a problem to be figured out and answered. For example, your usual approach to managing a difficult situation, such as identifying what needs to be done and then decisively proceeding immediately to resolve the entire matter quickly, often will not work the same way with grief. You frequently cannot control it in the same fashion. Yet you cannot avoid it either—many more problems will arise if you try to escape your grief. Also, the chaotic, unexpected, and intense experience of grief does not lend itself to the same logical and orderly processes of resolution as do problems you typically may encounter. Consequently, it may be quite frightening for you when your usual techniques don't work as you have come to expect. This can make you feel more powerless, vulnerable, and out of control, with additional secondary losses experienced since these coping and problem-solving strategies are less effective than usual.

There is another issue that can contribute to feeling that you are not sure of who you are anymore. This identity confusion, and the anxiety and insecurity it creates, comes from the altered sense of self that people experience after they lose someone integral to themselves and their lives. It develops from the sense of physically, as well as emotionally, losing a part of yourself that makes you be you. This comes not only from the sense of separation you feel from the person to whom you were so closely connected, but also from your own awareness of the loss of parts of your identity that had been validated by your relationship with her. For example, if you lose your life's companion through the death of your wife, you also lose that part of yourself that played the role of husband opposite your wife. This role irretrievably has been taken away. Even if you should remarry, that part of you that existed in the special and unique relationship you had with your first wife is no more. In this sense, part of you yourself dies in addition to your loved one. This makes some of your grief for yourself, as well as for your lost loved one. Losing this part of the self can make any griever confused about who he is anymore. This can last until such time as the processes of mourning have helped you to establish a new identity. (See chapter 14 for more on this.)

A final problem that contributes to anxiety and insecurity in grief, and fuels concerns about going crazy or losing control, is the absence of role models or social guidelines for mourners. American society has undergone so many social changes that death and the experience of handling it become increasingly remote. As a result, you may not know how you should act or feel. As human beings, when we are in confusing situations we tend to look to others to help indicate to us how to behave. Unfortunately, because of the social changes described in chapter 1, there are fewer people we can observe in the bereaved role. This leaves us with little knowledge about how to be a good griever. This ambiguity and uncertainty only increase your stress, anxiety, and insecurity.

This phenomenon explains why so many people pattern themselves on the behavior of Jacqueline Bouvier Kennedy following the assassination of President Kennedy in 1963. For many, she was their first role model of a mourner. The only problem is that what was right for her, as a specific individual in a given circumstance, was not necessarily right for another individual in a different circumstance. That is why it was helpful later for the nation to witness the responses of other famous people, such as Mrs. Coretta Scott King and Mrs. Robert Kennedy after the assassinations of their husbands and Prince Rainier of Monaco following the death of Princess Grace. These individuals all served as public examples of widowhood. At a time when American society lacked personal examples of how to respond to death, they gave us illustrations of how to behave. This was very important for individuals who were bereaved because they needed to have ideas about how to behave as a bereaved person and to know that it is a wearing and intense experience to lose someone you love.

The fear of losing control and going crazy actually are normal fears during grief. Certainly some individuals do have abnormal reactions that require psychiatric intervention. Much more commonly, however, people are afraid they are going crazy when in fact they are not. This is true despite the fact that if a person experienced the feelings and reactions that are normal in grief when he had not experienced a loss, he would be considered pathologically ill. The same symptoms that are normal in grief are abnormal in situations outside of grief.

Anger and Guilt

The two emotions in grief that cause tremendous problems because of society's attitudes towards them are anger and guilt. There are few things that can be said without qualification about the grief experience. However, one of them is that there *is* always some amount of anger and guilt after the death of someone you love. Your anger and guilt need not be overly intense, but some amount or variation of each of them is present in some fashion. For example, anger is not necessarily displayed through screaming rage but may be seen in milder forms such as irritation, irritability, frustration, intolerance, or annoyance.

Anger can be witnessed in terminal illness at the time of diagnosis, as are some of the other reactions in grief. Individuals whose loved ones died from a terminal illness may have experienced some of these reactions during the illness and therefore it may not be necessary to display them after the death.

Anger. Anger is always to be expected to some degree following a significant loss. It is a natural consequence of being deprived of something valued. If you try to take a bone away from a dog, he will growl and bite in an angry attempt to stop you from taking it away. How much more the human being protests against losing a loved one! Unfortunately, our society does not accept this anger very well. Therefore, both the griever and those trying to console him may have difficulty acknowledging and coping with this very natural, expected, and understandable emotion.

Ed lost his father suddenly, without a chance to say good-bye to the man to whom he was so devoted. When he heard his father unexpectedly had become seriously ill, he sped from one state to the next trying to reach his father before it was too late. However, after his mad rush he arrived at the hospital to find that his father had died shortly before and that his father's body had been removed moments prior to his walking into the room. Ed never had the opportunity to see or touch his beloved father until the wake. In therapy, Ed spoke of how his Irish Catholic family wanted to focus on all the good memories they had of the father. Crying was regarded as inappropriate, since they believed it indicated a lack of faith. Anger was unheard of. Family members were supposed to assuage their grief and dismiss their feelings by focusing on the good times.

One day in therapy it became strikingly clear that Ed was absolutely furious over the death of his father and the lack of opportunity to say good-bye. When his therapist interpreted that he was angry, Ed found it impossible to accept, pointing out the "inappropriate" and "unnecessary" nature of this emotion. Ed then was asked how he would feel if his car were stolen while he was in the therapy session. He immediately responded that he would want to destroy the thief and that the incident would confirm to him the degenerative nature of our society. He went on for several minutes in a heated tirade. When he calmed down, Ed was asked how he felt about his father being "stolen" from him. At that moment he finally could recognize that while he could allow himself to be angry over the loss of his car, he had not permitted himself the same luxury over the loss of his father. The analogy assisted Ed in realizing the appropriateness of his angry response to the death of his father and to his being "robbed" of the farewell he would have desired.

Anger does not have to stem solely from the death itself. It would not be unusual, for example, for you to be angry at your loved one for dying and "abandoning" you, leaving you behind to pick up the pieces or to carry on alone. Sometimes you might be angry at the deceased for her omissions or commissions while alive. Such anger may be quite difficult for you to admit, since in our sociey it is not socially appropriate to speak ill of the dead or, except in cases of suicide, to blame your loved one for dying.

Without question, there are many reasons for anger after you have lost someone you love. Only some of these are exclusively emotional reactions to your loss. Often anger is a result of the real-life circumstances of the death, as in cases of sudden or accidental death, homicide, suicide, children's deaths, or when the events of the death are unacceptable to you, such as when your loved one died in pain. For example, if your loved one has been murdered, one would expect you to be furious that someone would enter your life and arbitrarily take the life of the person you love. In these situations, you might well feel profound anger that is not easily channeled.

Many times your anger can get displaced onto other people, frequently without your conscious knowledge or intent. For example, you may find that you are venting your anger at God, the doctors, or others who have not had this kind of loss. You may even express anger at yourself through self-hatred, guilt, feelings of worthlessness, self-punishment, and self-defeating or self-destructive behaviors. Unfortunately, if your anger is not addressed and worked through, or if you cannot channel it in a healthy direction, you can become a very bitter, easily hurt person. You can develop an oversensitivity to real or imagined slights, and feel anger and envy toward those unaffected by the death.

On occasion, problems with anger develop when there is no one to direct it to, no particular person or object to focus it upon. You feel the emotion but lack a target for it. In such cases, you may turn it upon yourself, vent it indiscriminately toward anyone or anything, or erroneously feel you should not be angry. None of these will be helpful to you. You will need to identify your feelings, recognize you have a right to them, and find appropriate ways to channel them.

Anger and Loss of Faith. It is quite common to be angry at God, to lose faith in your religion or philosophy of life after the death of someone you love. The death precipitates a quest for meaning to make sense out of your loss. You may be among the many grievers who have a profound sense of injustice and disillusionment after the death. You may feel that you have played life by the rules but lost the game. Values and beliefs that once were comforting to you may now be useless.

The anger that results from your loss of faith in God or in your philosophy of life may be difficult for you to handle. This is especially true if you have considered yourself a religious person and/or saw faith as an important component of your life. It can be a major secondary loss for you if God, your religion, or your faith cannot adequately provide you with the answers to the question of why this death occurred. You may miss the faith that had given you comfort in previous times. If you also feel resentment that God permitted your loved one to die, you may find yourself experiencing intensified anger.

This distress over the failure of your value system, religion, or belief in God to sustain you in your grief can become a major stumbling block in your grief process, leaving you to cope with intense anger and a profound sense of betrayal. In particular, this will be true if any one or combination of them had been major supports in your life. Some people in this situation become very bitter. In time, a number of them can put the loss into a perspective that lends it some meaning. Others, however, are never able to recover their trust of value systems and remain chronically angry towards religion or authority figures.

Guilt. Guilt is the other emotion that can cause immense difficulties for you and those around you. In grief, guilt reactions are not limited exclusively to those who tend to feel guilty normally, such as those who are anxious or overly self-critical.

Reasons For Guilt. Guilt is a normal and expectable aspect of the grief experience for several reasons. First, human relationships always contain some measure of ambivalence, a mixture of negative and positive feelings. No matter how much you love someone, there are always little things that person does that annoy you, whether you admit it or not. You may be married to the very best person in the world but still hate how he forgets to put the cap back on the toothpaste, or get irritated when he scrapes his teeth on the fork while eating. Regardless of how good you or the other person are, there will always be times when the normal aspects of life cause you to irritate one another. Some people have more of these negative feelings in their relationship than others. These people are said to have more highly ambivalent relationships.

The second reason for guilt is that our relationships, as ourselves, are not perfect. Consequently, there always will be occasions when you can feel guilty for things that you did or failed to do. No matter how good, patient, and loving you consistently have been to someone, you can always remember the *one* time you were not so good, the *one* time you weren't as patient, or loving, or forgiving as you could have been. It is a cruel trick of human nature, but in the early phases of grief, people tend to recall everything that was negative in their relationship with the deceased, while failing to remember the positives equally as well.

In general, in the initial stages of grief you will probably dwell on all the bad things that you did in your relationship with the deceased, while overfocusing on all the good things that she did. You will only see your negative points and her positive ones. You will tend to remember your acts of omission and commission, concentrating on the "if onlys," "could haves," and "should haves," and obsessing over guilt-producing thoughts and feelings. Despite how positive your relationship may have been in reality, you will tend to remember the times it was negative. With time, the image of yourself and your loved one will be balanced out with the reality of the relationship and you will be able to look at both of you realistically, accepting the positive and negative aspects of each of you.

There are other sources of your guilt, too. Guilt is a normal reaction whenever you fall short of your self-image or violate a conscious or unconscious standard. This type of guilt is very frequent, as human beings tend to have unrealistic and inappropriate expectations and standards for themselves and therefore feel guilty whenever they fail to live up to them. For example, a daughter who feels she should never be upset with her mother will suffer from guilt after the mother's death when she recalls how her mother irritated her at times. Bereaved parents have particular problems of guilt. The emotion appears to be the single most pervasive parental response to the death of a child. This is because of the inappropriate social expectations society puts on them in their role as parents and the unrealistic standards by which they judge themselves. (See chapter 12 for more on this.)

You may feel guilty that you are still alive while your loved one has died. This is known as "survival guilt." You may feel guilt because of having postponed occasions for enjoyment with the deceased out of selfishness, feeling you could always make it up later. Guilt over such shortsightedness is very common. Your grief emotions themselves can prompt guilt feelings. For instance, you may feel guilty for having a normal sense of anger at the deceased for having died and left you or for having longed for the end of her lengthy illness. Crying over the death or experiencing other emotions of grief may be sufficient to cause you guilt if you regard such reactions as unacceptable losses of control.

Other responses associated with guilt include self-reproach and a sense of worthlessness. When extreme, they signify abnormal grief reactions that must be treated professionally. However, in mild and moderate amounts they are not uncommon in acute grief. They may be not only a form of self-punishment to expiate your guilt but also an expression of your anger that has been directed inward. They can be a reaction to the loss of someone whose support was important to you.

You might recognize that you have some sense of relief after your loved one dies. This is especially true if she had been suffering or there had been a long-drawn-out illness. Most grievers feel quite guilty about this. However, the relief is not usually a statement about your feelings or lack of feelings for the deceased. Most of the time it is your response to the alleviation of suffering and the end of your responsibilities. Some people feel relief because they themselves did not die or because their relationship with the deceased had been marked by a great deal of conflict or oppression and they are happy that the stress has ended. In most cases, the former is not readily admitted to, while the latter causes increased feelings of guilt and difficulty with mourning.

Illegitimate Guilt. In essence there are two types of guilt. Guilt that is out of proportion to the event is termed "illegitimate guilt." This is normal in grief. It is the natural consequence of a relationship that lacks perfection and contains ambivalence. The guilt comes from your unrealistic expectations and standards—for example, "I should have been able to protect her from death" or "I never should have felt any anger toward her during our relationship." Such guilt requires you to discuss with someone who will be nonjudgmental your guilty feelings and the acts, omissions, thoughts, or feelings that have generated them. You must examine the events rationally to determine if, given the amount of information available at the time, you did, in fact, act in the best way possible. Keep in mind that you are human and that humans make mistakes and have ambivalent relationships. You will need to see the positives that existed in the relationship and avoid overemphasizing the negatives. To eliminate the guilt, or to enable it eventually to turn only to regret, you will need to forgive yourself, find constructive ways to relieve your guilt feelings, and change any unrealistic standards or irrational beliefs that contribute to your guilt. It will help if others can let you talk about your guilt feelings without giving you premature reassurance that will block the expression of them.

Legitimate Guilt. This type of guilt occurs when there is a direct cause-and-effect relationship between what you did or failed to do and serious harm resulting to the deceased. In this situation, where your guilt is appropriate to the event, it must be acknowledged and plans must be made for restitution and expiation. This guilt can become destructive if you use it as self-punishment. When legitimate guilt warrants "punishment," you will need to do something constructive about it, such as doing something altruistic for others as a way of atoning. Guilt that cannot be expiated must be accommodated. You will have to learn to live with it and not continue to punish yourself. If not, you will be vulnerable to unresolved grief.

> Georgia was an alcoholic whose drinking resulted in the death of her son in an automobile accident. Her remorse and guilt were boundless as she continually tortured herself about the accident and the death of her child. In therapy she came to realize that this was just another way of feeling sorry for herself, as her drinking had been. She subsequently turned her energies over to working in an alcohol rehabilitation program, where she did her part to ensure that no such tragedy would ever happen again.

Guilt from the Experiences in Terminal Illness. When someone dies from a terminal illness, you can almost always expect to have experienced some amount of guilt during the illness. This stems from many of the feelings, thoughts, and behaviors that are a natural outgrowth of living with a dying person. (See chapter 7 for a further discussion of this.) Some of this guilt continues on in your grief after the death. For example, you may feel guilt if you recognize that during the illness you felt anger or other hostile feelings toward your loved one. Guilt can develop from the interpersonal conflicts that arose during the illness, when frustration, anxiety, and irritation are so much a part of everyone's experience. Normal reactions to the enormous tasks of contending with terminal illness usually prompt guilt, such as ambivalence about being in the situation and negative feelings about the demands that the patient and illness put upon you.

Guilt also may have been stimulated by your resentment of all the resources spent on the patient or your discomfort whenever you violated unrealistic expectations about devoting all your time, energy, and finances to the dying person without regard for your personal needs. It may have been fueled by the stressful "no win" situation of being forced to make choices about the incompatible responsibilities, roles, and tasks that arise during the terminal illness.

Guilt is not uncommon if you feel responsible for the illness in any way, either through heredity, omissions, or commissions, or because of your failure to protect your loved one from the illness. It might have been stimulated by any repugnance you could have felt when you confronted the ravages of the illness, for example, the scars, the smells, or the medication side effects. And, as mentioned above, you might also have experienced guilt when you wished that the end would come or were relieved because you yourself were not dying.

If you were provided with appropriate support and information during your loved one's terminal illness, you perhaps found ways to cope with your guilt during the illness. You undertook activities helpful both to you and to the dying patient. For example, you participated in her care, finished unfinished business with her, and gave her priority in terms of your time, attention, and actions. Such activities illustrated to you and others your concern for your loved one and atoned for any previous actions you regretted. Ideally, you expressed your negative feelings and were helped to understand your normal reactions in this situation. You were assisted in recognizing that angry feelings can coexist with loving ones, and that one sort does not preclude the other.

Separation Pain, Sorrow, and Longing

Acute grief typically includes painful yearning for your deceased loved one. You have excruciating loneliness for the person who died and for the unique relationship that has been lost. Your loss brings deep sorrow, with strong feelings of separation, sadness, and anguish. You ache and feel deprived. The intensity of these reactions might surprise and shock you. Unless you have lost other loved ones previously, you may feel that you have not contended with anything quite like this before. You may become fearful that you will be overwhelmed by your mental suffering.

You may feel your loss in physical terms, experiencing it as a physical emptiness or even as being "mutilated" or "wounded," as if parts of you have been ripped away. Such feelings not only reflect your sense of separation from your loved one but also your awareness of the loss of parts of yourself that had been formed by your relationship with the deceased. The yearning, aching, and pining that can accompany your separation from your loved one often are unparalleled in magnitude and urgency. Sometimes you may experience these feelings in your body as well as psychologically—a gut-wrenching, gnawing emptiness or sharp, intense pangs of grief.

A natural response to all of this is preoccupation with the deceased. This preoccupation often is manifested in obsessive rumination about your loved one, dreaming about that person, thinking you have seen him, or actively "searching" for the deceased and trying to recover him. For example, you may scan a group of people unconsciously hoping against hope to find your loved one still alive among them. Many mourners actually experience some type of visual or auditory hallucination of the deceased, or feel an intuitive, overwhelming sense of his presence. It does not mean you are crazy. It merely expresses graphically your intense wish to be re-united with the one who has been taken away from you.

These are all very poignant and painful feelings. For many people, this is the most difficult part of grief to cope with. The only thing that could help assuage these feelings would be the return of the deceased. You may desperately miss touching, smelling, hearing, and seeing your loved one. You might ache to be in contact with him again. Anything or anyone else is insufficient to salve this hurt, to fill this void. At this point, you might think that the pain will never diminish. It is overwhelming to think that you will have to live with this pain forever. You are frightened by the fact that you cannot see when it will stop.

There are no "tricks" to help you overcome these feelings. That will only come with time and continued grief work. Those who try to help bereaved individuals deal with separation and longing often recognize just how inconsolable you are. In fact, the experience of this separation and learning to live with it is what will allow you to cope successfully with the loss over time. However, it is a difficult time of missing your loved one, yearning and longing for his return, and attempting to deal with the anguish, deprivation, and feelings of separation that come with his death.

Disorganization, Depression, and Despair

Disorganization occurs when the absence of your loved one interrupts your usual patterns of behavior and your getting your needs met. It signals the breakdown of the old ways of being which had depended upon the deceased, and in turn leads to depression. It also develops as a consequence of the assault on your functioning caused by this major loss.

Depression and despair are common reactions to important losses. They are the emotions most people think of when they think of grief. There is a stereotypical picture of grief as a classic melancholic depression in which the mourner becomes unable to function and spends time sitting in the corner crying. In real life, however, people respond in many different ways. It is unrealistic and oversimplified to think that the depression of grief is expressed solely by sadness.

Frequently you may feel abandoned by your loved one, even though you know that she did not choose to die, unless it was a suicide or a death in some way intentioned by the deceased. However, even though you may know that your loved one did not choose to abandon you, the feeling of being "left" can bring up natural responses of abandonment, which in turn bring up old issues from the past about separation and abandonment. At times you may even get in a fight with yourself as you struggle to explain away these feelings. Usually, it is best for you not to argue with yourself about the feelings you experience, but merely to let them happen.

Besides feeling abandoned, you may feel sad, low, or blue. Pleasurable activities may no longer be enjoyable, and you may become apathetic and slowed down, with no energy or motivation. You may brood about the past and be pessimistic, if not hopeless, about the future. You may lament about your situation and how you have been victimized. Tearfulness and crying are not uncommon. On some occasions you may desperately want to cry, but find you are unable to do so. In your intense grief and depression, it will not be at all unusual for you to feel out of control, helpless, deprived, depersonalized, despairing, lonely, powerless, and vulnerable. You may feel that your life is meaningless and even that you, yourself, are worthless. Self-reproach, shame, and even guilt can occur. Feeling so inadequate frequently causes you to feel, in turn, childish, dependent, and regressed. While this is understandable in light of the major loss and the profound psychological injury you have sustained, you might begin berating yourself for feeling less than competent. This can cause you to become inappropriately angry at yourself. If you are like other mourners, too often you will underappreciate just how much you are affected by this traumatic loss. It is bound to set you back emotionally, physically, and socially for quite a while.

Confusion and Lack of Concentration

Don't underestimate your inability to concentrate or process information in your grief. You can expect to have some problems with memory and organization. These are natural reactions, despite the fact that you erroneously may believe you are losing control, since you feel confused and lack the decision-making abilities and incisiveness you once had.

You may find that your grief causes you to be highly distractible, befuddled, and disoriented. For example, on occasion you may find yourself lost in a fog, stopping at green lights, or arriving at a destination and not recalling how you got there. This can be dangerous both to yourself and others, so you must exercise proper caution when you find yourself in these circumstances.

Grief probably will cause you to be nonassertive and to lack clarity and certainty. You may be afraid to make choices, since you don't feel strong enough nor capable enough to trust your own judgment. All of this only heightens the anxiety and unreality of the situation for you. Such changes can cause you to feel helpless and dependent, almost like a child. As noted above, you might become very angry at yourself for not being able to see things more clearly. However, you will have to recognize the fact that grief affects you in all spheres—not just in your emotions. These problems in thinking and decision making are temporary and will pass with time and grief work. They do not indicate weakness or sickness.

You also will find that you are less effective and productive, which is a natural result of your grief process. For a while it will be impossible for you to function exactly at the same level after a major loss as before. You are just too overwhelmed with psychological, social, and physical responses to that loss. This is why it is so important for you to understand that grief can and usually does show up in *all* areas of your personal, work, and social lives. You cannot avoid your pain by throwing yourself into your work, for you will find that your work functioning, too, is compromised by your grief.

Because grief has such a profound impact on your ability to think clearly, it is not advisable to make major decisions too soon after an important loss. You may have to rely temporarily on other sources of support to help you solve problems, think through your decisions, and deal with your confusion and lack of concentration. You can solicit objective feedback from others you trust. Some of these supports you can give to yourself; for example, instead of relying on memory, you can use lists and agendas to keep your thinking straight.

Combined Anger and Depression

There are a number of responses to grief that are a combination of both anger and depression. These include irritability, anxiety, tension, and frustration. Also, there is heightened physiological arousal, which causes you to be jumpy, oversensitive, and overreactive. It interferes with your ability to relax, because there is a sense of being "geared up" or "wound up tight as a drum." You may feel very restless or sense that something is going to happen. You might wander about anxiously, going from one place to another without being able to feel content or relaxed. It is as if you are looking for something, but you don't know what it is. In fact, you are looking for your loved one. This is part of the searching behavior that normally occurs in grief in which you attempt to locate and retrieve the deceased. Your searching, which consistently is unrewarded since you cannot bring the deceased back, ultimately will help you to realize the finality of the loss. However, until that point, it also contributes to your emotional reactivity, since it both fuels your sense of loss and makes you angry because the search is unproductive.

Other common responses of this type include aggression, agitation, belligerence, and feelings of being overwhelmed and bombarded by feelings and events. You may tend to be hostile, intolerant, hypercritical, nervous, obstinate, and rigid. Very frequently, your physiological restlessness is an important indication that much is going on beneath the surface. When you are in this state, getting caught in a long line at the bank is intolerable. Or you may drum your fingers impatiently on the car dashboard if you get stuck at a red light. You may feel a great deal of emotional pressure inside and a need to keep moving.

Some people in this situation continue to keep their lives very busy in order that they not slow down and have time to think about their loss or feel their pain. Such individuals go from one thing to the next and are constantly on the move. They can never relax or let their guard down.

Diminished Self-concern

Accompanying your depression may be a lack of concern for yourself. When moderate, this appears as a disregard for personal matters because you are preoccupied with the deceased. Self-care may be permitted only as it benefits others; for example, "If it weren't for the children, I wouldn't even get up in the mornings." When taken to an extreme, this lack of concern is manifested in self-destructive behavior, even suicide. While many bereaved individuals have fleeting thoughts of suicide as a means of reuniting with the lost loved one and escaping the pain of grief, most do not act on them.

You must, however, take your suicidal thoughts seriously. Each one must be evaluated, especially if you are someone who has previously attempted suicide or who has past or present psychological problems. If this is the case, you will need to monitor yourself to make sure your diminished self-concern does not go too far. This is especially true if you have had problems with impulse control or acting out; if you have difficulty dealing with anger; if you feel hopeless, or overly depressed and dependent; if you believe you lack the resources you need to cope or do not have social support; or if you have made a concrete plan for suicide. If you feel that you will be unable to stop yourself from acting on any self-destructive wishes you have, then you should immediately reach out for professional help.

Obsession with the Deceased

In an effort to gain some control and understanding over what often appears to be a meaningless, unmanageable event, you may repeatedly review the death, trying to make sense of it. Also, you may attempt to restructure the situation so that it seems that you had some inkling that it was going to happen. For example, a widow may review the events in the weeks prior to her husband's fatal heart attack and "recognize" in retrospect the cues that then were imperceptible.

This retrospective reconstruction of events makes the situation more manageable. It gives you a perception of logical progression, control, and predictability, and retrospectively provides you with some anticipation and preparation, along with some sense of the death. This is especially important in circumstances of sudden death, when you must come to some cognitive understanding of what happened so suddenly to your loved one. However, the problem is that hindsight is 20/20, and you may erroneously hold yourself responsible for not having picked up on things before the death that, in fact, were not apparent. You may punish yourself unfairly for not having acted sooner to save your loved one.

Obsessive thinking after a loss gives you the opportunity to look at the death in every way possible to try to comprehend the event and its implications. At the same time, you are unconsciously hoping that the next time you review it the ending will have changed. This obsessive thinking usually excludes other concerns, except perhaps with the typical exception of worrying about how others in the family are doing in their grief. You are preoccupied with the internal reality of a severed relationship and with managing your reactions to this. Probably nothing else matters much to you at this point. Others who wish to give you support are often frustrated by your single-mindedness. They may seek to help you temporarily "forget," but find that you resist this.

Preoccupation with the deceased is a natural response to the loss. First, it is a wish to undo the loss. It allows you to "be with" your loved one even if only in your thoughts. Second, it is a reflection of the internal grief work being done. You are focusing attention on the deceased in an attempt to hold that loved one close in your heart and mind. This makes it akin to hugging someone and holding him tightly before saying goodbye and letting him go. This preoccupation with the deceased is often manifested in obsessive rumination about him, dreaming about him, thinking that you have seen him, or actively searching for him. This is accompanied by intense yearning, aching, and pining for what has been taken away from you.

As noted above, many mourners have visual or auditory hallucinations of the deceased, or feel an intuitive, overwhelming sense of his presence. A number report that this is a very comforting experience for them. You may try to create the conditions that will allow you to be reunited with your deceased loved one even if only in dreams or artificial connections. For example, you might hold a picture and hug it, smell the deceased's pipe tobacco, pore over old photo albums, reread old letters, and so forth. These are all examples of attempts to hold on to the loved one you do not want to relinquish. This is all right. It only becomes a problem when the demands of reality intrude upon this need to be preoccupied with the deceased and interfere with the process, or when the preoccupation absorbs too much of your time and energy and interferes unhealthily with other aspects of your life.

You may be concerned that you will not stop seeing your loved one dead or in the casket, and that you will be unable to remember him as he was while alive. Newly bereaved people often have some difficulty recalling memories from the past or the sound of their loved one's voice, his smell, or his touch. Frequently, this comes from your intense attempts at trying to reach out and recapture moments from the past that now will be lost forever. You may try to force yourself to remember every little detail that you can about the deceased; you may even be afraid that you will forget things about him. This is why some people are petrified to stop thinking constantly of the deceased. They fear that if they do not continually focus on him, their memories of him will fade. However, usually over time, with less of an attempt to force memories, these memories and recollections gradually will come back and are not restricted solely to the illness, the death, or the funeral rituals. Trying not to grieve, or not letting go of the deceased emotionally out of fear of losing memories, will only interfere with recalling the memories you seek to retain. Only in an atmosphere of free access to all thoughts and feelings about the person and the relationship, such as is provided by appropriate grief work, will you be able to remember your loved one the best.

Searching for Meaning

Very probably the search for the causes and meaning of your loved one's death will be quite important to you. For some, such as bereaved parents or those who have lost a loved one in sudden death or under traumatic circumstances such as suicide or homicide, it will be an essential component of the grief process. They can expect to be left with overwhelming questions that they may think about for a long time, if not forever.

Some questions about your loved one's death can be answered, such as questions about how the death occurred. However, questions pertaining to the philosophical reason why it happened and how it fits into the scheme of life are more difficult to answer. Why loved ones must suffer and die is a question that few of us can answer satisfactorily. Reasons that cannot be understood may have to be assimilated as just that—something that cannot be comprehended but must be accepted or at least tolerated. Accepting the fact that there is a reason, although unknown, can be a therapeutic step for some that helps them cope a little better with an unfathomable event.

The quest to answer the questions and make sense out of the death, and ultimately to find meaning in your new life, may result in a profound sense of injustice and disillusion for you if values and beliefs that once were comforting and promised security become hollow and useless. You may look at your principles and standards and wonder "What's the use?" You may become uncertain about what you believe or how you feel. The death can change your perspective on everything, and you may find life meaningless. Things that were important to you before may become insignificant. You may feel adrift without any emotional anchors.

These spiritual and philosophical crises can become major secondary losses for you. You will have to mourn them and try to discover new meaning in your life. For some the loss is permanent, while for others it is transitory. It will depend on how you can reconcile the death of your loved one, and the new life it brings you, with your other values, beliefs, and standards.

Identification

One way of holding on to parts of your lost loved one is to identify with him. It is a way in which you can keep him with you. In appropriate amounts, identification is not harmful. In fact, it was by identifying with significant others in our early lives that we took on many of the characteristics that make us who we are today.

After your loved one dies, you may consciously or unconsciously identify with that person. For example, you might consciously choose to be like your father and take over his household chores, or you may unconsciously become like him by picking up his interest in politics without ever consciously recognizing that this is a way to be like him or feel close to him. Sometimes identification is a way in which you can contribute to developing the new identity you need after your loved one dies. For example, in your desire to be a good parent to your children you may take on your deceased father's approach to child rearing if you feel he did a good job with you. (See chapter 14 for more on identification.)

However, when identification occurs too intensely (for example, you lose a sense of personal identity), when it is inappropriate to adult functioning (for example, the bereaved parent starts to act immaturely), when it occurs in areas where the mourner lacks competence (for example, the physically limited mourner tries to become the star athlete his brother was), or when it is incompatible with other roles (for example, the adult child becomes irresponsible like his father was and no longer assumes parental responsibility for his own young children), then the process has become unhealthy. If it is used to avoid dealing with the fact that the person has died, it is equally nontherapeutic.

Grief Spasms

A relatively common type of experience that might cause you great concern is the "grief spasm." This is an acute upsurge of grief that occurs suddenly and often when least expected. It interrupts your ongoing activities and temporarily leaves you feeling out of control. At times, such feelings may be experienced not as a spasm but as waves or pangs that produce painful emotional and physical sensations. They are normal for some time after the death, but you must stop your activities and deal with your feelings until you are in control again, or else you risk possible injury to yourself or others. Grief spasms or grief attacks, as they also are known, have contributed to automobile accidents, occupational injuries, and countless other mishaps. Small or surprising things can trigger these off—for example, moving the refrigerator a year after your child has died and finding a tiny toy that had become stuck behind it. This can cause a temporary, acute upsurge in grief with intense emotional reactions.

Social Effects

Your grief is manifested socially as well as psychologically. Your usual ways of behaving can be affected dramatically. Some of these social reactions may be seen in restlessness and an inability to sit still. You may be uninterested in your usual activities, or lack the initiative or energy to undertake them. You might find youself constantly bored or irritated with others. Without energy or concern for social relations, you may withdraw from your friends and their attempts to support you. You may lack all motivation and direction.

Although your great need for comfort may attract the consolation of concerned others, basically you are interested only in attempting to find and reunite with your lost loved one. You are preoccupied with your grief, and nothing else is as important to you. Other things are meaningless or trivial. You cannot be bothered with them. As a result, you may devalue all help offered, often driving away potential supporters. This focus on your lost relationship can cause you to neglect or be uninterested in other relationships, and the pain of seeing others with their loved ones may encourage your further withdrawal.

If you lack the energy to be involved socially with others, you may find it easier to decline social offers than to accept them. On the other hand, you might behave in an opposite fashion and become excessively fearful, dependent, and clingy. You may try to avoid being alone and surround yourself with others to distract yourself. Sometimes you may hide your grief fearing that others will get sick of listening to you and then they, too, will leave you. It is also possible that you can become distrustful of others or can get involved in self-destructive relationships as you act out your grief. Finally, you may get angry when people show concern because then you legitimately cannot say "everything in my life is terrible and the entire world is miserable."

Physical Effects

Although grief is usually conceived of as being an emotional reaction, you always have some physical reactions as well. Almost any type of physical symptom can be a manifestation of your grief. As human beings, our minds and our bodies are linked together. Medical evidence proves that stress in one area will cause stress in another. Also, the anxiety of losing your loved one, and the depression in reaction to the loss, each brings its own physical reactions.

For some people, physical manifestations of grief are the only way in which they allow their grief to be expressed. However, even if you are grieving appropriately on an emotional level, you can expect to have some physical responses as well. Usually you will have at least some symptoms in each area (psychological, social, and physical). The following physical symptoms are not unusual in grief:

Loss of pleasure

Anorexia and other gastrointestinal disturbances

Apathy
Decreased energy
Decreased initiative
Decreased motivation
Decreased sexual desire or hypersexuality
Physical exhaustion
Lack of strength
Lethargy
Sleep difficulties (too much or too little; interrupted sleep)
Tearfulness and crying
Weight loss or weight gain
The tendency to sigh
Feelings of emptiness and heaviness
Feeling that something is stuck in your throat
Heart palpitations, trembling, shaking, hot flashes, and other indications of anxiety
Nervousness, tension, agitation, irritability
Restlessness and searching for something to do
Shortness of breath
Smothering sensations
Dizziness, unsteady feelings
Chest pain, pressure, or discomfort

Frequently, physical symptoms are the only indication that grief still remains unresolved. Their presence is often the sole reason that individuals with unresolved grief are referred for therapy. Studies have demonstrated that bereavement is a great state of risk physically as well as emotionally and socially. You have lowered resistance and increased vulnerability to all types of illness after someone you love dies. It is as if your body is weakened by the stress of the loss and grief. For this reason, the importance of resolving your grief cannot be stressed too much. You will need to carefully watch your health and well-being in the months after a major loss. If you are concerned about a symptom, see your physician to have it evaluated.

As you have seen, grief affects you in many ways and in all areas of your life. In the next chapter, we will examine the factors that make your grief experience unique.

4

What Factors Influence
Your Grief

I T is a mistake to lump all bereaved individuals together. For instance, not all widows grieve alike merely because each has lost a husband. It is equally incorrect to assume that although two individuals lose the same person, they each have experienced the same loss. For example, although a bereaved couple have had the same child die, one spouse's reaction will not be the same as the other's. Each has lost a special relationship with the child that was unlike any other's relationship, and each is a different person. While the objective experience of the loss of the child is similar for both parents, the factors influencing both the griever and the loss situation will be different.

Too many people fail to understand that grief is very individualized and idiosyncratic. They tend to feel that all individuals who have experienced a similar loss grieve alike. In fact, as a mourner, you are more like yourself before the loss than you probably are like other bereaved people who have suffered the same type of loss. While it is very true that there are a number of universal elements in a grief experience, it is equally true that they will be experienced in very individualistic ways depending upon the psychological, social, and physical factors which influence your response to the death of a loved one.

Look at the list of factors below. Think about how each has influenced your own grief experience. Notice that at any point there are twenty-nine separate categories acting together to affect your grief. For this discussion they have been broken down into three main groupings: psychological factors, social factors, and physical factors.

Psychological Factors

Three sets of psychological factors influence your response to the death of your loved one:

1. The characteristics and meaning of the lost relationship
2. Your personal characteristics
3. The specific circumstances of the death

Characteristics and Meaning of the Lost Relationship

The first set of psychological factors that influences your grief has to do with specifically what the person and his loss mean to you.

The unique nature and meaning of your loss and the relationship that has been severed. Your grief depends upon what you perceive yourself to have lost. Each loss must be viewed from the bereaved person's own frame of reference. You cannot use your own standards to determine the impact of the loss on another human being; rather, you must comprehend what it means specifically to that mourner. For example, the loss of a pet may be painful to many people, but it may be exceptionally devastating to the elderly person to whom the pet has meant company and security. Or, you cannot automatically assume that a parent's death will bring more grief and a grandparent's will bring less. The death of the grandparent may carry more impact than that of the parent if the griever has had a more intimate relationship with that grandparent. Not everyone responds in a similar fashion to the same loss, in part because not all losses mean the same thing to all people.

The qualities of the relationship you lost. The nature of the relationship that has been severed and the strength of your emotional attachment to the person who died influence your mourning and your capacity to complete your grief work. For example, a relationship characterized by a small degree of attachment will be relatively easier for you to grieve than one that was closer, where you feel more is lost. Those who are strongly dependent upon an individual who dies often have more problems than others as they try to part with the lost relationship and establish new ones.

The role and functions that the deceased filled in your family or social system. Each person you love plays a variety of roles and performs a number of functions for you. After a death the losses resulting from your loved one's unoccupied roles and unfulfilled functions must be identified and mourned. They are important symbolic secondary losses. The number and type of these losses will affect you significantly. They will determine how much of a demand there is on you for grief, reorientation, and adaptation. Also, they force you to cope with a family or social system that is out of balance due to the unfulfilled roles, and this can complicate your grief. (See chapter 8 for more on this.) Finally, they affect the specific demands that may be placed upon you to fulfill some of the family roles and functions formerly belonging to the deceased. The more roles and functions your loved one played in your life, and the more important they were to you, the more loss you will experience and the more you will have to mourn and adapt. For example, the wife whose husband was her best friend, companion, lover, accountant, handyman, confidant, co-parent, social partner, chef, masseur, and travel coordinator loses much more when he dies than the wife whose husband was a lover but nothing else. She will have more to grieve and many more adjustments to make.

The characteristics of your deceased loved one. The age of your loved one, the type of person he was, and the interactional role he played for you (for example, spouse, parent, child, et cetera) will influence your grief experience. For example, losing someone you love who is your age, a good person, and intimately involved in your life will be more difficult for you than losing someone who was related to you but who was much older, disliked, and not well known.

The amount of unfinished business between you and your loved one. Unfinished business refers to those issues that were never addressed or settled in your relationship with the deceased. Were you able to express the things you needed or wanted to express to one another? Did you come to mutual agreement about your relationship before the death? Were there any loose ends in the relationship that had not been addressed, such as explaining why you had been so hurt or angry? Were past conflicts resolved? Were regrets and thank-you's stated? Did you get to say good-bye to each other? Such questions help reveal how much unfinished business remains between you and the deceased. The less unfinished business, the better. It means that there is less emotional baggage for you to cope with after the death when your loved one is no longer physically present to help you deal with it. You will have reduced anxiety because of it and less of a need to search for opportunities to achieve some sense of closure in the relationship.

Your perception of the deceased's fulfillment in life. The more you perceive the deceased as having had a fulfilling life, the more readily you can accept the death and complete your grief work. This is one reason why the death of a child is always so hard to cope with, since a child has not had the opportunity for the kind of fulfillment in life to which we think he should be entitled.

The number, type, and quality of secondary losses the death brings. The more secondary losses there are as a result of the death of your loved one, the greater amount of grief work is necessary for you because of the larger amount of losses to be grieved.

Your Personal Characteristics

The second set of psychological factors that influence your grief has to do with your own personal characteristics.

Your coping behaviors, personality, and mental health. These psychological attributes will influence your response to grief just as they influence all of your other responses in life. They are the tools that you use to attack the problems of grief work. To the extent that you have good coping behaviors, a healthy personality, and sound mental health, you have a better chance to resolve your grief successfully. Bereaved people tend to grieve in much the same manner as they conduct the rest of their lives. While it is true that people sometimes can change, most people tend to cope with grief by using the responses with which they have become familiar. For example, if you consistently have coped with crises by running away, the chances are that you will try the same behavior in your grief. On the other hand, if you tend to approach crises in a healthy, straightforward manner, you probably will have a similarly positive approach to your grief work. If you find you are using approaches that have not worked well in the past, you may be well advised to seek alternative ways of approaching your grief work.

Your level of maturity and intelligence. Maturity and intelligence have been found to be consistently and positively related with effective coping skills and with favorable resolution of loss. The more maturity and intelligence you possess, the better your chances for understanding the meaning and implications of this death and for utilizing healthy coping resources.

Your past experiences with loss and death. Your past experiences not only set up expectations but also influence the coping strategies you use. This influence can be either positive or negative. For example, if you have learned through your experience with previous deaths that intense grief will diminish if properly attended to, you probably will be more willing to yield to the grief process than someone who has learned to deny loss in an effort to avoid pain.

Your social, cultural, ethnic, and religious/philosophical backgrounds. These factors influence how you understand your grief, how you express it, and how you will deal with it. They shape the beliefs, meanings, and values you hold for life, death, and life after death. Consequently, depending upon the groups to which you belong, your grief work can either be helped or hurt. For instance, a person who comes from an Italian background that generally encourages the expression of emotion tends to have more support for the expression of grief than someone who comes from an English background in which emotions may be held more in check.

Your sex-role conditioning. Sex-role conditioning determines which aspects of grief expression are acceptable and which are unacceptable. In Western cultures, males traditionally are conditioned to be in control and to avoid the expression of feelings. This often makes it difficult for them to cope with sadness, loss, depression, and loneliness. It interferes with their ability to ask for help from others. Consequently, when a male is grieving he may experience conflict, as the expression of feelings necessary for grief resolution is often contrary to previous sex-role conditioning. Traditionally, women have experienced less conflict between their sex-role conditioning and the requirements for successful resolution of their grief. The feelings and behaviors most often prompted in response to loss are tolerated well in females. However, women tend to have relatively more difficulty than men in dealing with their anger and in assuming control and making decisions. Obviously, this is based on stereotype, and for this reason each person's unique background must be taken into account. (See chapter 5 for more on this.)

Your age. Your age is associated with other factors relating to your response to loss, such as the amount of past experience you have had with loss and death and your level of maturity and intelligence. For example, if a child is bereaved as opposed to an adult, there will be differences in the level of understanding, maturity of coping mechanisms, and access to resources. On the other hand, while an elderly person may have had much experience with loss and death and may be quite mature emotionally, he may find himself with physical disabilities that interfere with access to others and fewer opportunities for reestablishing a new identity after the death. Your age also is associated with particular developmental concerns, and these can complicate your grief. For instance, losing a loved one in adolescence is particularly difficult because it already is such a tumultuous and stressful time.

The presence of concurrent stresses or crises in your life. If you are forced to confront other crises at the same time you are trying to grieve, your grief will be complicated. For example, if you are unemployed, physically ill, getting a divorce, or struggling with a developmental crisis, you will tend to have a relatively more difficult time coping with your grief than if these crises were absent. These additional burdens can sap your energy and put extra demands on you at a time when you are already preoccupied and depleted.

Specific Circumstances of the Death

The third set of factors that psychologically influence your response to the death of your loved one pertains to the specifics of the death itself.

The death surround. This term refers to the immediate circumstances of the death. It includes the location, type of death, reason for the death, and your degree of preparation for it. To the extent that you can accept the death surround of your loved one, your grief will be easier to manage and resolve. When the circumstances of the death are unacceptable to you, the death may be harder to resolve. For example, it is usually relatively more difficult to cope with a loved one's death by murder than from an illness that ended peacefully at home, with family and friends present.

The timeliness of the death. This refers to your feelings about how acceptable the death was for this person at this specific time. Your perception of the acceptability may depend on several factors:

The age of your loved one (for example, the death of a young person is traditionally more difficult to cope with than the death of someone very old, for whose death you were more prepared).

What is happening in the relationship at the time of death (for example, it may seem especially unfair when a man dies immediately following the retirement for which he had worked so long).

The circumstances prior to the death (for example, you recently may have argued or reconciled with your loved one).

To the extent that you feel that the death was untimely, you will have more difficulty in resolving your grief because of your problems accepting the fact that the death occurred when it did.

Your perception of the preventability of the death. If you perceive the death to have been preventable, and assume responsibility for having failed to prevent it, your grief will be greater and you will experience more guilt, which will further complicate your mourning process. Sometimes your perception of preventability is based on a realistic appraisal of what could have been done. For example, the wife could have insisted that her husband be checked for his high blood pressure instead of going along with his denial of symptoms. At other times, however, your perception of preventability comes from unrealistic expectations you hold for yourself. For example, guilt over failure to prevent their child's death is very common in bereaved parents, as they erroneously feel that they should have been able to protect their child from everything. Whatever it stems from, if you feel that the death was a preventable one it is a harder loss for you to cope with. Since it was unnecessary, this is a death that did not *have* to happen. It could have been avoided.

Sudden versus expected death. When a death has been expected, even though it may put tremendous emotional demands on the individuals involved, people can begin to cope. When loss occurs, it has been prepared for. When the loss comes unexpectedly, grievers are shocked, and their ability to cope is seriously impaired. There are major differences among those who are bereaved from sudden versus expected deaths (see chapter 6 for more on this topic). To the extent that there was time for appropriate preparation, you will tend to experience relatively less of an assault on your ability to cope than when it is totally unexpected. This will put you in a better position in your grief work.

The length of illness prior to death. Too short an illness, as well as too long an illness, can make bereavement more difficult. In too short an illness, there is a lack of preparation. Those left behind appear to suffer just like those whose loved ones die from sudden death. If the illness goes on for too long, the care of the dying person requires large investments of time, effort, and emotional energy that can lead to progressively more social isolation, physical debilitation, emotional exhaustion, physical conflicts, and family problems. (See chapter 7 for more on this.) While this is something that cannot be changed after the death, the length of the illness does indicate the types of problems you may have to face.

Your anticipatory grief and involvement with your dying loved one. Your anticipatory grief and the type and amount of involvement you have with your dying loved one both affect your experiences during the terminal illness. Whatever these experiences are like, they will color your mourning following the death, since they will influence both what you need to deal with and how you cope with it after the loss. (See chapters 6 and 7 for more on this.)

Social Factors

There are a number of social factors that will influence your response to the death of a loved one.

Your social support system. This is a critically important factor. If you have a good social support system and the acceptance and assistance of its members, you will tend to fare better in your grief than someone who does not. Problems with grief usually develop if others place inappropriate expectations upon you or withhold nurturance and support.

Your sociocultural, ethnic, and religious/philosophical backgrounds. These will help or hinder your grief work because they influence your attitudes toward the expression of grief and determine the amount of support available to you. When these backgrounds bring attitudes that are consistent with what is necessary in mourning (for example, expression of feelings), they are most helpful to you. Also, they will influence your support system and the amount of support you receive. For example, in some religions the sadness over loss is well understood, whereas in others it is perceived as a lack of sufficient faith in God. The former would tend to encourage the healthy processing of grief, while the latter would discourage it.

Your educational, economic, and occupational status. In your grief, a lack of education, money, or occupational skills may magnify the stresses on you. They may compromise your ability to sustain and replenish yourself after the death, and can contribute to additional secondary losses. For example, if a woman is forced to get a job after her husband dies, she will be better prepared if she has a good educational background than if she is a high school dropout. Especially in cases where there are large bills as a result of medical care or funeral expenses, these social factors will not only play a part in getting your debts paid but also will have an impact on whether or not you can successfully meet present family needs.

The funerary rituals. These rituals will be truly therapeutic if they promote realization and confirmation of your loss, assist you in expressing your feelings and memories, and offer you social support. The absence of these rituals, or their inappropriate use, can be detrimental to the grief process. (See chapter 16 for more on this.)

Physical Factors

The third set of factors influencing your response to grief is physical factors.

Drugs and sedatives. In general, if drugs are used to keep you from experiencing your pain and realizing the loss that ultimately has to be faced after your loved one dies, they will be nontherapeutic for you. You need to feel your pain and express your emotions at the time when social support is available: during the wake, funeral, memorial service, or other leave-taking rituals. Otherwise you may have to confront your loss alone later on, when there may not be the social support that typically is available during the initial period following the death.

Nevertheless, there are times when drugs are a useful tool, such as when mild sedation is warranted to prevent exhaustion, severe insomnia, and illness. Medication can be helpful at these times because you need energy for your grief work. Also, there are other complications of the mourning process that may require medication. Notwithstanding this, too often drugs are prescribed indiscriminately in an effort to help you avoid the pain, and this often only ends up hurting you more.

Nutrition. You may not feel like eating, or, if you do, the food may not taste good or agree with your stomach. Despite this, you must maintain adequate nutritional balance and eating habits. Inadequate nutrition will only compromise your ability to cope with the loss, meet the continuing demands of your daily life, and overcome the physical symptoms generated by the stress of your grief.

Rest and sleep. Some degree of sleep disturbance is normal in the grief process. However, a lack of sufficient sleep may cause mental and physical exhaustion, contribute to your developing disease, and predispose you to unresolved grief. Similarly, excess sleep reduces the oxygen available for your brain and can interfere with your undertaking the important tasks of grief work. Medication may be warranted if the required energy to mourn is impaired. Without this energy, any bereavement experience is threatened.

Physical health. Grief assaults the body just as it assaults the mind. Your physical condition and the responsivity of your nervous system will influence how your body handles the stress of grief. A certain amount of physical disturbance is normal; however, physical symptoms must be cared for to preserve your energy for grief work and to reduce the potential for the development of serious physical symptoms. Tobacco, caffeine, alcohol, and other foods and drugs that adversely affect your nervous system will only hurt your ability to cope with the physical stress of grief and mourning. Poor physical health adversely affects psychosocial functioning as well.

Exercise. Adequate exercise not only keeps the body in good physical condition but also provides an outlet for the stressful emotions of grief. It offers you a reduction of aggressive feelings, a release of tension and anxiety, a relief of depression, and an increased sense of control. All of these benefits are desirable for anyone coping with the loss of someone they love. These emotions then will be less likely to be channeled into psychosomatic illnesses or other physical or psychosocial symptoms.

In summary, keeping these factors in mind as you progress through your grief—psychological, social, and physical—may help you understand what is happening to you in your unique grief experience and how you best can get through it.

Another factor may play a large part in your grief, depending upon society's attitude toward your relationship with the deceased or toward the deceased person himself. This is social recognition.

Social Recognition Of Death

When a loss is not socially validated—that is, not acknowledged by society as an important loss to be mourned—you are put in a difficult situation. Since the loss is not viewed as valid by society, you lack the social support necessary to face the pain and accommodate to it. Additionally, if the relationship that has been severed is not openly acknowledged, often there are no bereavement rituals to help you cope with the loss. You miss the confirmation, expression, and support they can offer.

Surprisingly, there are a number of situations in life where a person may suffer a major loss that cannot be acknowledged openly. Such a situation leaves you with little or no opportunity to publicly mourn that loss. This can occur for two reasons: either there is no recognition of the significance of the loss or the relationship was not socially sanctioned.

Many losses are not recognized socially. A primary example is the death of an infant. In this case, bereaved parents are often "comforted" by well-meaning others who tell them they are lucky they did not get to know the infant before they lost him. They fail to realize the attachment that existed from the time of awareness of pregnancy. There have been fantasies, needs, hopes, dreams, and expectations placed upon this child-to-be, all of which are profound losses in addition to the actual physical death of the baby. A similar case is that of abortion. Most of society feels that since a conscious choice was made to end the pregnancy, the parents do not grieve. This is completely untrue. Recent research documents the grief of many mothers who are profoundly affected by the decision to have an abortion, and who mourn as a result. (See chapter 12 for more on these losses.)

Numerous other relationships are not socially recognized as being significant enough for you to mourn. Relationships with friends, neighbors, colleagues, co-workers, former in-laws, and teachers—all can be exceptionally close, meaningful, powerful, and influential in your life. These people can range from being a confidante to being a pivotal person who can change your life. In the best of relationships, they may share your secrets, challenge your goals, support your dreams. By virtue of their not being embroiled in your own family, sometimes they can assist you in ways your own family cannot. They are close enough to be concerned, while distant enough to be somewhat objective. As noted before, whether or not this loss is perceived by others will not determine whether or not you grieve. Rather, it is the nature and meaning of this particular loss to you that will determine whether mourning is necessary.

The importance of a death in our life is not determined exclusively by bloodlines. For example, in many cases the death of your best friend may affect you more profoundly than the death of someone in your own family. However, this is not necessarily socially acknowledged. If a family member has died we typically receive help: time off from work; expressions of sympathy; offers of assistance; social support to cope; social recognition to confirm the relationship and validate the loss; and the opportunity to participate in mourning rituals after the death. However, if the person who dies is perceived "merely" as a friend, these therapeutic experiences often are missing. For instance, in many employment situations there are written guidelines delineating for whose deaths employees can receive time off from work. In some cases, while the death of a sibling is considered important enough that you would be granted time off, the death of an aunt or uncle is not. We know that the death of a friend or extended-family relative can be as much of a loss as that of someone who is more closely related. Yet, grief over the loss of these people is poorly tolerated and insufficiently supported by society. Those of us bereaved from these types of losses suffer as a result.

A second condition under which social support may not be offered is when the relationship between you and the deceased is not socially sanctioned. Lovers having extramarital affairs, cohabitant couples, ex-spouses, and relationships between gay men and between lesbian women are examples of nontraditional and socially unsanctioned unions that nevertheless can result in profound grief when one of the partners dies. These losses usually are not socially recognized or supported because the union is seen as illegitimate, has some stigma attached to it, is not valued by society, or is not seen as an intense attachment. Consequently, those bereaved from these types of losses may not have the opportunity or support to express their grief at the proper time. They can suffer intensified emotional reactions as a result. If there is guilt or ambivalence about having been in the relationship, experienced its strain, or lived as a minority, additional complications can arise.

There are many sad scenarios that develop in circumstances such as this. Here are some examples:

Imagine the feelings of the woman whose twenty-year love affair with a bachelor goes totally unrecognized when he dies suddenly of a heart attack and his widowed mother is regarded as the sole survivor.

Consider the reactions of the gay man who loses his lover following a relationship of forty years and is expected to act as if a "friend" has died.

Put yourself in the situation of a woman whose ex-husband dies, who has no input into the funeral arrangements of the man to whom she had been married for twenty-seven years and with whom she still had a respectful and close relationship. What must it be like for her to see all of the support given to his new wife of six months?

How must an elderly man feel when the woman with whom he has been cohabiting for twenty years, and with whom he has been pooling financial resources in order to exist above the poverty level, loses that woman? Not only may he not be accorded any status as a mourner, but her Social Security benefits stop and he is not "officially" able to qualify as her beneficiary.

In all of these cases, a close and intense attachment has been severed. If this is the case for you, you need to find social support to help you mourn. If possible, you should try to participate in any bereavement rituals or else create some of your own. (See chapter 16 for more on this.) If you do not, you may experience a more conflicted grief, with more distorted and intensified reactions. Realize that not only do you have to endure numerous secondary losses, but your dreams have been shattered as well. And you aren't even able to express what you feel! Such problems would make mourning difficult for any griever, regardless of the death's social recognition.

There are two other situations in which the death of a loved one typically is not socially validated and leaves the bereaved person without support. One of these is the death of a pet or companion animal. Unless you are an animal lover, you may be unaware of the intense and long-term attachment that can exist between a human being and an animal.

Pets have some of the very best qualities for a partner in a relationship. They are loyal, uncritical, nonjudgmental, relatively undemanding, and usually always there. Many of them are delighted merely to give and receive affection and companionship. They can be intuitive, caring, and engaging, often drawing us out of ourselves. For many people, pets serve as stabilizing forces within chaotic families, become critically important objects of love, and are the one for whom we first learn to be responsible. They are now being viewed as important in the development and socialization of children, and publications about the significance of pet–human bonding are appearing in the professional literature at an outstanding rate. These many special positive attributes of pets are what have led therapists to recognize their value for all people, but especially for the aged, the infirmed, and the mentally and emotionally ill.

Of course, any relationship such as this would generate profound grief at its severing. For this reason, the death of a beloved pet can strike humans at the deepest levels. Research and clinical evidence reveal that in many cases the loss of a pet is as profound and far-reaching as the loss of a human family member. Unfortunately, our society still tends either to encourage immediate replacement of the pet after death or to devalue the loss, saying, "It was only an animal." Sometimes even pet owners themselves tend to denigrate their loss. They may be embarrassed to express their full range of emotions or may chastise themselves because they think they are overreacting. This is unfortunate, since it robs them of their sense of legitimacy in the loss and inhibits full and necessary grief expression. The human–animal bond can be as intense and meaningful as any human–human bond, and it must be accorded the same respect, both in life and in death.

Finally, there are distinct social problems for grievers when their loss involves the death of a person who has been socially devalued for one reason or another. The person whose loved one was a criminal, an alcoholic, mentally ill, retarded, or an AIDS victim often is robbed of social support at the time of death. It is as if our society said, "This person is not valued very much by us, so it cannot hurt that much for you to lose him." However, while society may devalue some of those in its ranks, those who love them do not. Even in situations where there is a sense that justice has been served, grief exists. For example, the mother of the convict who dies in the electric chair loses a child no less than the mother whose teenager is killed in an automobile accident. While society may respond to the latter and not the former, this does not stop the parental grief of a woman who still has lost her child.

The lack of social validation of a death is particularly outrageous when social stigma has robbed the deceased of either what he should have been getting all during his life or during the illness that led to his death. The mentally ill, the retarded, and the physically disabled all too often experience discrimation throughout life. For many, although not all, this continues in death, when their survivors are not seen to have a necessity to grieve. Currently, those who die from AIDS or other diseases upon which society has put some moral judgment often leave survivors who are unsupported in their grief. This will be an increasingly major issue as these diseases leave more and more bereaved individuals who will have the same requirements for grief and support as does anyone who loses someone she loves.

In conclusion, as primary group interaction in our society declines, divorce rates increase, individuals get married later, and gays and lesbians reclaim their emotional and legal freedoms, we will see more of these nontraditional relationships. We will continue to see strong bonds between those not legally defined as close—for example, friends, neighbors, and co-workers. Divorce may end legal relationships but not necessarily bonds between former in-laws. Infants still will die. Pets will be lost. Extramarital affairs will occur. As a result, we will continue to see situations in which people have intense relationships that are not openly acknowledged or socially defined as important enough to mourn. To the person who is left surviving, the severing of any of these relationships is a major and traumatic loss which must be understood and responded to as such. Our failure to do so as individuals and as society only predisposes these people to poorer bereavement outcomes.

In this chapter, you have seen how your grief is determined by the idiosyncratic combination of the above factors coming together in your particular loss. In the next chapter, we will identify a number of general expectations you can have for your grief and will examine what happens when grief goes awry.

5

What to Expect
in Grief

GRIEF may have taken you by surprise with its intensity and mixture of feelings. You may find yourself wondering if what you feel is normal, and if your grief is progressing in a healthy manner. In this chapter we will try to give you some appropriate expectations for grief: how it may differ between males and females; how long it might take you to work through it; what times you can expect a surge in reactions; and what you can realistically expect from yourself. At the end we will talk about the various forms of unresolved grief and how they may develop.

Male and Female Differences in Mourning

The same passions in man and woman differ in tempo; hence man and woman do not cease misunderstanding one another.

— Friedrich Nietzsche

One of the main issues you undoubtedly will encounter as a mourner is that no one else mourns exactly like you do. While many of us pay lip service to understanding this, when it comes right down to it we *do* want people to grieve like we grieve. We want to know that we are doing it "right." We want others to have the same needs and desires that we have, so that it will be easy for us to understand and meet these needs. And we want other people to do the same for us. One cannot blame us for wanting things to be this way; we can only be blamed if we expect that they will be.

Problems Arising Because of Differences

It is not uncommon for a bereaved woman to be totally frustrated by her husband's not talking about a death, returning to normal routines of living sooner than she, and being uninterested in attending a grief support group. On the other hand, it is quite common for men to feel that women react too intensely, need to talk about the loss too much, and rely on others too heavily to help them cope with their loss. Why is there such misunderstanding? Can it be that there are separate processes of grief for men and women? Are men and women so different that they have totally distinct needs? Do men and women love differently, so that when there is a death their responses are dramatically incompatible? When compared to women, don't men have feelings? To these questions, only one answer is possible: No and yes.

No, men do not have separate processes of grief, totally distinct needs from women, different love, nor a lack of feelings. Yes, they do experience all of these differently from women, and they certainly express them to themselves and to others in a most divergent fashion from how women do. Men are on the very same earth as are women, and they undergo many of the same life experiences, but they do it in a dissimilar way and are not very verbal about it.

If you look at the traditional ways in which men and women have been conditioned, you will see the reasons for the differences in their grief experiences. This section looks only at the differences caused by sex-role conditioning. Personal and idiosyncratic factors will contribute to other dissimilarities as well (see chapter 4 for more on this).

Why is it important for you to understand the sex-role conditioning of men and women? Because one of the worst problems that occurs in grief, but is totally unnecessary, is the increased pain, misunderstanding, frustration, and secondary losses that you may have to experience if you fail to understand the difference between your responses and those of someone else you love who is a member of the other sex. For example, if you are a woman trying to understand the responses of your husband after the death of your child, it is very important that you recognize that his sex-role conditioning is going to make him grieve in a fashion that you possibly could misinterpret if you don't understand where it is coming from. Too often, wives feel that their husbands are insensitive and do not care about them or their deceased loved one. On too many occasions, men perceive women as being hysterical and overreactive. These misunderstandings can bring more pain at a time when you are already feeling too much of it.

Read about the differences between males and females below. Use them to understand how and why your loved ones of the opposite sex grieve as they do. They are undergoing the same experiences of grief and mourning but may be dealing with them in totally different ways. Be aware that traditional sex-roles are discussed below. To the extent that a person's experience has been unlike the traditional sex-role conditioning in American society, he or she would be expected to act in different ways.

Sex-Role Conditioning

As noted in chapter 4, there are many factors which influence your grief response. One of the most important ones is your sex-role conditioning, that is, how you have been taught to behave as a male or a female. In fact, it is so important that this section is devoted exclusively to looking at the traditional differences between the ways men and women grieve.

The information in this section is based on the traditional and stereotypical training of males and females in our society. To the extent that a man or woman has been raised with the ability to respond in a flexible manner, without regard to whether that behavior is appropriate or inappropriate for their traditional sex-role, we say that this person is "androgynous." This means that he or she can respond to a situation and react in the fashion that the situation demands, without worry over whether the response is masculine or feminine. For example, this is seen in the man who can allow himself to cry, which usually is prohibited in our society, and in the woman who is assertive and independent, traits which are usually seen as being more masculine. Our society is slowly becoming more androgynous. However, the traditional stereotypes still remain for many of us. They continue to have a strong influence on the ways we behave, and they are the basis from which we learn how to deal, or not to deal, with our feelings and experiences in life.

In very real ways, boys and girls still are raised differently, with dissimilar expectations and divergent sex-typed messages. These are learned by boys and girls from an early age and contribute to the development of specific gender identity as male or female. For example, by age four, children in our culture already know what toys little boys should play with (for example, trucks and blocks) and what types little girls should play with (for example, dolls and baby carriages). From age four to six, they already have associated goodness and competence with the male gender role, and niceness and attractiveness with the female gender role (Kohlberg and Ullman 1974).

All of these messages become a part of your identity, which in turn determines how you perceive yourself and the world; how you act in the world and communicate in it; and what you value and how you achieve it. Consequently, your attitudes and thoughts, your feelings and behaviors, your coping skills and even ways of life and death will be influenced by your perceptions and reactions as a male or female.

The Roles of the Male. From his very earliest days as a little boy, the male in our society is taught to be self-sufficient, self-reliant, and independent. He is expected to be able to do things on his own and not to need assistance from others. Often, if he cannot do something by himself he will not do it.

Along with this, the male is trained to control his feelings, his actions, and his environment. This especially means containing and repressing emotion. Consequently, a major part of the male image is to be noncommunicative about feelings and to exert emotional control. He is taught to have a stiff upper lip about his emotions, with the exception of the more powerful feeling of anger, which his male role can tolerate well. The strong, silent, macho image must always be acted out; most feelings, especially soft feelings of vulnerability, are not expressed. This necessarily will leave the traditional male with more difficulty experiencing closeness, vulnerability, intimacy, and open communication. It makes males less expressive than females in all areas of life, not only with emotional feelings but also in their physical health. It is for this reason that many males ignore physical complaints and refuse to seek rest or care.

Instead of verbalizing feelings, men tend to act them out. This is compatible with their sex-role conditioning because it allows them to be in control and fosters activity rather than passivity. For example, instead of discussing his feelings of discouragement at work, a male will be more likely to release his emotion through physical activity or by having a drink at the local bar. While both courses of action temporarily may make him feel better, they do not address the real problem and do not leave room for loved ones to help him with that problem. Such actions do not foster either effective emotional resolution or good communication with those close to him. In grief this can be a particular problem. Men actively may seek acting-out behaviors to turn around their feelings of being "victimized" or "acted upon" by the experience of the loss and the pain it brings. It also provides them with an escape. Overinvolvement in work or community affairs, extramarital relationships, and drug abuse are some of these common behaviors. The problems of this approach are quite numerous and devastating, often leading to additional loss upon loss.

Males in our society are socialized to be powerful and to act as pillars of strength. They are taught to be strong and aggressive in their actions, to take over in times of crises. They are expected to do, to produce, and to act. Consequently, passivity and reaction are looked on with disdain. Along with this comes the role of problem-solver, in which the male is expected to "fix" things. He changes what he does not like. He is expected to be the protector of and the provider for his family.

Often the male is socialized into being a loner who keeps his distance from people in order to appear rational and in control at all times. This contributes further to his inability to express needs even in very stressful situations. This is one reason why for too many men social support is minimal or an altogether deprived facet of their lives. This, along with the conditioning not to dwell on feelings or express them, makes a man much less able to be empathic than his female counterpart. He just does not know how to feel, intuit, or respond to the emotions of others, since such sensitivity is seen as unmanly.

In addition, the male is expected to be a competitor. He is supposed to be aggressive and to excel and be superior in what he does. He is socialized to compete rather than cooperate, and learns to evaluate his success in terms of external achievements as opposed to personal or interpersonal fulfillment. The notion of competition is taken into all areas of his life, which leaves many men uncomfortable with passivity and having a need to dominate every situation. Frequently, activities designed for leisure also become competitive, and there is a push to outdo everyone and everything.

Lastly, the male is expected to stay as far away from "sissy stuff" as possible. This translates into his being different from women in every way he can. There is a sense of regarding anything perceived as a weakness as "feminine." So, he will tend to deny his own feelings and needs emotionally, physically, and socially, along with those of others.

The Roles of the Female. In contrast, a woman has far fewer social roles, and she has a little more flexibility in them. She is taught to pay attention to all her emotional needs. She is encouraged to display and express them to others in her environment. Regarded as fragile, she is expected to be dependent and not self-reliant. At times, she is even taught to hide her capabilities in order to foster this image and not threaten men. She learns that it is acceptable, if not expected, to express her emotional complaints, as well as her physical symptoms. Regarding the latter, she has been taught to focus on her body as being one of her most important assets. This coincides with her focus of attention being geared to how she superficially looks and acts, as opposed to who she really is and what she can do.

A woman is raised to be more willing to share her fears and anxieties and to admit to problems without perceiving this as a threat to her gender role. It is permissible for her to feel both vulnerable and affectionate, and to be intimate, honest, and communicative. Emotional closeness is valued and desired. While the woman may submerge her own identity or individuality in order to receive support and direction from males, the one role she does not shirk is that of nurturer. In this regard, she focuses on the emotional needs of those she loves and pays attention to their physical comfort. She learns early on how to identify and respond to the feelings of others.

Male and Female Differences in Responding to Problems

There are a number of differences in responding to problems which stem from traditional sex-role conditioning. Men think differently from women. Men are more analytical and have faster reaction times. In contrast, women use their intuition more and generally are more empathic than men. In grief, men want to solve the problem, whereas women need to explore their feelings and have them recognized as legitimate by others. Consequently, a conflict may occur. For example, a man listening to his wife's expression of loneliness at missing their deceased child may attempt to problem-solve her dilemma. He will focus on the practical realities and try to make suggestions for easing the pain. He may suggest to her that she look for a part-time job or pick up a new hobby. However, his wife merely wants to share and express her feelings and to find out if her husband feels the same way. She wants to be listened to. She does not want the answers per se; she is not looking for a job or a new hobby. She wants emotional comfort and someone who can understand her pain. However, when she gets suggestions from him that are directed at something else besides her feelings, she feels misunderstood, frustrated, and alone in her grief. She wonders whether her husband has feelings about his loss, their deceased child, or her.

In this illustration, it can be seen that the man is focusing on one aspect of the problem and the woman is focusing on another. Their separate sex-role conditionings have prepared them each to respond to the issue in a different way. The male is responding to it in a way to problem-solve it, protect the woman, provide a solution, control the pain, and not require undue reliance on others. The female is seeking to express her feelings, get acknowledgment of pain, compare herself to others, and focus on her current experience. It is as if one is on an AM radio station and the other is on FM. They are both listening to the radio, but in totally different dimensions.

The difference is more than just a dissimilarity in approach. Because of her sex-role conditioning, the woman is better prepared to deal with grief. She is more open to feelings, both hers and others, and it is consistent with her training to express them. It is perfectly acceptable for her to seek out people with whom she can share these feelings. All of these avenues are precluded to the male in our society and can interfere with his successfully dealing with his grief. So it is not just that males and females are different in their approaches to the grief process; men are at a distinct disadvantage in terms of meeting the requirements for successful grief resolution.

Male and Female Differences in Having and Utilizing Social Support

Another very important way in which men and women are different is in the types of interpersonal relationships they have. This, too, will affect the way they experience and deal with their grief. Men do not tend to have close and intimate interpersonal relationships with other men. They more often have superficial "buddy" relationships which usually are structured around activities and not feelings. They tend to compete with one another in groups and usually do not admit to weakness. Consequently, in times of crises they have fewer support persons to turn to and little experience in sharing their feelings.

Alternatively, women are encouraged to be dependent and to look to others to assist them. The helplessness and powerlessness of grief is not incompatible with their role. They have always tended to have friends with whom they can share feelings. They have intimate relationships that afford them sources of consolation. They have had much training in being vulnerable and aware of the feelings of themselves and others, and disclosing these feelings is an important part of their communication patterns. This open communication ability is an important asset to women who are grieving. Since they do not have to hide their feelings, unlike their male counterparts, it will not be inappropriate or difficult for them to admit to their problems and to request assistance from others.

What Does It All Mean?

In essence, while the sex-role conditioning of the female prepares her to deal with mourning, that of the male tends to interfere with the successful resolution of grief. It stimulates denial, repression, and postponement of emotional reactions, a focus on practicalities rather than feelings, and a drive toward a quick return to normalcy. It prohibits admission of symptoms or reaching out for the support of others, and strives for control of an uncontrollable situation. It often encourages unhealthy acting-out behaviors. A woman can yield to the processes of mourning and not feel that she is unwomanly. However, if a man yields to the natural and necessary processes of grief, he will be confronted with an overwhelming conflict, since what is required in mourning is precluded by his sex-role conditioning and self-image. He will want to focus on managing and controlling his feelings, when what he needs to do is to identify and express them.

In grief, he has "failed" in all his roles. He cannot do anything that will change the fact of death. He cannot "fix" his wife nor his family. He cannot control his own feelings. He has been unable to win the battle of protecting his loved one who has died. Additionally, his grief work demands abandoning business-as-usual to pay attention to mourning; this often is too taxing for the male, since it is in direct contrast to his need to work and produce. He tends to feel that the best way he can provide for and protect his family is to be a pillar of strength for them, and often interprets this to mean not expressing his own emotions and not changing his usual routines.

Helping A Man. It is easy to see why there can be misunderstandings and conflict between men and women in their grief. Men want to "fix" their loved ones and help them figure out what must be done to ease the pain. However, for these loved ones, most especially women and children, what needs to be done is for them to experience their pain, express it, and reminisce about the person who died. The same things need to be done by the men, but they have difficulty doing it. If you want to help a male to grieve, it will be important to remember the following things in addition to general suggestions for resolving grief in chapter 14:

> Give the man "permission" to feel and express his emotions. This can be done verbally (for example, "You need to let out some of those feelings you've been bottling up inside") or nonverbally through a hug or a touch.

Convey to him that the expression of emotion in mourning is normal, necessary, and therapeutic. It is not "feminine," "sissy," or anything he should be ashamed of.

Help the man find the most comfortable ways for him to work through his emotions. For example, encourage him to work through his grief in behavioral ways, such as stacking wood and doing things that will give him a sense of productivity and physical relief. Recognize that he may never deal with his grief like a woman does; he may never be comfortable with deep discussion of feelings and long talks based upon the memory of the person who died. Find out what he can allow himself to do, and try to get him to channel his mourning into these courses of action.

Do not try to remake males into female mourners. This is unrealistic. Men may never cry as frequently as women do, but this does not mean they cannot express their sadness in other ways. For example, they can think about, verbalize, or in other ways give vent to their sadness, and they can do things in memory of their loved one. But they do not have to do it in exactly the same ways as women.

It is important that you not try to "de-condition" the man, only that you make him just comfortable enough with the necessary responses of mourning that his grief work can be addressed. For instance, a man may find it much less threatening to discuss his reactions to the death of his spouse in the context of a discussion of the family's responses rather than one focused on his own personal feelings.

Try to offer support to the male in ways that do not make him feel more weak or incompetent than he already may feel in his grief.

Keep in mind that the traditional male is in a "no win" situation as a mourner. If he gives in to his grief, he loses because he violates his sex-role conditioning and fails at the roles he has been assigned. If he does not give in to his mourning, the unresolved grief will cause him to lose, since it will bring so many additional problems.

You can be helpful by providing the male with the specific practical information which his new role as a bereaved person may require. For example, if he is a widower with younger children he may need direction in housekeeping; if he is a bereaved parent he may need help in dealing with his surviving bereaved children. This information can assist him in feeling a little more competent in a situation that is probably most difficult for him.

Helping A Woman. Women also need permission to grieve, but not in as broad-based a fashion as men. They already have internalized the requirements for grief resolution and so, frequently, do not require as much additional intervention beyond the usual as do men. They may have some difficulty dealing with the feelings of anger that grief can bring, and in coping with the independence and decision making that is necessary after the loss but which traditionally has been suppressed in women. Because this will be such a change in their role, they will need explicit permission to experience these new feelings and skills, and to incorporate them into their new identities.

Women will benefit a great deal from a realistic perspective on the socially conditioned male response. This will help them to understand it and not interpret it as a lack of love for them, for the deceased person, or for other family members. Depending on their particular loss, they will require practical information which may have been lacking in their upbringing—for example, on such topics as handling finances, dealing with school authorities, fixing household appliances, and so forth.

Bridging The Gap

What can be done to help deal with the fundamental conflicts between the sexes in terms of how emotional states and approaches to coping and adjustment are managed in grief? If each sex can understand the different approach of the other, there will be fewer misunderstandings and misinterpretations. Men must develop a more realistic appreciation for women's grief and their handling of it. They need to recognize that it will go on more intensely and for a longer time than theirs. They must acquiesce to the need women have for compassionate listening during their grief work and for dialogue with the men in their lives.

For their part, women will have to understand the way men approach and deal with grief in the context of their sex-role conditioning. They cannot expect to remake males into female mourners. Women need to recognize that men do grieve, but in their own ways, and these ways, if they are healthy, must be supported. The physical expression of grief through work and behavior must be recognized as a primary means of ventilation, although verbal ventilation needs to be encouraged as well.

Expectations for the Impact of Time and for the Course and Duration of Mourning

As mentioned previously, there are many false expectations in our society about the nature of the mourning process. To help yourself, you must be able to have a realistic view of how time affects grief, how that process will change during its course, and how long it will take.

Time

Very often, time is viewed as a healing factor in the grief. It is not uncommon to hear "Time heals all," "It just takes time," or "Time will ease the pain." However, time will be helpful to you in your grief *only* if you are dealing with the loss; not if you are denying, inhibiting, delaying, or otherwise not working through your loss.

In grief, time is therapeutic in that it can allow you to put things in perspective, adapt to change, and process the feelings and attend to the grief work. The passage of time, plus these experiences, reduces your pain. But if you seek to avoid your grief, if you try to circumvent the mourning process, time will be distinctly harmful for you. It will only increase the pressure and strengthen the resistance to healthy mourning, providing fertile ground for the development of other problems. If you have not attended to your mourning, your pain can be as acute and fresh years later as it was the day after the death of your loved one. During these years, other complications will probably have developed as well. It is similar to the healing of a wound. If your wound is cleaned and properly dressed, with time and treatment it will heal. However, if you ignore the wound, and it is not appropriately cleaned and tended to, time will only mark the progress of festering infection.

In contrast, the person who has successfully completed grief work still will feel a sense of loss, but time will have helped the healing and the pain will be more in memory than experienced at that moment. In sum, the passage of time can help you successfully adjust and adapt to your loss, but only if you are actively undertaking your grief work.

The Course of Grief

The intensity of your grief and mourning will fluctuate over time. You must be prepared for this and not let anyone misinterpret it to you.

There are numerous examples of how your grief and mourning vary over time. One example is the "six-month phenomenon." You may have been coping for some time immediately after the death of your loved one, only to experience a resurgence of grief months later. (The term *six-month* should not be interpreted rigidly since the phenomenon can occur anytime after an initial period of stabilization, usually, but not always, between four to nine months after the death. Six months is a good average of when it happens.) This is most often seen following sudden death, but also occurs after some anticipated deaths. You may find this experience to be quite disheartening and discouraging, and may imagine you are losing your mind, going out of control, or are backsliding in your grief.

Actually, however, you are merely coming out of the daze that you have been in through the early months following the loss. Now that everyday life has commenced, you are confronted with the painful reality of your loss in striking, unexpected ways. For example, a widow may only truly comprehend her aloneness when she struggles to put up the storm windows by herself the first autumn after her husband has died. Or, the implications about your being without your loved one forever may only hit you when the season changes for the first time after the death, when you have to go Christmas shopping alone, or when your daily routine settles in enough to emphasize your loneliness. Sometimes it occurs when you realize that you have a little more trouble than before recalling your loved one's voice, or in picturing him in a room. At these times, you have a more complete understanding of the ramifications of your loss as you see that life goes on without your loved one and that it will continue to do so. These observations make the permanence and finality of your loss much more real than before, and acute symptoms of grief temporarily may reoccur.

Usually you are not prepared for the impact of these experiences and mistakenly may believe that you are back to where you started in terms of working through your mourning. These intermittently acute realizations of the profound implications of your loss are not uncommon for several years after the death, depending upon who has died and what the circumstances were.

One woman reported how she finally really "knew" her loved one wasn't coming back and would never be part of her life as before, although the person had been dead for several years and the mourner had acknowledged that fact. One day she was washing her head in the shower when all of a sudden, from out of nowhere (she hadn't been thinking about it consciously), she experienced an intense stab of grief, just like a sword going through her heart. At that very moment she "knew" to the depths of her very being that there was no chance of her ever having her deceased loved one back. She hadn't consciously been hoping for this, but on some very deep, emotional level she had held on to some hope that it could happen. This is not unusual. She was a normal, healthy mourner and had been doing her grief work.

This example indicates both how hard it is to truly accept the implications of a major loss and how this process contributes to the highs and lows of the course of mourning.

It will be important for you to remember that your bereavement will not follow a decreasing linear pattern. It will not be static. Your grief will have many ups and downs, twists and turns. Some of these fluctuations are caused by anniversary reactions, holidays, specific life events you experience, and changes in the factors affecting your grief (for example, changes in your social support or the presence of other stresses in your life). They temporarily can intensify your grief. Some ups and downs will last longer than others—for example, for a few days as opposed to a few minutes or hours. Sometimes you will feel that you have a greater acceptance of the death than at other times. You can expect that some effects of grief will subside over a period of time and then increase again a while after the death. Fluctuation can be expected also over a shorter range of time. Even the person who is acutely grieving may not evidence it twenty-four hours a day, since mourning sometimes must be put aside for the ongoing demands of everyday life.

You may find it quite frustrating to have to experience your grief again after you have had a break from it. This fluctuation can be stressful, especially when you desperately want to return to normal and you had a small taste of it when you had your break. Nevertheless, grief changes; it ebbs and flows for some time. You need to recognize this without forgetting that at some point it will settle down for the most part, except for occasional upsurges.

For many mourners—especially sudden death mourners—this pattern emerges: You experience acute grief following the death. After this, you establish what you believe is a plateau or a new equilibrium; however, it is not permanent. You think you have your grief stabilized, but then experience the aforementioned phenomenon in which your grief is intensified over its previous lessening. Shock has worn off, and life has made you feel your loss more poignantly. When this is worked through, your grief starts to decline again. It may fluctuate thereafter, but often not in as major a fashion as in the six-month phenomenon.

Grief can flare up at other occasions, too, years after your loved one's death. Certain experiences later in life temporarily can resurrect intense grief from earlier losses. These new experiences in your life may give importance to aspects of your loss that were insignificant at the time your loved one died. For example, the woman saddened because her husband is not there to escort her daughter down the aisle at the daughter's wedding; the young adult who misses the presence of his brother at his college graduation; the young woman who recognizes she is now an adult and laments the fact that she never got the chance to know her parents as adults, since they died when she was so young; the woman who grieves for the loss of her mother when she herself becomes a mother—all these individuals are experiencing normal grief reactions brought about by certain specific events, changes, and experiences that poignantly illustrate to them the loss they have sustained. Your loved one's absence is particularly noticeable and difficult at these times. Within appropriate limits, these, like anniversary and holiday reactions, are normal and expectable.

Related to these later grief-evoking events are "correspondence phenomena." Here we see increased anxiety, along with other heightened emotions and upsurges in grief that can occur when you reach the age of someone who dies before you (for example, reaching the age your father was when he died) or when someone else reaches the age you were when someone died (for example, your child reaches the age you were when your mother died.)

The Duration of Grief

In general, people assume that they should be over their grief in only a fraction of the time it actually takes to recover. The duration of your grief is variable and will depend upon the particular factors influencing your individual grief response.

It was once believed that the normal duration of mourning was only six weeks. Now we know that some of the processes may take up to three or more years to be accommodated, depending upon who has died and the particular death, with most of the more intense symptoms of acute grief subsiding within six to twelve months. However, the saying "Once bereaved, always bereaved" still remains true. There are parts of the loss that will continue to be with you until you die. Also, there are aspects of the long-term mourning process which continue on for many years, if not forever. (See chapters 14 and 17 for more on this.) This does not mean that you will be in acute grief for all this time, just that some aspects of grief will take longer than others to work through. For example, after the first eight months of widowhood, you may not be experiencing the severe symptoms of grief you initially had, but it may take you another year or so to feel that you are as close to being back to your old self as you ever will be. And it may take another two years before you may be interested in dating again.

The duration of your grief, as well as which aspects are more easily resolvable than others, will depend upon you and the death you have experienced. This is why there is no set time period for how long it *should* take. What is an abnormally long grief experience in one person's situation may be fairly typical in another's. It depends upon you, the meaning of your loss to you, the circumstances of the death, your social support, and your physical state. Without information in all these areas, it cannot even be determined whether or not the course and duration of your mourning is appropriate. However, as long as your mourning behavior does not severely impair your ability to function (physically or psychosocially) for too long, is not harmful to your long-term adjustment, or does not represent more severe pathology, it can be viewed as not abnormal. This allows for a wide variety of reactions, fluctuating symptom intensities, and different durations.

Anniversary and Holiday Reactions

As explained above, most people incorrectly assume that grief diminishes with time and that once it declines it never erupts again; your symptoms decrease in intensity, going from high to low in a straight line. We know that this is not necessarily true. Research shows, for instance, that the mourning of bereaved parents can intensify again for a while after subsiding within the first several years. We also know that if you are bereaved from the sudden death of a loved one, you may feel that you have achieved a new balance and then, around four to nine months following the death, can either undergo an increase in symptoms or, at the very least, have experiences which suggest to you that you are backsliding in your grief. These are two special types of cases. There are others as well which illustrate that specific bereavements do not necessarily only diminish over time. However, there is a general phenomenon that almost all bereaved individuals experience. These are anniversary and holiday reactions.

Anniversary reactions are brief upsurges in your grief that occur during certain times of the year (for example, during anniversaries of important events, birthdays, or holidays) or in the presence of certain stimuli (for example, a special song, photograph, or location). Some of these anniversary dates pertain specifically to important events related to your loved one's death. You may become depressed on the anniversary of the death or on the date your loved one received her terminal diagnosis. Birthdays and wedding anniversaries also may be occasions on which you experience temporarily intensified grief symptoms.

These are the days on which you are most reminded of your loss by the painful absence of the person you love who cannot be there with you to celebrate. For some, the birthday of the loved one is more difficult to cope with, while for others the anniversary of the death is harder. You will need to discover which dates and holidays are the most difficult for you personally and then plan accordingly. The most important thing for you to remember is that these reactions are normal, within limits. As long as they do not unduly interfere for too long with your functioning or reduce your ability to have enjoyment and gratification in life, these intermittent pangs of grief do not have to be incompatible with your recovery. If you become overly symptomatic or your defense against these anniversary symptoms starts to require too much effort, then the reactions have gone outside the normal limits.

All of us have an unconscious time clock within us that keeps track of anniversary dates whether or not we consciously recognize it. It is very common for someone who is experiencing an inexplicable increase in symptoms to realize later that it is the anniversary of a significant event. It is important that you know that this is a common phenomenon. It does not mean you are regressing. It also is important to recognize that you may need some support at these times, and that you plan how to get it. For example, one widow recognized that it was too painful to spend New Year's Eve alone, so she began inviting other widows and widowers to her house each year in order that they would all have others with whom to spend the holiday.

Holidays are especially hard for the bereaved. In our society you are supposed to be together with your loved ones at holiday time. This is why you might experience so much anxiety when anticipating the first holidays without your loved one, and why your grief may increase intermittently when they arrive. Usually, however, your anticipation is much worse than the actual holiday.

Especially in the first few years, you may be uncertain about how to spend these days and whether to continue certain family rituals that would have taken place if your loved one were alive. Remember, there are no right or wrong answers about what you should or should not do during the holidays after your loved one dies. You may want to continue the traditions (for example, you may have a big Thanksgiving dinner or put up the Christmas tree), or you may want to change them if you feel they will be too painful without the presence of your loved one (for example, you don't hang stockings on the mantelpiece at Christmas or you make only a brief appearance at the traditional neighborhood New Year's Eve party.) (See chapter 18 for a full discussion of how to cope with the holidays.)

Appropriate Expectations You Can Have for Yourself in Grief

Taking all of the information you've read so far, the following is a list of appropriate expectations that you can have in grief. Evaluate yourself on each one and see if you are maintaining realistic expectations for yourself.
   You can expect that:

Your grief will take longer than most people think.

Your grief will take more energy than you would have ever imagined.

Your grief will involve many changes and be continually developing.

Your grief will show itself in all spheres of your life: psychological, social, and physical.

Your grief will depend upon how you perceive the loss.

You will grieve for many things both symbolic and tangible, not just the death alone.

You will grieve for what you have lost already and for what you have lost for the future.

Your grief will entail mourning not only for the actual person you lost but also for all of the hopes, dreams, and unfulfilled expectations you held for and with that person, and for the needs that will go unmet because of the death.

Your grief will involve a wide variety of feelings and reactions, not solely those that are generally thought of as grief, such as depression and sadness.

The loss will resurrect old issues, feelings, and unresolved conflicts from the past.

You will have some identity confusion as a result of this major loss and the fact that you are experiencing reactions that may be quite different

You may have a combination of anger and depression, such as irritability, frustration, annoyance, or intolerance.

You will feel some anger and guilt, or at least some manifestation of these emotions.

You may have a lack of self-concern.

You may experience grief spasms, acute upsurges of grief that occur suddenly with no warning.

You will have trouble thinking (memory, organization and intellectual processing) and making decisions.

You may feel like you are going crazy.

You may be obsessed with the death and preoccupied with the deceased.

You may begin a search for meaning and may question your religion and/or philosophy of life.

You may find yourself acting socially in ways that are different from before.

You may find yourself having a number of physical reactions.

You may find that there are certain dates, events, and stimuli that bring upsurges in grief.

Society will have unrealistic expectations about your mourning and may respond inappropriately to you.

Certain experiences later in life may resurrect intense grief for you temporarily.

In summary, your grief will bring with it, depending upon the combination of factors above, an intense amount of emotion that will surprise you and those around you. Most of us are unprepared for the global response we have to a major loss. Our expectations tend to be too unrealistic, and more often than not we receive insufficient assistance from friends and society. Your grief will not only be more intense than you expected but it will also be manifested in more areas and ways than you ever anticipated. You can expect to see brief upsurges of it at anniversary and holiday times, and in response to certain stimuli that remind you of what you have lost. Your grief will be very idiosyncratic and dependent upon the meaning of your loss, your own personal characteristics, the type of death, your social support, and your physical state.

Unresolved Grief

In some cases, mourning does not go as well as we would hope. You may not pay attention to the loss, or process all the feelings in a timely manner. Usually this is the result of your attempting to deny or avoid the pain of grief and the realization of what the implications of the loss are for you. It also is an attempt to avoid letting go of your lost loved one. Unfortunately, although your motivation is understandable, you cause many additional problems for yourself by not coping actively and thoroughly with your loss.

Unresolved grief is indicated in three ways (Siggins 1966):

1. An absence of normal grief
2. The prolongation of normal grief
3. The distortion of normal grief

This means that if there is no normal mourning, if it goes on for too long, or if it is abnormally distorted, then something has gone wrong.

There are a number of ways in which the typical process of grief can be sidetracked. These are termed "unresolved" forms of grief because in each there has been some disturbance of the normal progress toward resolution. They are listed below. Knowing these forms is important, because what is helpful in one form may be harmful in another. The same helping techniques have different impacts depending on the particular type of unresolved grief to which they are applied. (The following descriptions of forms of unresolved grief have been taken from the analyses of Averill [1968], Parkes and Weiss [1983], and Raphael [1983].)

Absent Grief. In this situation, feelings of grief and mourning processes are totally absent. It is as if the death never occurred. It requires either that you completely deny the death or that you remain in a stage of shock.

Inhibited Grief. In this form of unresolved grief, there is a lasting inhibition of many of the manifestations of normal grief, with the appearance of other symptoms, such as physical complaints, in their place. You may be able to relinquish and mourn only certain aspects of the deceased and not others—for example, the positive aspects but not the negative ones.

Stella came to therapy because her deteriorating physical condition suggested a significant depression. She was compliant and easy to please in treatment. Investigation revealed that her estranged husband had committed suicide several years earlier. She had attended to the tasks of the funeral and then resumed her life as if nothing had occurred. There were no behavioral expressions of any grief and no internal processing of her mourning. Shortly afterwards Stella developed severe stomach difficulties, and the next several years were devoted to focusing on her physical complaints.

Delayed Grief. Normal or distorted grief may be delayed for an extended period of time, up to years, especially if there are pressing responsibilities or you feel you cannot deal with the process at that time. A full grief reaction eventually may be initiated by another loss or by some event related to the original loss. For instance, a pet's death can trigger a response for a loved one who died years earlier but who had never been mourned because you felt you had to be strong to take care of other family members. Meanwhile, only an inhibited form of grief may be present.

Randi was a high school senior when her mother died suddenly following a successful heart operation. Her father also had died unexpectedly the previous year. Randi was always the domestic one, and she took over the task of managing the house and paying the bills for her two siblings and herself. She also was the "strong one" and never took time to grieve. Several years after the death of her mother, Randi entered nursing school. One day she went to give a cardiac patient an injection, but instead of seeing the patient in the bed she "saw" her own mother. This initiated an acute grief reaction.

Distorted Grief. In this form of unresolved grief, there frequently is an exaggeration or distortion of one or more of the manifestations of normal grief, while at the same time other aspects of your grief may be suppressed. Two common patterns are extreme anger and extreme guilt (also known as "conflicted grief"). Extreme anger is often associated with your having had a dependent relationship with the deceased or with deaths that are sudden and unexpected and for which someone is blamed (for example, a medical caregiver's negligence, or where the deceased died violently, such as through murder, accident, or disaster). Extreme guilt is often associated with your having had a markedly ambivalent relationship with the deceased.

Felicia's ten-year-old son died from acute appendicitis eight months prior to her referral for therapy. Felicia was an overemotional woman who for years had become hysterical whenever she had to contact the pediatrician about her son. She had strongly ambivalent feelings toward her son because his father deserted her when she discovered she was pregnant. At the time of the appendicitis attack, the pediatrician had heard Felicia exaggerate her son's symptoms once too often and consequently responded too slowly to save the child's life. Felicia's grief continued unabated as she constantly blamed herself for not convincing the pediatrician of the gravity of the illness, and she was filled with self-reproach for the resentment she frequently had felt for her son.

Chronic Grief. In chronic grief you continuously exhibit intense grief reactions that would be appropriate only in the early stages of acute grief. Mourning fails to draw to its natural conclusion. There is an inability to relinquish the deceased, and it almost seems that you keep the deceased alive with your grief. Intense yearning is symptomatic of this grief. Such mourning typically occurs after the loss of dependent and irreplaceable relationships, deaths that are unexpected, and deaths of children. It usually indicates that you had extraordinary, and possibly abnormal, emotional investment in the deceased.

> Bill was a shy, insecure man who was devoted to his wife and built his entire emotional world around her. She handled all the family finances, organized their social schedule, and raised the children independently. Most of his social contacts with others were through her. After she died, he was both deeply depressed and isolated. He went through only the minimum attempts at communicating with others, being fearful of them. He spent most of his time alone and arranged for a housekeeper to handle the domestic duties and take responsibility for the children. Six years after the death he still had made no changes in his personal or social worlds.

Unanticipated Grief. This occurs after a sudden, unanticipated loss and is so disruptive that your recovery usually is complicated. In unanticipated grief, you are unable to grasp the full implications of the loss. Your adaptive capabilities are seriously assaulted, and you suffer extreme feelings of bewilderment, anxiety, self-reproach, and depression that cause you to be unable to function normally. There is difficulty in accepting the loss, despite your intellectual recognition of the death, and the death may continue to seem inexplicable. Grief symptoms persist much longer than usual. Avoidance and anxiety eventually lead to states of anxious withdrawal since the world has become such a frightening place. (Note that this is different from the unanticipated grief response which, in and of itself, is a normal reaction following sudden death [see chapter 6], and not a specific form of unresolved grief unless it progresses to the state described here and lasts beyond reasonable expectations for this type of loss.)

> Jane's husband was hit by a drunk driver after he had stopped to help a motorist change a tire. Jane was completely overwhelmed when informed of

the accident, and this feeling stayed with her for several years. She could not believe that the death had actually occurred, and she frequently had to remind herself that her husband was not going to return. Many of her grief symptoms persisted for an abnormally long period of time. Although she was able to go through the motions of putting her life back together again, Jane became chronically anxious and apprehensive, always awaiting another trauma to befall her. Jane dated, but she was never able to make a commitment to another man for fear that he would be taken from her too.

There is another form of grief that is not unresolved but is often mistaken for it. This is *abbreviated grief,* a short-lived but normal form of grief. It may occur because of your immediate replacement of the lost person, as when you marry a new spouse right after the first one dies, or because you were not that attached to the deceased in the first place. Often it occurs when a significant amount of anticipatory grief has been completed prior to a death—for example, after a long illness in which there was time to finish unfinished business and gradually prepare for the loss. After the actual death occurs in these situations, you grieve, but much of your grief work has been accomplished already. For this reason your bereavement period after the death, while painful, can be relatively shorter.

> Becky's mother succumbed to cancer after an illness of several years. Becky had gone through a long process of anticipatory grief during the illness and consequently, after a short but intense grief reaction at the time of her mother's death, was left with few acute symptoms. Becky was able to pick up her life because she had received therapeutic help during the illness that had allowed her to continue to maintain some outside interests that could sustain her after the death. She had been as prepared as possible for the emptiness that would ensue when she would no longer have someone to care for, and had made appropriate plans to occupy herself with other caregiving functions. Although she missed her mother deeply, Becky's acute grief was not long-lasting.

As can be seen in all of these forms of unresolved grief, there are elements of what is normally seen in acute grief. With the exception of the unanticipated grief syndrome, in which selected aspects of normal grief become generalized and chronic, what makes these forms of grief different from normal grief is that some of the symptoms of normal grief that ordinarily would be present are denied or repressed and/or there is an extraordinary attempt to hold on to the lost relationship by not dealing with either the implications of the loss or the feelings it brings up.

Reasons for Failure to Mourn

There are a number of specific reasons why people fail to resolve their grief work in a normal fashion. In this section we will identify the issues which can interfere with your grief resolution. Much of this discussion is based on the excellent work of the Massachusetts psychiatrist Aaron Lazare (1979).

There are persons who do not permit themselves to grieve because of specific psychological fears that interfere with the process. For example, some people will not grieve for fear of losing control or appearing weak to themselves and others. Other people have expressed the concern that if they started to cry the tears would never stop, or have believed that they could not grieve because their loved one had been such a large part of themselves that they could not bear to recognize the loss and deal with the death. Still others are afraid to give up the pain, since it binds them closely to the deceased. There are individuals who do not grieve or get on with their lives because of some unspoken but powerful contract with the deceased. For instance, they tell the deceased and themselves, "I will never get over losing you and will *never* allow myself to be happy again." Some mourners are afraid to review their relationship with the deceased for fear of discovering some feelings in the relationship that would be unacceptable to them, such as anger or guilt. Others do not grieve a present loss because it resurrects the pain of a past loss or because they are too overwhelmed with a number of simultaneous losses to deal with any of them.

It is not uncommon for people to have difficulty with grief because of their social conditioning. As noted earlier, males may find that social conditioning interferes with the expression of feelings and types of behaviors that are necessary in grief (for example, expressing feelings and needing social support). In contrast, women traditionally have had more trouble dealing with anger and with decision making because they are conditioned to be sweet, passive, and dependent. Any particular fear, conflict, issue, or conditioned response that interferes with your yielding to the normal process of grief will create a resistance to mourning. It will need to be recognized and worked through if your grief is to be resolved.

Besides individual psychological causes for resistance to mourning, there are several social causes. When a loss is not socially defined as a loss, the social support for grief work is inadequate or nonexistent. This typically occurs in cases involving symbolic psychosocial losses; it also occurs after deaths in which the relationship was not socially recognized. For example, if you lose a lover, a friend, or a pet, the death may go unrecognized and unacknowledged by those you know. (See chapter 4 for a discussion of this topic.)

At other times, important social support isn't available because people are so distressed by the death that they shy away. This is seen after "socially unspeakable" losses such as suicide, murder, and the death of a child. In all of these cases, you do not have the support and assistance necessary to get through the painful process of grief. When this happens for the reasons just mentioned, or for others such as geographical distance, you lose a vital aid to handling the difficult issues demanded in grief work. Research repeatedly shows that a lack of support usually leads to difficulty in grief resolution. Problems also may occur as a result of inappropriate expectations held by others. In some situations, the grief is not addressed because of the mourner's reluctance to give up the attention or reinforcements she may have been getting as a grief-striken person.

Bereavement as a Health Risk

Studies of physical illness, along with investigations of mortality rates, indicate that bereavement can escalate into a serious health risk for you as a bereaved person. For this reason, the importance of adequate resolution of your grief work cannot be stressed too much. Certainly, some degree of physical distress is a normal component of acute grief; however, this does not mean you should take it lightly.

While health problems are *not* inevitable, the potential for serious harm is there if you do not pay attention to your grief. Interestingly, only some of the evidence suggests that bereavement illnesses are caused directly by your responses to the death itself. Much of it supports the idea that your adaptation, reorganization, and adjustment after the loss, and the psychosocial and physical situations existing following the death, can be just as important as the actual death in influencing your health. This suggests that the ongoing state of mourning, occurring after the decline in acute grief, is also a time of physical vulnerability to the bereaved, and that you would do well to monitor your health during this time as well.

This concludes the section of the book devoted to learning more about grief in general. In the following section, we will investigate the experiences of grief caused by different forms of death.

PART

II

Grieving Different Forms of Death

6

Sudden versus
Anticipated Death

O NE of the most important considerations in the death of your loved
one is whether or not you expected the death to occur. Had you
anticipated the loss of this person at this time?

I have seen bereaved individuals argue over which type of death is worse:
a sudden death, such as an accident or heart attack, or an anticipated death,
such as a death from terminal illness. Although it is unwise to compare
different types of death, bereaved individuals seem sometimes to need to
point out the special problems they have as a result of the type of death
their loved one experienced. For example, someone whose loved one died
in an automobile accident may say that her loss was worse and may challenge
another whose loved one died from a terminal illness by saying: "At least
you got to say good-bye. You were prepared. You were able to be with
your husband when he died." In contrast, the person whose loved one died
from a terminal illness may say: "At least you did not have to see your
husband suffer and waste away. You did not have to deal with his painful
recognition that he was dying and would never see our children grow up.
You did not have to wait for it to happen."

It does not help to compare losses in order to decide which is the "worst";
all losses are painful. The deaths of those we love, no matter how they
occurred, will leave us bereft. What we do know is that the difference between a sudden death and one that has been anticipated is not in the amount
of pain that the survivor suffers but in the impact it has upon that person's
ability to cope and to go about the rest of her life.

An example will illustrate how the differences in coping are affected. Sup-
pose you are standing on a street corner and you see someone approach you

as if he were going to hit you. If you decide you can't run, the usual response is for you to ready yourself for the assault. You steel yourself against the oncoming blow. You assume a fighting stance. You position yourself so that you will have the leverage to move to avoid the hit and then shift your weight so you can retaliate. You put up your fists to defend yourself. When your assailant knocks you down you are ready for it and, despite the pain of the blow, get up to defend yourself. This is like the situation of an anticipated death.

In contrast, imagine that you are standing on a street corner minding your own business and all of a sudden someone comes from behind you and hits you. The blow comes from out of the blue and you are knocked to the ground. Before you can respond to this, you have to figure out: What happened? What am I doing on the ground? Where is this pain coming from? What do I have to do now? This is what happens in sudden death.

The pain of the blow is the same in both instances. In each situation you are knocked to the ground. However, if you had seen the blow coming, you'd have prepared for it and understood what had happened when you were hit. You could then direct your energies toward coping with the attack. In sudden death, this preparation and comprehension is missing. As a result, the ability to cope with the situation—that is, to decide what to do in response to the blow—is compromised since the shock and unpredictability of it has stunned you so much. You are at a relative disadvantage to the person who had seen the blow coming and could prepare to defend himself.

Sudden Death

In both sudden death and anticipated death, there is pain. However, while the grief is not greater in sudden death, the capacity to cope is diminished. Grievers are shocked and stunned by the sudden loss of their loved one. The loss is so disruptive that recovery almost always is complicated. This is because the adaptive capacities are so severely assaulted and the ability to cope is so critically injured that functioning is seriously impaired. Grievers are overwhelmed.

If you are such a griever, you probably are suffering extreme feelings of bewilderment, anxiety, self-reproach, and depression, and you may be unable to continue normal life. You had no preparation and no time to gradually absorb the reality that the world was about to change dramatically.

Instead, there was a sudden destruction of the world you used to know. There was no gradual transition nor time to make changes in yourself, your expectations about your life, or your world. In sudden death you are called upon to face a massive gap between the way the world *should* be, with your loved one alive, and the way the world *is*. The person whom you loved, and who provided you with security, is taken away without any warning. This is a major violation of your expectations. Your sense of the world and of control is assaulted.

This is not to say that these issues are not confronted by those whose loved one's death was anticipated. The difference is that they have had a valuable period of anticipation that placed the death in the context of events that were predictable and made sense. Although they experienced pain when their loved one died, they could see what caused the death. Ideally, they had been preparing for the death and dealing with their feelings about it. They were able to finish unfinished business with their loved one, to say "I love you," and to do the things they wanted to do for the person before he died. While there certainly are many problems and emotional demands associated with losing a loved one in an anticipated death (see section below), at least when the death comes, the grievers' coping capacities have been directed toward dealing with that expectable end. The loss makes sense.

After a sudden death, the loss doesn't make sense. The critically important understanding of what happened is missing. The sudden shock of losing someone we love without warning so stuns us that we cannot comprehend what has transpired. Consequently, if your loved one died suddenly, you may be unable to grasp the situation and find it difficult to understand the implications of the loss. Accepting that the death occurred can be difficult, even if you intellectually recognize that it happened. The death may continue to seem inexplicable for a long period of time. You repeatedly will have to go over the story of the accident or of the heart attack to try to make sense of the loss after the fact.

Because you were not prepared for the death and it had no understandable context, you will try to deal with your lack of anticipation by putting the loss into a series of events. You may find yourself looking back at the time leading up to the death and searching for clues that could have indicated what was to come. For example, one woman looked back on the days preceding her husband's sudden fatal heart attack and "perceived" warnings she had missed initially. This tendency to reconstruct events in your mind in order to allow for some anticipation of the death is quite common. It is an attempt to restructure what happened so that it seems you had some inkling that the death was going to occur: "He really didn't look that good in the last few weeks as I look back on it now" or "You know, he was visiting his sisters whom he had not seen in a long time. Maybe he knew that something would happen." This retrospective reconstruction of events makes the situation more manageable. It gives a perception of logical progression, of control and predictability, and retrospectively provides you with some anticipation and preparation.

However, problems arise when you hold yourself responsible for not perceiving cues that were actually either imperceptible or nonexistent prior to the death. Frequently grievers react emotionally and respond to what they perceive as unmet responsibility. One woman felt inordinate guilt for many years for not recognizing that her mother had been having some difficulty climbing the stairs. After her mother died suddenly from a burst aneurysm, the daughter felt that she should have recognized the mother's impairment and known that this meant that something was wrong with her. However, unless this woman had been a physician and had run tests on her mother, there really was no way she could have known.

For survivors whose loved ones die suddenly, grief symptoms tend to persist longer. The physical and emotional shock that is a normal part of acute grief appears to be more intense and long-lasting. This may further demoralize you as you are trying to understand what happened to you and to cope with a drastically altered world, in addition to dealing with your feelings of loss and grief. You have the same grief tasks as all mourners, but you must cope with extra stresses that leave you relatively more depleted and disadvantaged.

If you have lost a loved one from sudden death, you know that you had no chance to say good-bye and no opportunity to finish unfinished business with your loved one. Most probably these are major issues for you. The lack of time to bring this important relationship to a positive close causes much anguish to those of us whose loved ones die without warning. We wish that we could have known in order to say and do what we wanted to; we wish we could have just one more brief moment with our loved one to tell him we loved him, apologize for ways we might have hurt him, explain why we treated him the way we did, or let him know what he meant to us.

You may feel a profound loss of security and confidence in the world. After all, you have been taught a dramatic lesson: Loved ones can be snatched away without warning. You may always await another loss to befall. Research has shown that widows whose husbands died suddenly are slower to move toward remarriage, since they are unwilling to risk future unanticipated loss again for themselves and their children. Avoidance and anxiety eventually can lead to states of anxious withdrawal since the world has become such a frightening, unpredictable place.

In some ways, the consequences of losing a loved one to sudden death can last a lifetime. While for some mourners this can be evidenced in chronic grief or persistent anxiety in which security and confidence never totally return, for others the consequences are less dramatic, though no less powerful. The best example I can give of this is a personal one. All of the deaths in my husband's life have been anticipated deaths. When I am a little late returning from work my husband automatically assumes that I have been held up on the telephone or have run overtime with my patients. Unless I am dramatically late, he is not unduly disturbed and assumes I will be home soon. In contrast, I have a much different response when he is later than expected. This is because all of the important deaths in my life have been sudden, unexpected ones. As a consequence, when he is later than usual I automatically assume that something terrible has happened. I experience a considerable amount of apprehension. What makes me different from someone who has not worked so hard on these issues is that I will not immediately jump to call the hospitals or the police. I will remind myself that statistically the chances are that he is all right and that there are reasons for his delay. Nevertheless, I am concerned.

Does this mean that I love my husband more than he loves me because I am more concerned when he is late? I think not. What it reveals is the scars of sudden death. I have been taught all too well that the people I love can be snatched from me without warning, and that death doesn't always happen to someone else.

This awareness that you can lose someone without warning does not have to be negative. It can prompt you to deal with your loved ones on a timely basis. It can help you not to put off until tomorrow those things you should say and do today. It may assist you in making sure you don't have too much unfinished business with the people you love. If your loved one died from a sudden death, you know that tomorrow is promised to no one. This awareness also can help you keep in mind what is important in life, so you don't get lost in trivial matters and lose sight of those things that are most important to you. It is an ironic but positive consequence of sudden death that it can make you appreciate life more than you ever would have if you had not undergone such a traumatic experience. This does not mean that you would seek out such a loss in order to teach yourself such a lesson, but it does let you know that you can pull something meaningful out of such a tragedy.

Again, it is important to remember that I am not saying that there is a difference in the pain of loss or the tasks of grief for those who lose loved ones suddenly versus those who lose them after a period of anticipation. The main point is that an unanticipated death so profoundly affects mourners that it is extra hard for them to adjust. They have less to work with for some time because of their lack of preparation, and this affects them in all spheres: emotionally, cognitively, physically, and socially. However, while sudden death survivors are at high risk for unresolved grief, they *can* work through their additional problems to resolve their mourning successfully. It just will take longer and demand more from them and from those who seek to comfort them than if they did not have to deal with these additional burdens.

Anticipated Death

In the previous section, we looked at the quality of the sudden death mourning experience and the demands placed upon you as a mourner. In this section, we look at mourning in anticipation of a loss and at the unique demands of this type of grief. You will see that although anticipated death does not leave you with the same confusion and assaulted capacities as does sudden death, it is not without its own problems.

Why Anticipatory Grief Is Important

If your loved one died suddenly, you can do nothing to change either the dying experience or the situation, since your loved one already is dead. You must cope with an event that has already occurred, a fait accompli. You cannot do anything to make a difference at this point. Your grief and mourning will consist of dealing with this fact, picking up the pieces after the death, and coping with the altered life that remains. In contrast, in anticipatory grief, you have the golden opportunity to say and do things during the illness that may help not only you, your dying loved one, and other family members, but which may create a more positive bereavement experience after the death for those of you left behind.

It has been well documented by research that your experience in your loved one's dying process will have a profound effect on your grief after his death. To the extent that your experiences with him and your mourning in anticipation of his death are healthy, you will have a better bereavement experience after his death than you would have if the predeath experiences were unhealthy. In this sense, you can do something during the illness about what you must contend with after the death.

Both you, as a family member, and your dying loved one will mourn in anticipation of the death. Your loved one will mourn for all that has been and will be lost, including himself. (Further discussion of the experience for the dying patient is outside the scope of this book; see chapter 20 for references on this topic.)

The rest of this discussion on anticipatory grief pertains to you and others who love the dying person. You can expect that your grief will be influenced not only by the type of person you are but also by who and what you are losing, how you are losing it (that is, the type of illness and death involved), how your loved one and other family members respond, and the social and physical factors influencing you in this situation.

Anticipatory Grief Involving Past, Present, and Future Losses

In contrast to the implications of the term *anticipatory*, which suggest that it is solely a future loss that is being mourned, in anticipatory grief there are losses in three time frames which are being mourned: past, present, and future. This means that the grief that you experience during the terminal illness of your loved one actually is stimulated by losses that have already occurred in the past and those that are currently occurring, as well as those that are yet to come. For illustration, let us consider the case of Mrs. Jones, whose husband is dying from cancer.

In nursing her husband through his final bout with cancer, it is not uncommon for Mrs. Jones to grieve over the vibrant and healthy man she *already has lost* to cancer and to mourn their altered relationship and life-style, and their dreams for the future that will never be realized. It is not unusual for her to remember the activities they shared when he was well; to recall how, in contrast to his present state, he was strong and independent; to grieve over the fact that so many limitations have been placed on their lives; and to mourn for all that has been taken away by the illness.

Each of these losses is a fait accompli. This is what is meant by mourning over losses in the past. This past may be recent, as in the case of Mr. Jones's altered life-style, or in the more distant past, as in the lost opportunities Mrs. Jones regrets in light of the limited time she has left with her husband. You can see that even though the subject content of the losses may pertain to the future (that is, in terms of the hopes, expectations, dreams, and plans held for it), the loss is one which already has occurred. Even in the shadow of the ultimate loss of death, there are other losses that cause grief.

In addition, Mrs. Jones grieves for the *ongoing losses* she sees. She witnesses her husband's progressive debilitation, increasing dependence, continual uncertainty, and decreasing control. A fundamental part of her anticipatory grief is for what currently is being lost and for the future that is being eroded. This is different from grief about what will happen in the future. It pertains to mourning over what is slipping away from her right now, for the sense of having her loved one being taken from her, and for what the increasing awareness of Mr. Jones's impending death means to her at this very moment.

Mrs. Jones also grieves for *future losses* yet to come. Not only is Mr. Jones's ultimate death mourned but also the losses that will arise before his death, for example the fact that she and Mr. Jones will be unable to take their annual vacation this year or that she knows he will lose his mobility and become bedridden. Mourning is not limited exclusively to losses that happen prior to death; it also may focus on losses that will happen after the death as a consequence of it: the loneliness, the insecurity, the social discomfort, the assaulted identity, the economic uncertainty, the life-style alterations, the fact that he will not be present at their daughter's wedding, and so forth.

Anticipatory Grief Does Not Have to Mean Premature Detachment

As you can see, Mrs. Jones is not focusing solely on her husband's eventual physical death. She mourns for what has already been lost, what is being lost, and what will be lost in the future. Some people get concerned that this mourning could mean that Mrs. Jones necessarily will pull away from her husband and withdraw her emotional attachment to him too soon before the death. This "premature detachment" occurs when people mourn too successfully in the sense that they grieve the loved one and withdraw their emotional investment in the person prior to that person's actual death. We see this in people who abandon their loved ones in institutions or after illnesses have gone on for too long. Certainly this is a serious concern. It is not fair to those who are dying to be mourned so effectively that we no longer have a connection with them even when they are still among us. However, this does not have to happen. You can grieve the loss of your loved one in the future and still be involved with him in the present.

This is the key to healthy anticipatory grief—to start to grieve the loss of a loved one in the future without separating prematurely from him now.

Like Mrs. Jones, you can start to withdraw your emotional investment in the hopes, dreams, and expectations of a future that would include your dying loved one. You can start gradually to detach yourself from the emotions you have placed in the expectation and desire for this person's being available for interaction with you after the terminal illness. In essence, you must recognize and prepare for the future in which you will be without this person physically. But you can continue to be involved with him in the here-and-now. Continued involvement with your loved one and maximizing whatever possibilities are left for living together for as long as possible are not inconsistent with anticipatory grief. We can mourn the future without relinquishing the present.

Mutually Contradictory Demands

Finally, a critically important task in anticipatory grief is for you to balance the mutually contradictory demands of the process. You are being pulled in three opposing directions:

1. You move toward your dying loved one as a consequence of directing increased attention, energy, and behavior toward the person you love during his illness.

2. At the same time, the status quo is being maintained, as your ongoing involvement with the dying patient continues on as many levels as possible; in this regard, you stay the same with your dying loved one.

3. Opposite to this, however, you are starting to move away from your loved one, beginning to withdraw emotional energy from the image of him as someone who will be present in your future, and from the hopes, dreams, and expectations you had for him and your relationship in the future.

This leaves you to balance the mutually conflicting demands of simultaneously holding on to, letting go of, and drawing closer to the dying patient. While you are managing this juggling act, you also are trying to contend with the many competing demands placed upon you in your loved one's terminal illness (see section on illness in chapter 7 for more on this).

Your anticipatory grief will bring up reactions similar to those outlined for postdeath mourning elsewhere in this book (see chapters 2 and 3). However, the anticipatory nature of the grief adds a different dimension to the general grief experience. It may be helpful for you to see your anticipatory grief as being made up of three sets of processes which interact with one another. They occur inside of you, between you and your dying loved one, and among your family and friends.

Individual Psychological Processes. On the individual level, healthy anticipatory grief involves four sets of psychological processes. They overlap and are not exclusive of one another. They include: awareness of and gradual accommodation to your loved one's dying; emotional processes; thought processes; and planning for the future.

Awareness of and Gradual Accommodation to Your Loved One's Dying. Through these processes you start to comprehend that your loved one is dying and begin to prepare yourself for it:

Developing a progressively deepening awareness of the seriousness of the illness and its implications through your dawning realization that hopes about recovery will not be actualized

Gradually absorbing and coming to terms with the reality of the impending death

Rehearsing the death and its consequences as you attempt to adjust in part in your mind to the death of your loved one

Becoming partially socialized into the bereaved role through this time of anticipatory bereavement

Emotional Processes. These processes arise naturally as you contend with your loved one's dying and your feelings about it:

Confronting the need to manage the stress and emotional reactions to the experience and incompatible demands of your loved one's terminal illness.

Mourning past, present, and future losses attendant to the terminal illness and death and the unrelated losses that have been revived in this loss situation. This also refers to experiencing, managing, and coping with all the associated emotions and reactions of grief and mourning.

Experiencing and coping with the separation anxiety and fear brought about by the threat of permanent loss.

Gradually withdrawing emotional energy from the image of your dying loved one in the postdeath future, and from the hopes, dreams, wishes, expectations, and plans that accompanied it.

Recognizing your separateness from your dying loved one, and learning to tolerate the awareness that he will die while you will continue to live.

Doing what you need to do to maintain some confidence in the face of the profound threat of losing your loved one. This includes doing things to help you to master the situation, such as seeking information and participating in care. It also involves having strategies for maintaining emotional and personal balance, affirming life and its meaning, and revising your values, goals, and philosophy of life in light of your loved one's illness and death (Futterman and Hoffman 1973).

Thought Processes. These are processes which may go on in your mind as you face your loved one's dying:

Experiencing heightened preoccupation with and concern for your terminally ill loved one

Starting slowly to incorporate changes in your identity, roles, experiences, beliefs, assumptions, and expectations that reflect the current situation and will begin to prepare you for a world without your loved one

Striving, through all your senses, to "take in" your loved one in order to emblazen these perceptions in your mind and senses for the purpose of later constructing a mental and sensory image of your loved one to keep with you after the death

Reviewing the past and attending carefully to the present in order to crystalize memories to keep after the death

Bargaining with God or fate for a reprieve from the illness, for more time with your loved one, or for a different type of illness experience

Recollecting previous losses, griefs, periods of vulnerability, and other related experiences that have been revived by this loss

Contemplating your own ultimate death

Developing a philosophy about how to cope with your loved one's remaining time. For example, should you exert as much pressure on both of you to experience and squeeze as much out of remaining life as possible? Or, should you take a more natural and passive attitude in which you will take what comes without the stressful burden of rushing to make all the last times memorable and meaningful?

Planning for the Future. These are some of the issues you must plan for when your loved one is dying:

Considering what the future will be like without your loved one, and experiencing associated reactions to it

Anticipating and planning for future losses and changes, both before and after the death of your loved one

Anticipating and planning for practical and social considerations that need to be addressed both before and after the death

Interactional Processes with Your Dying Loved One. Anticipatory grief involves numerous interactional processes between you and your dying loved one. By preparing for the ultimate loss of your loved one through anticipatory grief, you will become aware of any unfinished business remaining with him. And by interacting with him you will be able to finish your unfinished business, which in itself is a crucial part of anticipatory grief. There are three interrelated subprocesses incorporated here: directing attention, energy, and behavior toward your dying loved one; resolving your personal relationship with your dying loved one; and helping your dying loved one.

Directing Attention, Energy, and Behavior toward Your Dying Loved One. These are ways in which you can attend to your loved one during his illness:

Remaining as involved as possible with your dying loved one, avoiding withdrawal and promoting whatever continued communication, interaction, dignity, control, living, and meaning remain available

Directing increased attention to your loved one and being hyperalert to cues about him

Focusing your energy (physical and emotional), behavior, thought, and resources (emotional, physical, time, financial, social) on caring for your dying loved one

Balancing the incompatible and conflicting demands of simultaneously holding on to, letting go of, and drawing closer to your dying loved one

Assigning your loved one a considerable degree of priority in terms of giving him consideration, fulfilling his wants and needs, planning activities, and so forth

Responding to your loved one in ways that make allowances for his deterioration, loss, and disability, without supporting any of his inappropriate or prematurely regressive defenses

Possibly doing painful things (for example, taking your loved one for an uncomfortable medical procedure) or omitting pleasurable ones (for example, refusing to buy his cigarettes) for your loved one's own good that signal debilitation and/or the terminality of the illness

Resolving Your Personal Relationship with Your Dying Loved One. These are ways in which you can come to closure with your loved one about your personal relationship:

Finishing unfinished business with your loved one

Specifically informing him or reinforcing what your loved one means and has meant to you, providing other personal feedback, and stating promises and intentions for the future

Recollecting your mutual relationship and sharing memories from common experiences

Planning the future with your loved one so that you do not feel that such plans are betrayals after he dies

At the appropriate time, saying good-bye to your loved one and providing permission to die

Helping Your Dying Loved One. As your loved one is dying, these are some of the ways you can be helpful to him and make the process better for him:

Identifying, anticipating, and meeting the needs of your dying loved one

Attending to the last wishes of your loved one

Acting to facilitate the kind of death your loved one would want

Assisting your loved one with his own anticipatory mourning, problem-solving of specific fears and concerns, completion of terminal illness tasks, and finishing of unfinished business with others, so that he can achieve a sense of closure that can give him a feeling of peace and the ability to let go when the time is appropriate

Promoting a context of open communication to the fullest extent possible

Acting to minimize your loved one's psychological, social, and physical suffering and losses

Providing the psychosocial support and acceptance necessary for your loved one to cope with, express, and manage the feelings, thoughts, fears, concerns, and needs caused by his illness and impending death

Taking over necessary body and ego functions for your loved one without making him feel ashamed, devalued, or having to undergo unnecessary loss

Joining your loved one in the process of reviewing his life

Working with your loved one to determine how he wants to be remembered, and trying to bring this to fruition

If desired by your loved one, preplanning with him the type of funerary rituals preferred

Family and Social Processes. Anticipatory grief stimulates a series of family and social processes. These show that the dying of your loved one takes place in a social context which in itself is affected by his loss.

Your family starting to reorganize itself without your loved one being available to fill the same number and types of roles in the same manner or extent as previously

Individual mourners beginning to assume and adapt to new roles and responsibilities because of the incapacitation and future absence of the dying loved one

Making plans with other survivors-to-be for what will happen later in the illness and after the death

Negotiating relationships with people you must deal with outside of the family

Networking with other people, institutions, and organizations to get the best services and provide your loved one the optimum treatment and quality of life possible

Working with clergy and funeral service personnel to arrange for postdeath rituals to meet your loved one's preferences

As you can see, anticipatory grief is a complex set of processes that may be called forth during the terminal illness of your loved one. It entails mourning not only over future losses, but over past and present losses as well. It does not have to result in premature detachment from your dying loved one and, in fact, has the potential for and capability of supporting and stimulating your continued involvement with your loved one for as long as possible.

When an "Anticipated Death" Is Actually a Sudden Death

Because of the profound influence that the suddenness of unanticipated death has upon a mourner's grief, I find that if I had but one question to ask of a mourner, it would be whether or not the death was anticipated. However, this brings up an important issue: We cannot assume that a death has been anticipated merely because it occurred in a situation where we think the mourner *should* have been prepared. A person's anticipation of death depends upon that person's perspective in the situation and not on whether we or society think that the death has been anticipated. This is seen when death occurs suddenly in the context of an ongoing terminal illness or during a recuperation from serious illness or operation.

Whether a death is considered sudden or anticipated is not determined by the length of time the mourner knew the loved one was dying, but rather by its timing for her, given that particular mourner's state of mind and circumstances.

A.J. was an elderly male whose physical abilities had been declining for several years. Upon what proved to be his final admission to the hospital, he was diagnosed as having a debilitating neurological disease that was expected to be terminal within six months. His family was attempting to cope with this news and making plans to bring A.J. home to die when they were notified that an undiagnosed aneurysm had burst and A.J. had died. To the family this was a completely unexpected and unacceptable death. They responded with many of the same reactions witnessed in families of accident victims. Not only was the death untimely in terms of what the physician had told them, but they also felt robbed of the opportunity to take A.J. home, participate in his care, finish unfinished business, say good-bye, and engage in many other important processes of anticipatory grief.

In contrast to the family, friends perceived this as a death that was expected. They had known of the continuing decline of A.J. over the previous several years and had assumed that the death was a natural consequence of this. Their expectation was that the family knew that A.J. would die soon and that the family had been prepared for the death. They failed to appreciate that it was the "wrong" death occurring at the "wrong" time. Unfortunately, because others' viewpoints were totally different from that of the family, the family never received appropriate support. Friends never realized the type of loss nor its impact. Additionally, those friends had unrealistic expectations for the family's bereavement and recovery, since they were based on an incorrect assessment of what the family had experienced.

As illustrated in the case above, when families have been informed that a loved one is dying they start to have certain expectations about the course and type of death their loved one will experience. When these are violated, for example, when the person dies suddenly from something unrelated to the illness, there actually is a sudden death for them. Most of society would not validate it as a sudden death. From the outside it would seem that the family would be prepared for the death, since they had known that their loved one was dying. However, because that person died from something other than what was anticipated, the death is a sudden death for the family. This is why we cannot assume that awareness of a terminal diagnosis means that any death that occurs is an anticipated one. It only would be "expected" if the death were consistent with the expectations the family held for it.

Such a situation also can arise following the death of someone who was recuperating from an acute illness in which there had been an initial expectation that the person would die, but who had been considered to be back on the road to health.

Eileen was a fifty-three-year-old woman with a history of cardiovascular problems. Following three serious heart attacks, a stroke, the development of three heart blockages and an aneurysm, it was determined that she required open heart bypass surgery. Her family was prepared for the very worst. To their joy, Eileen survived the painful surgery. She was recuperating in perfect fashion when, ten days following her surgery, she unexpectedly experienced massive gastrointestinal bleeding. This so destabilized her blood pressure that she developed a ventricular arrhythmia and suffered a myocardial infarction that killed her. The family was in total shock. Because of her positive recuperation they had dared to raise their hopes again about her survival, after having worked diligently at keeping such hopes moderate and realistic before and during the operation. They were particularly outraged and bitter that these hopes had been resurrected only to be dashed by her death, leaving them with "so much farther to fall" when she died suddenly. Their expectations had been that the danger had passed and, consequently, when Eileen died, her family responded to it as a sudden, unanticipated death. Also, the family felt exceptionally angry that Eileen had had to endure the pain of the operation only to die so soon thereafter. It seemed senseless and cruel.

Friends of Eileen's family appeared not to recognize that there had been a dramatic shift in hopes and expectations during the ten days following the operation when Eileen had been improving. All they had known was how seriously ill she had been and that the operation was risky. From their perspective, the death was expected, and they responded as they would have if Eileen had died during the operation itself. This failure to take into account the changes that ten days of positive recuperation had made in the hopes and expectations of the family left the family without adequate support and understanding by their friends. Everyone responded as if it were an expected death for which the family had prepared, and they expected the family to act accordingly.

In this case, the sudden death occurred in the context of a situation in which a patient had been seriously ill and now was improving. If you looked at the situation from the outside you would think that the family should have been prepared; however, the ten days of positive convalescence had changed the family's hopes so that they expected that she would survive. For her to die suddenly in this situation was as dramatic to them as if she had been a completely healthy person and had died suddenly in a car accident. Also, they now had a great deal of resentment that Eileen had had to suffer great pain for no reason.

Both of these situations illustrate that even in the context of a terminal illness or a recuperation, a death that is unanticipated or different than expected by the survivors will be perceived as a sudden death. They will suffer the reactions of unanticipated grief as a result. Furthermore, they are vulnerable to difficulties because of the circumstances of the death, most notably that society will expect them to be prepared when they are not. Again, this means that any death must be viewed from each individual's perspective, not just from objective data. Just because the loved one was dying does not mean the death was anticipated. The mourner's expectations and the subjective timing of the death for the mourner must be taken into account.

Whether or not your loved one's death was anticipated will have a profound impact on your ability to cope with your grief. In the following chapter, we will examine specific causes of death and learn how they present additional issues that combine with the anticipation issue to influence your grief experience.

7

Cause of Death

WHETHER a death was sudden or anticipated influences *how* you will cope. This chapter covers *what* you must contend with, given the way the death occurred. Five categories of death are discussed, along with specific issues that can complicate the mourning of survivors. These are only brief overviews of these types of bereavement. Chapter 20 lists available resources which discuss each type of death in depth. The issues of mourning that these types of deaths share either with sudden or anticipated losses or with death in general are not repeated here. I will identify only the more distinctive concerns, assuming that you will combine them with the others found in most deaths.

Accident/Disaster

Both of these types of events can lead to either a sudden or an anticipated death. For example, a person can be killed instantly in a car crash or can linger for months. In cases where these events lead to sudden death, you can expect to experience all of the sudden death survivor reactions of unanticipated grief. Even if death does not occur immediately, you undergo reactions similar to unanticipated grief responses at the time of serious injury to your loved one.

Several issues are important in accidents or disasters that result in death. If your loved one has died in one of these types of events, you will be concerned about the issue of preventability. We cope better if the death is not considered as preventable than if it is. For example, those who lose loved ones in natural disasters (for example, earthquakes and hurricanes) fare better than those whose loved ones die from disasters that are the result of avoidable human error, such as airplane crashes. The central issue here is blame and responsibility. If your loved one dies in an earthquake, there is no one to blame; however, if she dies as a result of an airline pilot's error, then there is someone to hold responsible. This puts the event in the realm of having been preventable—it could have been avoided—and means that you must cope with anger at the person responsible. It also means you probably will spend great time and effort looking for the "cause" and attempting to determine who or what is to blame, trying to find some meaning, and striving to regain some sense of control. You will have to cope with its being a senseless and unnecessary death, and also deal with your feelings about the unfairness and injustice of a loved one's dying in a situation that did not have to occur.

This does not mean that if your loved one died from a natural event for which there is no human culpability you will have no anger or issues of blame and responsibility. It is better than knowing that someone needlessly caused your loved one's death, but this doesn't mean you will not seek a cause, attempt to determine blame, try to find meaning, or strive to regain a feeling of control. Losing a loved one from a natural accident or disaster has its own type of stress because it may be difficult for you to cope with having no one to blame, no particular target to focus upon. You may feel that it would be better if there were someone toward whom you could vent your anger, since it is so hard to direct it toward agents such as fate, God, or the weather.

The absence of a specific target may leave you feeling that you should not be angry, or that you have no recourse but to turn your anger in on yourself. You may feel frustrated and powerless. Some people actually assume the blame themselves because they find it easier to deal with a traumatic event's being their responsibility, and thus within their control, than to cope with the fact that it was a truly random event over which no one had any control. They need to maintain a sense that the world is not so random and unpredictable. It is their way of looking for some control. Truly random events are frightening to all of us because we cannot protect ourselves against them.

If your loved one dies from an accident or disaster, you will have to cope with the sense of unfairness and injustice that such deaths bring. Like the issue of randomness just discussed, the fact that your loved one died solely because she was in the wrong place at the wrong time, or because she chose the wrong airline carrier, can be enraging to you and leave you feeling impotent in your ability to protect your loved ones as well as yourself. The fact that it often doesn't make sense, or that there is no reason why the person you loved was killed under those circumstances, can interfere with your ability to perceive the death as timely, acceptable, or appropriate—and this can contribute to problems in resolving your grief.

As often happens in sudden death, the circumstances of the death may seem unacceptable to you. For example, if your loved one was dismembered in an automobile accident, you understandably may have many feelings about the fact that you were not with her at the time of death and that you do not know whether she suffered. Violent, mutilating, and destructive deaths often leave survivors with a greater sense of helplessness and threat. You may experience intense feelings of vulnerability and fear after losing a loved one in this kind of death. You can feel quite insecure and unprotected for a long time.

If you were not present when your loved one died, you may imagine the worst for your loved one; it may be more painful for you than it actually was for her. Many mourners replay scenes they believe to have taken place when their loved one died. This can be most distressing and can constitute a major stumbling block in grief if not adequately worked through. Sometimes accurate medical information can be helpful—for instance, to know that your loved one died instantly and didn't suffer, or that she had no awareness of what was happening. On the other hand, such comforting information may be missing, which means that you will need to find a way to cope with your unanswered questions and concerns about the final moments of her life.

Other dimensions of these death events that can influence your mourning are the legal and insurance proceedings that can ensue. Conflicts in this area could well interfere with your bereavement. For example, when a loved one dies from a physician's malpractice or from another's drunk driving, grief is often put on hold until the legal proceedings are completed. For some, this contributes to a delayed grief reaction. For others, these proceedings themselves are therapeutic, since they afford a way to channel the rage and give it a focus. For still others, they provide a vehicle for achieving some meaning. If some good can come out of their loved one's death—for instance, better drunk driving legislation—then the death may seem less meaningless.

If you believe yourself to be responsible for your loved one's death through what you did or didn't do, your grief can be complicated by guilt. You may interrogate yourself endlessly, searching for whether you had any responsibility in the death or guiltily obsess about your decisions, omissions, or commissions related to the death; for instance, "why did I let her borrow the car?" or "why didn't I go visit her, instead of suggest she fly out here?" You will need to address this emotion in order that it not interfere with the rest of your grief (see chapters 3 and 15 for more on this). Another problem is that you may correctly or incorrectly perceive others to blame you for the death. You may feel accused, or as if you are an outcast because others avoid you since you remind them that they could be victimized in this way too. You will need to be realistic about the blame you accept, and not internalize the attitudes of others.

Homicide

Usually, in homicide, death occurs fairly suddenly, although certainly there are cases where the victim lives long enough for loved ones to anticipate it. Nevertheless, as in the death events above, when the assault occurs and the victim is wounded the family experiences shock and all of the other responses of sudden death grief, even if death does not take place immediately. After the death, acute grief often goes on for an extraordinarily long period of time.

In homicide there is no question that the death was preventable. Someone wanted to hurt your loved one. Someone made a choice and reached into your life and robbed you of a person you loved. No matter what rationale the murderer may have had, to you it is a senseless and unnecessary event. In such cases, no death surround is acceptable; no death is timely; no death is anticipated. The problems that each of these brings to any death situation individually are compounded when added together in murder.

You must contend with all of the same issues noted above regarding accident or disaster. (Please read that section first.) For example, as with accident or disaster deaths, you may have the same concerns about not being with your loved one at the time of death, worrying about what the last moments were like and whether she suffered beforehand or was terrified. Like accident/disaster survivors, you will have many feelings about the randomness of the event, or, if the murderer was someone your loved knew, anger and distress that your loved one was involved with that person. You may have guilt for not having intervened in the relationship, especially if you think you could have done something to prevent the murder. You also may feel guilty for what you did or didn't do that put the victim at the scene of the murder.

There is incredible rage at the violence and your helplessness, as well as at your loss. You will need time and support in learning how to channel it so that it will not become destructive to you. Your desire for revenge and retribution must be focused constructively, so as not to bring additional pain to you or your loved ones by getting yourself in legal trouble. You already are going through enough.

The violent and traumatic nature of the event usually complicates your mourning and subsequent adaptation; it also can interfere with your receiving social support from others. Coping with this additional injustice and unfairness takes major effort, as does coping with your increased vulnerability, paranoia, and anxiety after this type of death. Feeling out of control, which in itself can be worsened by the frustrations of the criminal justice system, is one of the most difficult aspects of this type of bereavement. Further, the drains on your personal, economic, social, and physical resources can be mammoth as a consequence of this type of death and how you feel you must respond to it.

People whose loved ones have been murdered will tell you that they are victimized not only by the death but often by the criminal justice system, private investigators, insurance companies, and the media as well. Although this is not the place to discuss in detail the problems of negotiating the criminal justice system (see chapter 20 for specific references to resources on this topic), it must be mentioned that being involved in this system will add much stress to your grief. Some survivors feel they should not intervene in the system but should let it take its own course. Others feel compelled to intervene on behalf of their loved one. In those situations where you have a desire or need to participate, you must recognize that grief over the death of your loved one often truly cannot begin to be resolved until there is some resolution of the legal conflict. This can make it very difficult for you, since grief that is not being dealt with only causes you further distress.

In this situation, where it is not uncommon for your grief and mourning to be shelved partially or totally because of your need to focus on the legal battle, you must recognize your relative disadvantage and act to counteract it. You will need to capitalize on whatever support you can muster to help you deal with that portion of your grief which you can manage now, while simultaneously coping with the legal process. While that process may be necessary as a way to work through your grief, it is a most stressful and victimizing experience that adds to your burden. This is not to advise you not to get involved in legal proceedings but only to alert you to the areas of vulnerability such involvement can create and to urge you to prepare for it.

Suicide

A suicide is one of the most difficult deaths to cope with. Not only is it a sudden death, but it also involves a conscious choice on the part of your loved one to choose death over life. The deliberateness of this act fuels intense feelings of rejection, abandonment, and desertion in those left behind. This can contribute to a profound shattering of your self-esteem, with strong feelings of unworthiness, inadequacy, and failure. Like homicide, this death was not inevitable. It was preventable. You must recognize that you are particularly victimized by this type of death, and are susceptible to intensified and conflicted bereavement reactions.

After a suicide you may feel exaggerated emotions of anger and guilt along with the other sudden death bereavement reactions. Not uncommonly, the anger is quite intense. It may be directed at your loved one, at yourself or at other people and things. It may come from your acute shock and grief. It may come because you feel betrayed and rejected. It may come from the conscious decision your loved one made. Or it may come from the fact that she is now at rest, but you have been left behind to pick up all the pieces and to cope with the intense pain and stigma of this type of death. You may be uncomfortable with your anger at the one now dead, but you must recognize that this is normal in this situation, and you will need to deal with it, not deny it. (See chapters 3 and 15 for more on coping with anger and guilt.)

Like anger, intense guilt is quite common in this situation. It, too, is worse than usual because you may assume that you could have done something to prevent the death. Despite the fact that none of us is responsible for, nor in control of, the choices of another adult, when someone we love commits suicide we tend to think we could have prevented it. You will have to recognize the limits of your ability to have prevented this suicide. Although you may disagree with the action of your loved one in ending her life, it was her choice. Frequently it is the last and only option that a suicidal person sees. That she took that option is a statement about the deceased. It is not a statement about you.

Hindsight is 20/20 in this situation. You may look back in time to discover hints or clues about the impending suicide that now make sense to you in light of the death. Usually at the time they occurred they were unrecognizable. Nevertheless you may be inclined to assume unrealistic guilt for not responding to them. Try to be realistic about what you could have expected yourself to have noticed at the time with the information you had available. If you feel you need to punish yourself, or if you see youself being destructive or sabotaging your own actions, go for professional help. All of the other normal reasons for guilt will be more bothersome to you after this type of death as well, since you may find yourself susceptible to every kind of guilt because this is a death that didn't *have* to happen. Learning to work through your guilt will be a major issue for you in this bereavement. Make sure you pay sufficient attention to it.

You may be quite confused about the death and why your loved one chose it. The normal need to know why the death occurred will be intensified in suicide. Unfortunately, many people in our society look at a suicide and come, quite erroneously, to the fearful question which you may be struggling with yourself: Didn't you love the person enough to be able to keep her interested in living? What is wrong with you that the person chose death over life with you? Because of this attitude, social isolation can result. Don't accept responsibility for the actions of your loved one, and don't buy into the guilt or shame that may be attributed to you by others.

Also, don't deny yourself the social comfort and company you need in your attempts to cope with this loss. Unfortunately, suicide survivors often feel embarrassed. Many refuse to ask for the support of others. At times, they may be reluctant to place obituaries in the newspaper or to hold funeral rites for the deceased. Nevertheless, these activities are quite important to all survivors and should be encouraged. Your activities following the suicide should be kept as much as possible like those following a normal death. It is important that you not let guilt, shame, or social stigma deprive you of this.

In mourning your loved one, you will need to come to the point where you can remember her realistically, with all her positive and negative aspects. You may need some assistance in doing this if the suicide has interfered (either positively or negatively) with your developing a truthful image of this person. The lack of this can complicate your grief.

You may wonder whether suicidal behavior is inherited, or whether it is contagious. You may even start to develop a fear of your own self-destructive impulses, especially when your feelings of guilt and anger are so strong. This is normal. However it is important to remember that suicide is a conscious choice; it is not a disease that can be transmitted.

Especially if your loved one had been suffering physically or emotionally, you may feel relief after this suicide. This also is true if the relationship had placed great burdens and worries on you. It is possible to be relieved that something is over and yet still grieve for it. Relief at the time of death does not mean that you did not love the deceased; it means that you appreciate the termination of stress and pain.

There is one situation in which your feelings about your loved one committing suicide may be somewhat lessened. This is when the suicide was consciously and freely chosen as an alternative to debilitating illness. In this case, the suicide may have been planned and, therefore, expected. There is then some time for experiencing anticipatory grief and finishing unfinished business. You do not experience the death as a sudden death. You have more of a sense of control and an answer to why the death occurred.

Acute Natural Causes

In these situations you must contend with all of the usual reactions to sudden death. However, you are spared from having to deal with the issue of a personal agent responsible for the death, such as in suicide, homicide, and sometimes in an accident or disaster. In these situations the death comes suddenly from natural causes, as when your loved one dies in her sleep or from an acute heart attack. You may identify causes responsible for the death, but usually they are indirect. Even so, if one has been identified, there will be normal feelings of anger about it. For instance, a bereaved widow may blame her husband for his forty-year habit of smoking cigarettes, or a widower may believe his mother-in-law encouraged his wife not to diet and hold her responsible for the high cholesterol that contributed to his wife's fatal heart attack.

As in other deaths, you may have a tendency to blame yourself if you feel you did not do something that could have prevented the death. However, it usually is less intense than if it were a situation in which the death was completely preventable. In many instances of this kind of death, the deceased is the one who had the ultimate responsibility for acting or not acting in a particular fashion that contributed to her death.

Often the death surround in these situations is more acceptable, or at least less distressful to you. It is much easier to accept the death of your loved one if she dies in her sleep in her own bed than if she is murdered in a bank robbery. Despite this, people certainly can die from acute natural causes in ways that are difficult for survivors to cope with. For example, the husband who has a sudden heart attack, loses control of his vehicle, and smashes into a telephone pole dies in a way that most probably is unacceptable to those left behind. Yet, although your sense of preventability and acceptability for a given death may vary, more than in other cases of sudden deaths you well may feel a sense of consolation that the deceased did not suffer.

Chronic and/or Terminal Illness

The death of your loved one from an illness can offer you circumstances that are a blessing, a curse, or a combination of both. This will be influenced by the characteristics of your loved one's particular illness—its length, its type, the amount of pain involved, and the type of treatment necessary. It also will involve your own specific reactions to the illness and the death it brings; your loved one's knowledge of and response to her illness and ultimate death; the characteristics of your family and each individual member's responses to the illness and impending death; and the social, financial, and environmental factors that affect you and your dying loved one during the illness.

If your loved one's illness permitted sufficient time and circumstances for appropriate anticipatory grief, you probably had the opportunity to prepare emotionally for the loss, to finish unfinished business with your loved one, and gradually to absorb the reality of the death and its consequences. (See chapter 6 for more on the processes of anticipatory grief.) You directed your coping mechanisms toward the expected end. You were spared all of the problems of sudden death. However, given the nature of today's illnesses, you very well may be carrying scars long after the death.

These scars come from the difficult experience which you may have had to endure as your loved one was dying. In most cases, you were forced to witness the progressive debilitation of someone you love without any power to stem the inevitable course of loss and death. Doubtless you suffered, too, as you watched your loved one in physical and psychological pain and struggled with her through the uncertain up-and-down course that many illnesses bring. With modern technology, terminal illnesses no longer progress in a steady, downhill course. More often, what happens is that a patient feels fine one day and is quite ill the next. And, as advances in medicine continue, the interim between diagnosis and death becomes longer. This period of time brings to you, your dying loved one, and other family members a number of problems that not only encumber you during your loved one's illness but also leave you with emotions and consequences that affect your grief after the death. The special problems of terminal illness include:

Numerous remissions and relapses, with the many psychological reactions that arise to each

Lengthened periods of anticipatory grief

Increased financial, social, physical, and emotional pressures

Long-term family disruption

Progressive decline of your loved one, and the emotional responses of you and other family members to this decline

A longer period of uncertainty

Intensive treatment regimens and their side effects

Dilemmas about decision making and treatment choices

In most cases, dying is a gradual process. Few people become bedridden or die immediately, as was the norm in the past. During times of remission, your loved one probably still wanted to work, play, relate to others, and be involved in social activities. She continued to want and need honest communication and interaction. You were called upon to provide this. At the same time, however, you had to deal with graphic reminders of what was to come during times of relapse. Probably this often left you in a difficult place, trying to ascertain what was needed and attempting to respond to a shifting medical scenario. It put enormous demands on you. The uncertainty of some situations, the certainty of others; the inconsistency of the illness or its relentless and persistent consistency; the steady debilitation or the up-and-down nature of the loss of control; the wish that the end would come, and the fear that it will—these are but some of the pressures that may have placed uncommon stress and demands not only on your dying loved one, but also on those of you who were concerned about and involved with her.

This is why the period of time from diagnosis until death is so complex and burdensome. Although it offers more time for preparation and provides the opportunity to avoid the negative consequences of sudden death, it has another side: The extra time often is filled with a painful witnessing of progressive debilitation over which there is no control. During a period in which you may have experienced intense emotional reactions, you also were faced with the stress of demands for major changes in your family and for investments of yourself, your time, and your finances. All of this stress contributes to what commonly is seen in families of the terminally ill—psychological conflicts, emotional exhaustion, physical debilitation, social isolation, and family discord. All of these will have an impact on what you have to cope with after the death, since experiences with your loved one prior to the death influence what you are left to deal with after she dies.

Other problems probably arose during the illness as well. It is exquisitely difficult to strike a delicate balance between coping with the terminal illness of a loved one while continuing to take care of the rest of your family. Most probably there often were opposing tasks with which to contend, clashing responsibilities, and discordant roles to play. For example, you were expected to remain involved with your loved one, yet to start to recognize she would one day be gone. You were expected to balance supporting her increased dependency with supporting her continued need for autonomy. You were expected to focus on your loved one as a living person while remembering that she was dying. You were expected to redistribute family roles and responsibilities so family life could be maintained, and yet you were expected not to do anything that would call attention to or cause more losses for your dying loved one. While immersed in caring for your loved one you also were expected to care for yourself and others, too. All of these stresses probably left you with the normal feelings that most family members have during a loved one's terminal illness: guilt, anxiety, sorrow and depression, and anger and hostility.

How you felt about what you did during your loved one's terminal illness profoundly will affect your grief after the death. As terminal illnesses become longer, family members are presented with increased stress and demands. Their resources are depleted, and they live with painful and negative emotions. This is likely to cause problems in grief after death. For example, if your loved one died after a terminal illness you may find that you are guilty when recollecting the times you wanted to be alone, or when you felt angry for the demands that caring for her placed upon you. You may feel guilty over the relief you might have felt when the death finally came. You may have felt guilt from recognizing that you were angry at your loved one, or because you were disgusted by the sights and smells of the illness. These are just some of the normal circumstances in a terminal illness that can prompt additional problems in grief after the death.

After your loved one dies you may find that you are so emotionally and physically exhausted that you do not have the energy to grieve. Or you may feel excruciating loneliness and hurt if you have been involved in the care of that person. The loss leaves you with more memories to disengage from after the death. If you were living with your dying loved one and had a daily routine that centered on her, you may be confused about what to do when there is no longer a dying person who needs you. You may have given up social interests and professional concerns in order to center your attention on your loved one, and when that person is no longer alive you may be at a loss not only for her but also for how to fill your time and for what to be besides a caregiver. You will have to develop a new pattern of life, with changes in your routine and roles.

If you have anticipatorily grieved the death of your loved one during the illness, you may find that at the time of actual death many of your emotions already have been worked through. This may reduce the amount of mourning you display publicly. Many times mourners feel guilty or ashamed because their reactions are less than they expect. Sometimes they receive disapproval from others who feel they are not grieving as they should. In most cases this is because much of the grieving has taken place during the illness. You have been dealing with the death through your grieving of the little losses that take place throughout the entire illness: the limitations of the illness, the diagnosis of a shortened life expectancy, the relinquishing of a job and responsibilities, and the progressive debilitation. All of these losses can help to prepare you for the ultimate loss in death. If you have been paying attention to them and grieving them as they occur, you may not need to have as dramatic a reaction after the death. Much of your grieving has taken place in advance of the actual death. This is the reason why you may have only an abbreviated reaction. Do not think you are bad or that you did not love the person who died.

If your loved one has died following an illness, recognize that it probably has taken an extraordinary amount out of you in terms of time, energy, emotion, physical stamina, family stability, and even finances. Depletion in these areas will make it more difficult for you to cope with your grief. For this reason, it is critically important to give yourself what you need to replenish yourself following such a demanding and stressful time.

This chapter concludes the section devoted to what you must contend with in different types of death. In the next section, we look at how the family responds to the loss of one of its members and examine the impacts of the losses of different people.

PART

III

Grieving and Your Family

8

Family Reorganization after the Death of a Family Member

W HENEVER a family member dies, there is a process that a healthy family undergoes in response to the loss of one of its own. This process is called "role reorganization." It occurs because the family needs to get itself back into the rhythm and balance that was lost when the family member died. Many times families are not even consciously aware of what they are doing, but it is a critically important process nevertheless.

The family is a system in which the sum (the family) is more than the total of its parts (the family members). This means that the family is more than merely a collection of its individual people. It is above and beyond this. The family system is something which takes on its own life and its own characteristics and does not just reflect the individuals within it.

There are two important principles in family systems. The first principle is that anything that affects your family will affect its individual members, and anything that affects the individual members will affect the family. If a family is distressed because one of its members is seriously ill, this will affect all of its members. For instance, the father may be preoccupied when he tries to function normally at work. Conversely, if work problems are distressing the father, it will affect the family, because he will be acting differently due to his concerns over problems at work.

The second principle concerns balance. Like any other system, your family works to maintain itself on an even keel; it struggles to maintain its equilibrium. To keep the family functioning on track, each family develops specific roles for each person and establishes rules, communication patterns, family expectations, and patterns of behavior which keep the family operating in a consistent and stable fashion. They are determined by that particular family's beliefs, values, ways of coping, and relationships within the family.

The methods of keeping a family operating as smoothly as possible differ from family to family. What might work for your family may be totally wrong for another. Each family has its own unique and characteristic style. Having set ways of doing things does not mean that the family is without problems. It merely means that the family and its problems most probably will continue to operate in the same old ways unless something forces them to change.

Like systems, families require the ongoing support of each individual component (family member) to keep the system operating in balance. When an element is added or taken away, the system becomes unbalanced and there is a struggle to reach balance again. Therefore, whenever anything changes in the usual and customary ways in which a particular family operates, whether because of problems inside the family (for example, the death of a member) or outside of it (for example, external stress put on the family), the family must move to compensate for these changes. It is similar to a balance scale, where if something is added to one side it alters the other side by the same amount in the opposite direction. If the scale is ever to become balanced again, something must be added to one side or subtracted from the other. When the family experiences some type or degree of change, it, too, must adjust itself to accommodate to that change and get back into equilibrium.

What does all of this information on family dynamics have to do with grief? Very simply, it helps us to understand what happens—indeed, what *must* happen—in families after somebody dies.

When a member of your family dies and no longer can fulfill his assigned roles or obligations, there is a shift in the balance of your family. One element has been removed and the entire family system is thrown into disequilibrium; something has to change. Your family focuses on reestablishing balance in the system. This will affect not only the family as a whole and its individual members but also the various relationships that exist within the family. Power, responsibilities, and roles will be reassigned as a result of the family's struggle to reestablish stability in the face of your loved one's death. Your family's unique ways of functioning determine how it will respond to the demands for change.

Some of the reassigned roles and responsibilities are easy to see. Everyone in your family has a number of obvious roles to play to help the family run smoothly. For example, if the one who died is the one who cooked all the meals, then someone else will have to be reassigned that chore. Or, if the one who died is the one who always took out the garbage, someone else is going to have to assume that responsibility or else the house will become a dump. This is what is known as "role reorganization" —roles are reorganized and reassigned to different people in order that essential family functions can be carried on to ensure that the family continues to operate.

Some roles and responsibilities are not so clearly apparent. They may or may not be explicitly assigned, but all family members know that they exist. This is seen, for example, in the case of the family "troublemaker." This is the person who constantly gets into trouble. Everyone pays attention to him instead of looking at the more upsetting problems in the family. Very often a child will take on this role and serve the purpose of taking attention away from one or both of the parents' problems. If this child dies, someone else in the family will have to cause trouble if the family wants to keep the focus off the real issues. If this does not happen, and if the customary methods of keeping things running in the same old way do not work, the family is thrown way out of balance and suffers severe problems. This does not happen only where there is a negative role such as "troublemaker" to be reassigned. It happens as well when there are positive roles left unfulfilled by a family member's death.

After your family member dies, the degree of role reorganization that will be necesssary depends on the number and types of roles that particular family member fulfilled. For example, in traditional families, if the person who dies is the father, chances are that there are a large number of roles to reassign if the family is to function. Among others, these could include the roles of provider, protector, maintenance man, and the numerous roles inherent in being a husband and a father. Additionally, each role has its own nature, meaning, and role-fulfilling aspects that will be different to individual family members. This means that what one child needs to fill in for her father will be different from what another child needs. The family needs someone to assume the father's functional roles, but the individual family members will need more than that depending upon the nature of the personal relationships severed by the death. In contrast, if an infant dies, there will be fewer roles to reassign in order for the family to function. However, don't look solely at mere number of roles. The role of being the infant and embodying parental hopes and expectations, and of being the object of love and focus of family attention, is a critical one, and its absence can strike at the heart of a family, even though the family is more affected behaviorally by the death of the father.

Suffice it to say that in each family the deceased's roles will need to be fulfilled in some way, or the family will be thrown out of kilter. Sometimes this ends up being a positive thing, because the family may go for help and/or find new ways of functioning that are better than before. Yet, many times problems just continue unabated. In either case, whether it is or isn't resolved healthily or successfully, the period of reorganization prompted by a family member's death is most stressful for all concerned.

Lastly, you should be aware of the serious consequences of roles that are not reassigned suitably to family members. If you give someone a role that is inappropriate for them (for example, expect a child to take on her deceased sister's personality), inconsistent with their preparation (for example, ask a little boy to be the "man" around the house), or incompatible with current roles (for example, you expect the mother to be home with the children and at work simultaneously), you are only asking for further problems. New role assignments can constitute either secondary losses (for example, the person is robbed of his identity) or secondary gains (for example, the person finally gets some recognition that formerly may have been withheld) for individual family members.

In role reorganization you must evaluate not only what roles need to be reassigned but also whether the reassignment is as healthy as possible for all involved. It will be important to keep in mind that each bereaved family member has to cope both with the complexities of the grief process itself and with an altered, out-of-balance system and new role responsibilities and demands.

Special Family System Issues in Grief

A problem that can complicate the family reorganization process stems from the volatility of the grieving family and the need for compromise among family members in their grief. Both issues arise because of the very special nature of the family system.

The "multiplier effect" exists in all families. This is when the grief of one member triggers the grief of another. Having so many acutely grieving people under one roof is such an intense situation that, at times, it is a wonder that the whole situation does not blow up with the accumulation of grief and pain. In contrast, at other times, the presence of a sense of community, shared loss, and strength in numbers is quite comforting and supportive.

Family members must recognize the necessity to weigh the needs of a particular family member versus the needs of the family as a whole. A delicate balance must be struck. For instance, what should be done when one member finds it too upsetting to look at the photographs of the deceased that the rest of the family wants to hang on the wall? How should the family respond when two out of the six members find it too painful to put up the Christmas tree, but the others need to put it up? Yet it is not right for family members to hide their grief in an attempt to protect one another or promote false unity. This will only fuel the volatility, increase the chances for communication problems and unmet needs, and force the grieving underground, adding to the potential for unresolved grief.

There are no right or wrong answers in these situations; families must learn to compromise. There is the best chance for success in this if communication among your family members can be open and honest, each person's needs are recognized as being just as legitimate and important as everyone else's, and there is a commitment to the survival of the family, with compromise valued and assurance that in other situations one's needs will take precedence.

As with married couples who have lost a child, family members must not expect each other to have the same needs, to grieve in similar fashion along an identical course, or to assume that each has lost the same relationship. They must allow for personal differences, recognizing that the individual factors of each particular person's grief will influence that person's reaction to the death more than will her presumed similarity to other family members, or the fact that they all have lost the same person. Lastly, family members will need to understand that while their closeness may be supportive in their grief, it also can make them likely to displace blame, anger, and other hostile feelings onto one another, to avoid communication for fear of upsetting the other, or to place irrational demands on each other. As a family, and as individuals, your family members will need to minimize this as much as possible, be gentle and patient with one another, and have the proper perspective on what grieving the death of your loved one will mean.

After a family member dies, the surviving family must reorganize itself to survive and must cope with the stresses of containing different grievers, each with diverse, idiosyncratic needs. It is a mammoth task. In the following chapters, we will look at some of the special bereavement issues brought up by the deaths of different people in the family.

Loss of a Spouse

Unless a couple dies together at the same time, widowhood will be the inevitable conclusion of all intact marriages. Despite this inevitability, however, most of us are unprepared for it.

The comments in this section are based on the death of a spouse where the marriage had been ideal. To the extent that your marriage was not ideal, you can expect to be different from the bereaved spouses described here. Marriages run the gamut from a relationship in which there is only sharing of daily activities to a relationship in which each spouse is integral to the other, sharing all aspects of their practical, social, and intimate lives.

Depending upon the relationship you had in your marriage, the loss of your spouse is a major loss in your life. This is because the person with whom you have built and are living your life frequently plays a number of roles for you. This person may have been your friend, partner, confidante, lover, roommate, sounding-board, the person with whom you made decisions, with whom you set family policy, and with whom you divided family labor and worked toward goals. Therefore, contingent upon the number and type of roles your spouse fulfilled for you, the loss of your spouse can be expected to bring a number of secondary losses as well.

Depending upon your relationship with your spouse and the manner of death, you can expect that your grief will follow the typical responses to loss outlined elsewhere in this book (see chapters 2 and 3). However, there are a number of special issues you must confront, and these are discussed below.

Changes in Your Identity

For most of us, our relationship with our mate is a critically important and exclusive one. It is a central part of our self and our being in the world. As a result, one of the major roles your spouse had was as someone who affirmed your identity, someone who helped you define who you are in many ways. For example:

Emotionally (for instance, if your spouse knew you were a sensitive person and conveyed appreciation of your sensitivity to him and others)

Physically (for instance, if your wife had been the only person in your life who could remember what you looked like without the beard you've worn for the last forty years)

Behaviorally (for instance, if your spouse knew that you were clumsy at times and was always there to offer an arm to steady you)

Socially (for instance, if you and your spouse enjoyed a fulfilling social life with your married friends)

Psychologically (for instance, if your spouse knew of your secret wish to have been a dancer and watched old movie musicals with you so that you could enjoy the dancing)

Your senses of self and security will be affected profoundly when the person who helped support them the most dies. The loss of that special validation can change you because you lose someone whose relationship with you causes you to be you. This can be quite disorienting.

Simply by undergoing many years of experiences together, you and your spouse have developed ways of doing things, perceiving things, and feeling and thinking about things that helped to define who you are. When you lose that person, you are bound to feel tremendously thrown off balance. There is an insecurity due to the absence of a support that told you, whether positively or negatively, who and what you were.

If you lived with your spouse for some time, it is most probable that your spouse helped you to define the world and the things in it. Although spouses certainly may differ from one another in many areas, they also tend to have many things in common, some of which brought them together in the first place. So, when you lose your spouse, you may lose a person who perceives the world in the way that you do, along with a partner with whom you defined your world and self. For example, you may have lost someone who was as disgusted with local politics as you are, you may have lost a person who shared many of your opinions about your common friends, and so forth. Of course, not all spouses share the same thoughts or feelings. What is typical is that spouses usually know one another's thoughts and feelings. With the death of your spouse, you most probably have lost someone who really "knew" you. Often it means losing the person who has known you longer and/or better than anyone else alive. Spouses provide one another with a strong sense of history. To lose a spouse means to lose a person who can reminisce and bring you back to "the old days." Or it may mean losing the person with whom you have shared very special times, such as the birth of your children.

As with other major losses, after the death of your spouse there are other ways in which identity changes. Some of this is discussed in previous chapters (see chapter 3 on grief manifestations and chapter 14 on resolution of grief). With regard to spouses, there is a special transition that must be made. Whereas once there was a "we," now there is only an "I." This not only happens to you psychologically, as you struggle to cope with losing the interactional part of yourself that was created by the unique and special relationship with your spouse (for example, being the wife of your husband); it also happens socially. Marriages are a social unit, and now one-half of that social unit is gone. You may have been used to operating as a couple, and now you must operate as an individual. This has many implications for you, ranging from whether or not you will get an invitation to a dinner party if everyone else is in couples to whether or not you still can dine at the Faculty Club if you are the widow of a deceased faculty member.

You will have been used to psychologically operating in the world as one-half of a pair. For women, as we will discuss below, this is true in more areas of their lives than for men. Also, redefining their identity may be more difficult for women because they traditionally have been socialized to be too passive, which will lead to insufficient tools for the development of required new social roles and relationships. However, for each sex, when there has been a relationship of some duration in which the partners had some investment in one another and shared their lives, the death of one is bound to make the other feel as if something is missing as the other continues on in life. This can cause significant fear and anxiety, along with feelings of vulnerability and insecurity.

Unless you have had time to anticipate and rehearse new roles because of the length of your spouse's illness, you may have many new tasks to learn as you attempt to get used to life without your mate. These will depend on the division of labor you had in your marriage. It also will depend on the presence of any remaining children or other dependents, as well as on your stage in life. Many women, as a result of their traditional sex-role conditioning, have been accustomed to relying on their husband for financial advice, home maintenance, auto repair, and other financial and practical assistance. As will be seen below, to the extent that a particular woman is unfamiliar with these matters or cannot address them, she will have to learn how to deal with them when her husband is gone.

Correspondingly, many times husbands are unfamiliar with child rearing, domestic chores, and housekeeping management. They may not have much experience chauffeuring the children to extracurricular activities or running their own social lives. After the death of his wife, a widower will have to develop skills in these areas.

Basically, new tasks must be undertaken and new skills must be developed by you, as a widowed person, if these tasks and skills previously had been assumed by your deceased spouse and continue to be necessary for your family's survival. Children still must be fed, lawns still must be mowed, and a family must continue on despite the loss of an important member.

In some areas, there are no new skills nor tasks required, but only the hard, but necessary, process of reacting to your mate's death, achieving appropriate emotional independence from this person, and recognizing that you now have a new status as a widowed person. Males and females tend to vary in their success at accomplishing this grief work.

Sex Differences in Bereavement

The research available on sex differences in bereavement following widowhood is mixed in conclusion. (See chapter 5 for a further discussion of this.) There does seem to be a general trend, however, indicating that males suffer more physical problems and are more vulnerable to death and disease, especially those under the age of seventy-five and particularly within the time shortly after the death. Yet widowers seem to form new relationships more often and sooner. It appears, therefore, that widowers make faster social recoveries but slower emotional recoveries because of their problems with expression of grief. And despite their increased morbidity and mortality in the year following the death of their spouse, long-term adjustment for males seems to be better than for females.

Women seem to be at greatest risk for physical problems during the second or third year following the death. This indicates that while both sexes are affected at the time of the death and shortly thereafter, widows experience additional difficulties as time goes on, while widowers find a decrease in stress over time. Research indicates that widowed females are less likely than widowed males to achieve a satisfactory long-term adjustment to their widowhood.

If you are a woman, the chances are that you will have more difficulty coping with the death of your spouse. This is the case for several reasons. First, as a woman, your mortality is lower than for men. Therefore, you statistically can expect to survive your spouse, especially if you married someone older. Second, remarriage rates are higher for widowed men than for women. Because there are fewer men available to remarry, more women remain unmarried, with the expectation of finding eligible men diminishing with advanced age. This is why most older men in this country are married, while most older women are not.

Women tend to have more social and practical problems after widowhood then do men. The traditional sex-role conditioning of women emphasizes family and home. If you were raised traditionally, you may not have fully developed the needed competencies to socially and financially manage your career, your family, and your home simultaneously. Consequently, the death of your husband may leave you with serious financial problems and difficulty with securing a well-paying job because of absence from the labor market, economic discrimination toward women, and disproportionate employment in low-jobs. Statistics indicate that at all ages widowed females are more likely to live in poverty than widowed males.

There are a number of reasons why a woman experiences more change than a man following the death of a spouse. Men traditionally have defined themselves largely by their occupational roles. In contrast, women have defined themselves first as wives and mothers and only secondarily by their working roles. Typically her name comes from her husband, for example, "Mrs. John Smith." As a result, when your husband dies you lose more of your identity and experience more secondary losses. Traditionally, you also lose a social link between yourself and society, since for many women social status has been dependent upon the husband. If you had devoted yourself exclusively to your roles as wife and mother, or if your traditional upbringing focused on the importance of marriage and your role in it, you have lost the object of your work and the purpose of your role as well. Of course, the changes you experience after your husband's death will depend on the extent of your involvement with him, the strength of the bonds between you, and the number of roles he played for you.

Your task as a widow will be to develop a new identity that recognizes your new status. This is not different from what bereaved men have to do, but it is more difficult. It has been said that widows must move from seeing themselves as a person's wife to accepting themselves as a widow, and then move on into independent life as a formerly married woman. Relinquishing the investment in your role as a wife is a very difficult process and one you will most probably resist. For those of you who regard the loss of your husband as the loss of the best part of yourself, the task can seem monumental. Even for those of you who had a stronger sense of yourself as a separate individual, the loss of a partner in a couple-oriented society will have a strong impact on your identity. For this reason, you will have to seek new friends to support your new identity, ones who understand what you are experiencing.

As you will doubtlessly discover, too often widows are the victims of stigmatization and alienation. They tend to be socially ostracized, since they make others feel uncomfortable. They can be very threatening to those whose husbands are still alive. Unfortunately, it is not uncommon for best friends to drift apart after one of them becomes widowed. The friend who is still married may be less inclined to include her former friend in social events. In contrast, widowers are perceived as less of a threat. They have more women available to choose from for remarrige, since women tend to live longer and men tend to marry younger women. As a result, the social life of widows tends to diminish, while it can expand for widowers. This lack of social contact is as harmful for widows as it is for any bereaved individual. For them as for anyone else, it is important to have social support in undergoing the difficult processes of grief and making the transition from a couple to an individual person.

Loneliness

It is the loneliness that is most difficult for many widows and widowers to endure. The sense of being so incomplete can be devastating. As a result, some rush too precipitously into new relationships in an attempt to compensate for their loss. While it is important to maintain social contact and to develop relationships that support your new identity as a widow or widower, it is equally important to take the necessary time to grieve and to establish some kind of equilibrium before you focus on establishing new relationships. You may find that you need to develop new relationships which can support the new, widowed "you," as opposed to relying exclusively on old relationships where people are used to seeing you as one-half of a couple and may be threatened by you if they still are married.

The absence of your mate may mean that you are not only lonely emotionally and socially, but physically and sexually as well. Research has made it very clear that human beings need to have physical contact and to be touched. Sexual expression is an important part of this aspect of life. In our society, where widowed women have less opportunity to remarry than men, the absence of a rewarding sexual life may be quite distressing, especially if one existed previously in the marriage. How you will eventually solve this problem is an individual question. However, it may be necessary for you to develop a new system of values for this particular situation or you may become quite frustrated and unsatisfied with your celibate life.

Resumption of dating and remarriage does not always occur without difficulty. Frequently there are problems with children who for personal or economic reasons resent their surviving parent's involvement with someone else. Both widows and widowers need to ensure that a remarriage is based on a healthy decision and reflects appropriate compatibility. Marriage stemming exclusively from loneliness, the desire to avoid grief, or a need to replace the lost spouse can be detrimental in the long run. This does not mean that new and healthy relationships cannot be forged; it only means that they require appropriate time and consideration. (See chapter 18 for more on resumption of dating.)

In situations where you are handicapped, infirm, or elderly, being alone can be a matter of serious practical consequences. You may have been quite dependent on your spouse physically and socially as well as emotionally and financially. This may mean that the death of your spouse compromises your own health and safety. It will be important that you ask concerned others to help you assure your adequate survival. Don't be afraid to reach out for this assistance to people you know or to appropriate community resources.

Adjusting to Widowhood

To adjust, besides working on your grief, you will need to evaluate your personal situation. You must identify the roles and functions previously assumed by your spouse that will have to be adopted by you or someone else in order to continue with as similar a life-style as before. For example, you may discover that you need assistance with financial planning or with some domestic tasks. You will need to identify your strengths and weaknesses. Then you will need to capitalize on your strengths and compensate for your weaknesses as you start to operate in the new world without your spouse. Whether or not other widows or widowers have difficulties at the same times or in the same areas as you do is irrelevant. You must focus on what is causing your problems and what you can do to cope with them.

Widows especially will need to assess their educational, occupational, and social skills and gear their plans and education to what they will need to know and do in order that they and their family can survive. Some of this may entail a loss of their traditional sex role, moving from being a passive woman to being an independent and self-sustaining one. In and of itself, this must be recognized as possibly being a major secondary loss that will have to be dealt with. For widowers, there is usually less of this involved.

One of the major problems in adjusting to widowhood stems from having to shoulder responsibilities alone. The physical and emotional fatigue can be enormous. In no way is this more burdensome than with the responsibilities pertaining to minor children. Single parenting is not easy under any circumstances; it is particularly overwhelming when you are simultaneously struggling to cope with the loss of your loved one. You must be careful about not placing inappropriate expectations on your children to take care of you (be they minors or adults). You should not depend on them too much; yet you should not bar them from your life nor live exclusively for them either. Both you and your children have separate, although interconnected, lives to lead. With your minor children you will need to have the proper perspective on your abilities to parent and mourn at the same time. You will have to do the best that you can under the circumstances, be realistic about what you can expect of yourself, and tap into other resources to help you help your children and yourself (see chapter 13 for a full discussion of this).

Despite the many social problems of widowhood, it has been found that many widowers and widows eventually seem to adjust to their change in status. Some even derive a good deal of pleasure and independence from their new lives, feeling more competent, active, and free. Self-help groups can be quite important in your adjustment, as members can be models for you, teach you necessary new skills, help you solve problems, give you advice, and provide you social opportunities to experience a new widowed role.

An important point to keep in mind is to avoid making decisions precipitously. As much as possible, maintain the status quo for a while to spare yourself the problems caused by hasty decisions. For some widows, especially those concerned about financial survival, it may be quite difficult not to immediately take some action designed to protect your family. If you believe this absolutely must be done, make sure you talk with several trusted people who are qualified to advise you in the specific area. However, many more problems are caused by decisions made in overreaction to initial fear (for example, selling family possessions, moving, or putting your house on the market) than are caused by taking some time to make sure the decisions are warranted and will help, not hurt, the family you love.

The death of your spouse confronts you with the loss of a significant part of yourself, someone who was crucial in helping you define yourself and your world. More than many other losses, it can prompt the need for major identity changes and assumptions of new skills and roles that may challenge much of your previous sex-role conditioning and experience.

10

Adult Loss of a Parent

I N today's society, in the cycle of human development, it is normal and natural to lose your parents when you yourself are an adult. The death of parents is the single most common form of bereavement for adults. Depending on their ages and on yours, death is usually more or less expected. In contrast to the death of a child, it is consistent with the laws of nature. In contrast to the death of a spouse, it usually does not deprive us of our primary sources of companionship and identity. And in contrast to the loss of a brother or sister, it is usually less threatening to us personally.

Nevertheless, the death of a parent is not insignificant. Despite your expectations and those of society to the contrary, the loss of your parents has profound implications for you. Although you may be an "adult child," you are still the child of your parents, and this role will determine a number of your issues in whatever grief you experience over their deaths.

Factors Influencing Your Grief

Your response to the death of your parent will, of course, be influenced by a number of factors (see chapter 4 for more on this). Without question, the importance of the loss will be determined by the meaning of the relationship and the roles your parent played in your life at the time of death. Those of you whose relationships were negative, unsatisfactory, or highly ambivalent will have a different grief response from those who basically had a positive relationship with their parent. For illustration purposes, this chapter will examine the loss of the more-or-less ideal relationship with a parent. If your relationship departed from this, you can expect to have correspondingly different grief experiences. It is assumed that you are familiar with the general issues and responses of grief discussed in chapters 2 and 3 of this book, and therefore this chapter will highlight only those that relate specifically to the adult's loss of a parent.

One of the most critical factors influencing your grief will be your age and that of your parent. There is a major difference between losing your parent when you are in your twenties and she is middle-aged and losing her when you are in your seventies and she is quite elderly. Your dependency on and need for her, the quality and stage of the parent–child relationship, her involvement in life (yours and hers), and your connection to her naturally changes over time and will influence your grief. So, too, will your sense of the psychological acceptability of her death at that time.

For example, in your twenties and thirties you are experiencing transition and change in your life. You often still are struggling to separate from your parents and to be independent. At this stage, despite possible physical and financial separation, there is usually not complete psychic separation. You still are attempting to consolidate your own sense of identity. At the same time, you are building your family and your career, often while your parents are still actively enjoying theirs. You may be relying on your parents for support and advice with both. They may be helping you with the stresses of having your first child, or assisting you financially in purchasing your first house.

The death of a parent at this point can be particularly poignant. Not only is there regret that the parent is robbed of the many more years he or she could have had, but there is also the sense of your being robbed of a significant person who could help you and validate you in the important areas of development of the twenties and thirties.

In contrast to that developmental period, your years of the forties and fifties are marked with relative stability. At this time, you give career and family responsibilities primary focus. Developmental concerns of mid-life are prominent as you confront your own aging-related issues—issues of meaning, identity, mortality, and reordered priorities. While it is true that these issues can precipitate crises, they also can lead to growth, rediscovered or newly identified parts of the self, and greater personal satisfaction. The middle years are often the most success-filled and enjoyable. Many of life's uncertainties have been resolved. There may be new freedom with increased financial income and children leaving home. Throughout all of this, there is often an ever present concern about the aging of your parents and a continually sharpening awareness that their time is limited.

Throughout these years and in the decades thereafter, your parents may become increasingly dependent upon you. Role reversals or dependency shifts may occur, and you may find yourself caring for the ones who once cared for you. They may require increased time and assistance from you psychologically, socially, physically, or financially. This usually is not without some conflict, since, in addition to coping with your own mid-life concerns and your own aging, you still have continued responsibilities to family and career. To lose a parent at this time will present you with the necessity of reconciling these normal, but uncomfortable, feelings (see chapter 7 on grief after long-term illness, since these same issues apply). Your parent's death also will foreshadow your own as you contend with your own declining abilities and advancing age and as your expectations of your own future death are tied to your family history, in terms of longevity and type of death.

The age and life circumstances of your parent also will affect your grief. If your parent was enjoying life and feeling fulfilled, no matter what her age her death may seem untimely. If your parent was senile, or in pain, or was waiting for death, it may seem a blessed relief when she finally dies. Again, this must be viewed from your own perspective. Age alone does not in and of itself make death "okay." One woman suddenly lost her ninety-eight-year-old, sound-of-mind, and relatively healthy mother. She was absolutely furious when friends told her she should be pleased that her mother had lived to such a ripe old age—she felt her mother should have had at least another five years, since her grandmother had been one hundred and three when she died.

Another factor that is particularly important in this type of loss is whether this is your first or second parent to die. If it is the first parent, you may be inexperienced with death and grief. It even might be the first time you have had to confront the fact that, most probably, you will someday be living without either parent. Also, you usually have to be concerned about the impact on your surviving parent. You may have increased responsibilities now for this parent, potential problems with siblings about the family division of labor and responsibilities, and new emotional issues or conflicts about the nature and extent of your duties and continuing relationship with your surviving parent. For instance, you need to figure out what is appropriate and realistic for you to do to try to take away your parent's loneliness for his or her spouse. If you had a more positive relationship with your parent who died, you may have to struggle with feelings that the "wrong" one died, and the "wrong" one was left behind.

Regardless of age or circumstance, when your second parent dies you already have had some practice. You already might have learned that your subconscious, childish belief about your parents' immortality has to be relinquished. However, the death of your second parent casts you in a totally new category—you are now an orphan. The many implications of this are discussed below, after examining the inappropriate expectations which both you and others may hold for yourself in this type of bereavement.

Inappropriate Expectations for Grieving

As adults we often surprise ourselves with the intensity of our feelings of grief when our parent dies. We do not expect the loss to produce such serious effects. Some of us erroneously think that because our feelings of attachment to others—our spouse and our children—are so strong, we will not grieve much when our parent dies. Attachments to others may help us deal with our grief, but they do not make it unnecessary when we lose a parent.

Certainly you may regard your current relationships with your spouse and children as your primary emotional investments. Your feelings, thoughts, behaviors, and energies may be directed towards them. You may have decided that, if necessary to choose, they are the ones whom you must accord first priority over your parents. Nevertheless, unless your relationship with your parent is one from which you have already emotionally detached yourself (and this does happen in some cases, whether in addition to or following from geographical distance), the death of a parent will affect you to a greater or lesser extent depending on the factors surrounding it and you.

You may think that because you are an adult you should not be doing so badly, you should not feel so much like a child. However, feeling regressed and childish is a normal response to loss, and it is to be expected here, no matter what your age. Because of society's attitude that it is expectable and acceptable for the old to die and for parents to predecease their children, you might think that something is wrong for you to be so distressed. You may think that you are handling your parent's death poorly because you are finding yourself actively grieving and focusing on "the old days."

These are all natural responses to the death of a parent. Regardless of your age, your other attachments, or your other responsibilities, you still have lost your parent. It is no wonder that you may feel less than strong, or immature. You have lost the person to whom you were a child. Even if you are among the most powerful people on earth, you are still a child vis-à-vis your parent. Some childish feelings inevitably get resurrected, however, briefly, when your parent dies. You may find it easy to deny your grief and childish feelings because of the responsibilities and activities of daily living which occupy you. Society will help you do this because it does not define your parent's death as a major or disruptive loss. Yet the fact remains, especially when this is the death of your second parent, that this is a loss which must be grieved and which brings with it a number of implications for you.

There may be some feelings of guilt on your part if you feel that pressing responsibilities at home or work interfere with your grief. You might remember how your parent always put you first, and be distressed that you are not putting your grief over your parent first now. Or you might be underestimating the impact of the grief you feel. Consistent with society's attitude that this is not a "high grief loss," you still may expect yourself to be a fully functioning adult in all areas of your life and not give yourself the required time or permission to grieve over the death of your parent. In such an instance, you can set yourself up for problems, just as does any mourner who pays insufficient attention to the grief work that is required after a particular loss. And, just like that mourner, you can expect that most probably the reactions will emerge in some other, less healthy ways.

The Parent–Child Relationship and the Meaning of Its Loss

Our relationship to our parents is a relationship unlike any other. No one else knows us and our past in the same way; no one else can be as uniquely important. With the loss of a parent, we have to make some major adjustments in the way we view the world and ourselves.

Parents' Unique Role in Our Lives

For better or worse, parents are a part of their children. Whether we choose to be like them, whether we consciously decide to be the opposite of them, or whether we unknowingly pick up some of their good or bad traits—all of us have parts of our parents as parts of ourselves. This is the way that human beings develop.

Our parents helped us to form our images and sense of ourselves. They influenced what we think and feel about ourselves: how much we like

ourselves; to what extent we think we are good, worthwhile, or competent people; and how much we value ourselves. Also, they helped to determine how we see the world and the others in it. By the ways they treated
us, our parents (or those who acted in parental roles even if they were
not our biological parents, such as adopted parents or the persons who
raised us) gave us the self-concept through which we evaluate everything
and everyone in the world. Our feelings, thoughts, hopes, desires, attitudes,
values, and morals, which guide everything we do, have been profoundly
influenced by our parents. These are not only the parents who do or did
exist in real life, but the "parents" who exist in our hearts and in our
minds. These are the parents we carry with us forever.

For most of us, when we lose our parents we lose the figures who for
a very long time, if not always, had been the most influential and powerful in our lives. While at the point in time at which they finally die their
status might not be equal to that earlier period, the fact that they once
were such extraordinarily significant people in our lives (either positively
or negatively) makes their deaths special.

For us, their children, parents play a number of roles. This continues
throughout childhood and often beyond. Ideally they are protectors, providers, problem solvers, advisors, nurturers, and comforters. They are self-
sufficient and in control of what happens to and for us. They can "fix"
things so they are right for us. Their loss, even if it occurs long after they
have ceased playing these roles for us and when we might resent it if they
tried to, frequently stirs up for us feelings about losing a person who holds
this type of valued role(s). For example, we may have long ago stopped
needing them as protectors, but to varying degrees their deaths may bring
up feelings of being vulnerable in the world, of being like a little child
without her mother.

This can happen with regard to all the roles our parents play or did
play for us, as well as with regard to the expectations attached to the
role of parent itself. As noted in chapter 12 on parents who lose children,
the social and personal expectations for parents are that they are all-loving,
all-good, all-concerned, totally selfless, and motivated only by their children
and their children's welfare. They are to have perfect and unconditional
love for their children. Although this is unrealistic, this is what we, as
children, universally long for from our parents. Some of us learn to temper
this with a little more realism; others hang onto this desire forever and
judge parents and others negatively when they fail to live up to this
expectation.

Some of your losses, therefore, stem from your recognition that with the death of your parent, no one will ever love you or be as concerned about you in quite the same way. In essence, this is true. The feelings of attachment for a child are different from any others. Losing the person from whom these feelings came will deprive you of someone who loves you in a very intense and unique way. The comment from a fifty-year-old man who had just lost his second parent, his mother, describes it aptly: "No one ever loves you like your mother. I will never be loved that way again in my life."

This man is absolutely correct—no one ever again will love him like his mother. And no one should! He will be loved as a spouse, a father, a sibling, an uncle, a friend, and all the other roles he has in his life, but unless he has another person who filled a maternal role for him, he will not be the recipient of that kind of love. Since that type of love is idealized not only by us as children, but by artists, poets, philosophers, and all others in society, we must expect to have some feelings of grief upon losing it. Such a loss need not only occur at death, however. It also can occur, for example, as Alzheimer's disease robs the personality of our parent and takes her from us long before she actually dies.

So with the death of your parent you may feel the loss of the perfect and unconditional love that only a parent is supposed to be capable of supplying. You lose someone to validate you and your accomplishments in the way only a parent, to whom you have wanted to prove yourself, can. If you do not feel you have already done so, you also lose the opportunities to prove yourself once and for all. Our parents, besides being our caretakers, usually have been our primary providers of praise and the permission givers in our lives. Even when we mature enough not to require this from them, seldom does recognition from others mean more. Just look at the people to whom works of art, scholarship, and charity have been dedicated. Parents are right up there.

Loss of Ties to the Past and Childhood

Unlike most other people in your life, your parent usually always has been there in some fashion. This is not to say that the relationship has been good or that you were never abandoned by your parent. Unhappily, these things do happen. What it refers to is the coincidence of lives. For example, by definition, unless she died at your birth your mother has been in existence from the time of your beginning until the time one of you dies.

While others may have been born and died since then, until her death she always existed somewhere in your life. This consistency obviously is destroyed with her death. For those of us for whom the relationship was more positive than negative, and for whom it was a present aspect in our lives, the removal of the longest consistent element in our lives brings many reactions.

Some of these reactions center around losing your connection to the past. Your parents interpret life to you, life in general and the life of your family. They are roots back to your ancestors, both biologically and psychosocially. They help you to see events in the context of the family. They are the keepers of tradition. They help you make sense of your present in light of your past. They may remind you that this is not the first time you have felt this way, and then they tell you a story about yourself that you had long since forgotten which puts things into perspective for you.

Your parents go all the way back with you. They may be the only ones around who have known you all your life, the only ones who remember that you used to be a skinny, gawky kid who had a beloved puppy named Duchess. They may be the only ones around, besides yourself, who can remember what you looked like before you grew your beard and moustache. For some of us who have no brothers or sisters, gave up our maiden name at marriage, or who have no children, our parents may be the only others with our same last name, with our same heritage, with the same knowledge of "the old days," and with the same memories of co-history as we have. They are or were the primary interpreters of you. When they die, we lose all of this. Like a community or institution which loses its archives in a fire, we have been stripped of a form of documentation of our lives and our history. We also have lost the direct links to our past and to unremembered parts of ourselves.

Loss of a Buffer Between You and Death

When your parents die, there is a buffer gone between you and death. A barrier has been removed. You are now the older generation. You may feel vulnerable because death seems closer. There is no longer a generation between you and it, no longer an insulating layer of people through which nature must pass before it is your turn to face mortality. Along with this, you may be dealing with the loss of constancy. Your parents have always been alive. Now these always-have-been-there elements in your life have been removed. It places you in a different relation to life than ever before.

With the weight of being the oldest generation, and with the awareness that you no longer have your parents to fall back on or to buffer you from old age and eventual death, you may think of youself in a different way. For some of us, this is the first time we no longer think of ourselves on some level as children. We perceive ourselves truly as adults because there are no longer any parents to be children to. Consequently, a more mature stance can be a result of the death of our parents.

Becoming an Orphan

By the same token, the recognition that you are an ophan once your second parent dies is a profound realization. A "given" is taken away. Our very foundations can be shaken. And this makes sense, because our parents served as our foundations. Never before have we been in the world without at least one of these two people. Despite intellectual recognition to the contrary, you may feel that this is the first time they let you down, the first occasion they abandoned you. You may feel insecure, vulnerable, anxious. You are on your own with respect to not having parents for the first time in your life. Depending on the relationship lost, you have lost direction, guidance, and security.

The death of our second parent may mean you no longer can go "home" either physically or psychologically. For some, this is a major loss. "Home" had continued to be a place of comfort, a refuge where you could be yourself without the pressures of the world impinging. If the death of the second parent means losing the house, person, or environment that signalled "home," it can be a major secondary loss for you which can cause feelings of rootlessness and insecurity.

This does not mean that you cannot function. It does not mean that you fall apart. It does not mean that your grief will be overly intense or overly long in duration. These dimensions will be determined by the specific constellation of factors describing you, your parents, and their particular deaths. What it does mean is that you will have to contend with a new set of circumstances in and a new relationship with the world. You will have to redefine your sense of self to accommodate the fact that there are no parents to be a child to; no parents to act out certain roles with and for you; and no parents to embody anymore to any extent the fantasies about and the aspects and attributes of the universally wished-for perfect parent.

Loss of Future Opportunities

Depending upon the age of your parent and the circumstances of the death, you may be particularly disturbed by the fact that this death has robbed you of a very special friend. In many parent–child relationships there is a gradual change in the quality of the association as the child becomes an adult. The connection is now more reciprocal, with sharing of mutual interests. As the parents relinquish their caretaking duties as the child matures, there is usually less conflict and fewer power struggles. Many adults report how their parents have mellowed or, to their amazement, gotten so much smarter than they ever were before. While certainly some of this may be true, in many cases it reflects the normal developmental easing of tensions that can occur when the child feels secure enough in her own right that she does not require former amounts of approval, permission, and dependence.

With decreased parent–child conflict, with increased understanding of one another assisted by your having your own family and/or mature responsibilities, and with your parent treating you as an adult, the relationship may be the very best it has ever been. Now that much of the normal difficulty between generations has been bridged, you may feel deep regret at losing your parent. You may wish that you could have had more of this, and feel a sense of violation that it was taken away at the time it was so pleasurable.

With the death of your parent you lose opportunities also to atone or make up for unpleasantness in the past or to have further contact in the future. Along with this, you may feel quite grieved over the fact that you couldn't have helped your parent in the way you would have liked. You may recall how this person always would help you out, how she consistently took care of you first before herself, how he could always fix what was wrong. Now you are in a position where you would want to return the favors—to help her, to take care of them, to correct it so he doesn't have to die. Your sadness and frustration at not being able to make it "all better" for your parents, as they so often did for you, can be quite painful.

On the other hand, there is a reaction which some adults experience upon the loss of their parents which often is not addressed: the sense that "Now it's over." It is not that you are unmoved by the death of your parents. Rather, the worry over their eventual deaths is now gone. You no longer have to face the uncomfortable thought that "One of these days I am going to lose my parents." It finally has happened, and you do not have to deal with the anticipatory anxiety anymore. Your fears about how you would react are quelled. You have already undergone the feared experience, and its potential occurrence can no longer frighten you.

As with other loved ones who die, when you grieve the deaths of your parents you grieve not only for them but also for yourself, for what you have lost with their deaths. This may also specifically involve grieving over the fact that your parents will miss seeing you achieve and be successful. It often entails sadness at the fact that your parents will miss seeing their grandchildren grow up, along with regret that your children will not have future experiences with their grandparents. In cases where your parents were providing tangible and practical assistance, such as financial resources or babysitting services, their losses will be felt in these areas too.

If Your Relationship
with Your Parent Was Negative

Despite personal and societal wishes to the contrary, not all parent–child relationships are primarily healthy and positive. In these cases, grief can be expected to be more complicated because of the ambivalence that is present. In some cases there is no grief, only relief. When the death of a parent ends a relationship that is painful, when it offers you the chance to be free of conflicts and other negativities which the parent brought up for you, you may have more to celebrate than to grieve. You may have new freedom and new chances. You may be out from under a burdensome relationship. You may not have to contend anymore with the person who saw you as bad or as a failure.

Some of these negative holds your parents had on you can be perpetuated if you fail to detach yourself from them. For example, some of us fear growth and change if it is not sanctioned by our parents. Or, because of psychological concerns about what it would mean if we were to do better in our lives than our parents, some of us hold ourselves back and sabotage our successes in life. Some of us feel guilty that we really did outlive the parents we may have cursed and wished dead for so long.

In these situations, if you cannot work through the self-defeating and unhealthy ways in which you continue to let your parents affect your life, it will be necessary for you to seek professional help. Sometimes this will be merely to help you see that the images and messages you have internalized about your deceased parents are frozen in your mind, and that, unlike normal human beings, they do not change and develop over time. You may need to be reminded that death has robbed both your parents and your internalized images of them of the opportunity for further growth. They may be inappropriate to current situations and to the age you are now. This is because we change constantly, but they are frozen at the time of death. It will be important for you to reevaluate them in this perspective and to decide whether to retain or change them for your greater benefit.

Sometimes the aging of our parents, and their illnesses and declining physical abilities, only serve to increase the conflicts that were there already. This, in and of itself, may increase the problems you may have with them and present you with more ambivalent feelings to contend with when they are gone. Frequently, adult children are put in the position of caring for an ill or elderly parent. This means that they will be subject to the inordinate stresses, strains, and conflicts which are found in families whose loved ones are dying from a long-term illness (see chapter 7 for more on this). You understandably may have many feelings about the demands this can place upon you in all areas—psychologically, physically, socially, and financially. You and your family may experience psychological conflicts, emotional exhaustion, physical debilitation, social isolation, and family discord in caring for your ill or aging parent.

After these types of death, along with the normal responses to loss you may feel relief from the demands. However, you also may feel increased guilt and anger. This is especially true if, against your wishes, you either had to take your parent into your home or you had to institutionalize your parent. As with any terminal illness, when taking care of one who is aging there will be conflicts about whose needs to meet, frustration with clashing roles and responsibilities, and the stress of balancing the incompatible demands of anticipatory grief. All of this will put you in a position that will very likely lead you to be exhausted and resentful at the time of death. While this is quite normal, you may either not be aware of it or may judge yourself very guilty as a result. Or, you might be one of the adult children who devote most of your time and resources to caring for your parents. You even may not have gotten married in order to be their caretaker. After their deaths, you may be forced to confront what will happen to you now that the purpose and focus of your life is gone. It can be a major period of readjustment.

Whether or not the negative feelings in your relationship with your parent comes from long-standing problems between the two of you or whether they are relatively recent and caused by the normal stresses of illness and aging, it still will be necessary to grieve the loss and to come to grips with what it means and what the implications are for you. This grief may be more or less intense depending on what the death of this parent in this fashion at this time means for you.

Social Support

Since many of the people in your life may not have seen you actively involved as the child of your parent, they might not be able to appreciate what this loss means to you. For example, unless your friends were aware of your type of involvement with your parent, they may be unable to see precisely what it was that you lost when your parent died. Especially in this mobile society, where it is highly likely that your friends never even saw your parents, might not even have remembered if they were alive, much less knew them to share more completely in your grief, you may greatly miss the support of others who had known both you and your parent for some time. Therefore it is quite probable that this will not be the type of community-recognized or shared loss it might be, for example, if your spouse died.

Your spouse and children may or may not feel the loss. It depends on the type of relationship they had with your parent. For some children, the death of their grandparent is a nonevent. They know that the death has occurred but cannot really feel much about it because of the lack of relationship with their grandparent. While they may be quite affected by their own parent's distress at the loss, they may have little to grieve for themselves. Do not expect your children to mourn those they never knew, despite what the loss means to you.

With your spouse there is usually more knowledge of your parent, but again, depending on the relationship, there will be differing types of grief. For some, the death of a beloved in-law can be just as hard, if not worse, than the death of their own parent. It will depend on what the in-law meant to them. The death of your parent can be perceived as a blessing or a relief.

In any event, it is important for you to recognize that the death of your parent, unless that parent was an integral part of your own family of spouse and children, most probably will not be viewed by them in either the same fashion or with the same importance as it is for you. You could expect to see more understanding and greater similarity of response (although family members' responses are always idiosyncratic, depending on the factors involved) if your parent had been more a part of their lives. Although your parent may have been the most influential person in your life, and for years was the closest person to you, an essential part of your existence, that parent may have been no more than a peripheral figure to the others who are so close to you now. It is strange that those who are the closest to us are not the closest to each other, but this is not uncommon in this day and age.

Changes in Family Relationships

The death of the first parent usually means some reorganization in your relationship with your surviving parent. Regardless of the quality of the relationship, it will need to be readjusted to reflect the fact that your parent is not one of two parents anymore, but your sole surviving parent. You will need to perceive and relate to this parent as an individual, who is no longer one-half of the parental unit.

For some of you, this may be the first time you have considered your parent as a distinct person outside of the parental role or the marital pair. This can give you the opportunity to assess who and what he or she really is. This may mean you now can relate to your parent in a more positive fashion (for example, "I can see that she is vulnerable and no longer has the power over me she once did. Therefore, it's a little easier to be sympathetic to her now"), although sometimes it can be more negative (for example, "Without Mom here to soften things, I can see just how miserable my father really is").

One of the most frequent consequences of the death of a parent is a change in relationships with brothers and sisters. You may find that during the illness or aging of your parent, or after the death, you had different relationships with your siblings. These changes can be for the better or the worse. They stem not only from reactions to the events during the illness and after the death but also from the role reorganizations and reassignments that occur after a death in any family (see chapter 8 for a discussion of this important process).

If one of you felt you had more than your fair share of the burden of your parent, or if you feel that your older sibling is now trying to act as if he or she is your parent, there is bound to be resentment and anger. The stress of a dying or dead parent or what to do about the surviving parent can put enormous strains on sibling relationships. Old conflicts, long-buried or still seething; sibling rivalries, new or old; and unresolved issues around power, control, and favoritism can erupt. Perhaps your parent kept the peace. Or perhaps you and your siblings kept the infighting to a minium to protect your parent. When these reasons are gone, and replaced by concerns about money, estate disposition, and "who's done more for whom," many secondary losses can occur in addition to the loss of your parent. Unfortunately, the death of a parent has not infrequently provoked serious family estrangement.

However, all the changes need not be negative. Oftentimes siblings are able to work out their differences, if they have them, and to pull together for the surviving parent and the family. You may even end up being closer to a sibling than before. The shared loss of your parent may help put previous conflicts in perspective. You may recognize that the value of keeping together with your siblings, and of keeping in contact with those who shared your past at the earliest and most formative times of your life, is worth the effort to do so.

The death of your parent may surprise you with the reactions it stimulates. Despite social expectations to the contrary, the adult's loss of a parent can have profound implications because of the significance of the role a parent plays.

11

Adult Loss of a Sibling

THERE is no other loss in adult life that appears to be so neglected as the death of a brother or sister. Rarely has it been the subject of investigation or discussion. Nevertheless, this is a loss to which most of us are repeatedly exposed. While we have only one mother, one father, and one spouse (at least at any given point in time), it is not uncommon to have several siblings. Therefore we are more exposed to sibling deaths than to other losses.

Social Expectations

There is a general social expectation that the death of a brother or sister in adulthood will have little or no disruptive effect on us. Yet few adults have no contact with their siblings. This expectation seems to be based on the presumption that child and spouse loss are the most distressing. Usually, if given the opportunity to think about it, people also can understand an adult's bereavement after a parent's death. In contrast to this, however, there is a failure to appreciate the significance of brothers and sisters in adult life. While the effects of childhood sibling bereavement have been investigated, there has not been the same degree of interest in adult sibling bereavement.

The Sibling Relationship

There are special characteristics unique to the sibling bond. It is a relationship that can be quite profound, either positively or negatively.

Brothers and sisters influence each other's identity in fundamental ways. Just the existence of an older sibling, regardless of the relationship that exists, has a number of implications for the younger siblings in terms of (1) birth order; (2) parental attention, affection, and expectations; and (3) the world the younger siblings are born into. The research on birth order and its influence on self-concept, personality, and all subsequent life experiences is quite striking. It demonstrates clearly the impact of brothers and sisters on our lives, and this is without taking into consideration the precise relationship that exists among them.

When these relationships are taken into account, even more dramatic influences are apparent. As we naturally seek security, attention, and love from our parents, it is only normal that we perceive our brothers and sisters as competitors for these precious parental commodities. Sibling rivalry is not something that requires much explanation, at least not to those of us who have siblings! Along with this, just living together in the intimacy of family life will put us in positions with our siblings where normal feelings of tension and aggression are bound to erupt. Yet siblings are also often sources of affection and security as well as of conflict. For this reason, ambivalence about siblings is not uncommon.

Sibling relationships may be close and intimate, distant and formal, or anything in between. By its very nature, the sibling relationship is ripe for ambivalence. How much will depend on a whole set of variables outside the scope of this book. What is important to remember is that sibling relationships are often marked by attachment as well as antagonism, caring as well as competition, and loyalty as well as lingering resentment. Certainly one of the primary factors influencing your grief response over the death of your brother or sister is the type of relationship you had with him or her.

Meaning of the Loss

Let's assume that your brother or sister was raised with you, that you had the same parents, and that you were close enough in age that you had normal sibling contact. If your circumstances were different, the following comments will be less applicable to you.

When you lose a brother or sister in adult life, you experience many of the same losses as you would if you had lost that sibling in childhood. However, despite the fact that you are more mature and have access to the resources you require, you have the disadvantage that there is less social recognition of the loss as an important one. Like those who lose parents in adulthood, unless your sibling was very much a part of your family's life, this death may not have the same impact on other members of your immediate family as it does on you. While your sibling may have been a pivotal person in your life, he or she may have been insignificant to others who now are quite important parts of your life. For this reason, your family may not understand your grief or help you with it in the way they could if someone they knew well had died. They may not understand what the loss means to you or why it affects you like it does, since they did not know you when your sibling was more a part of your life.

The death of a brother or sister means that you have lost someone who was a part of your formative past. This person shared common memories with you, along with critical childhood experiences and family history. This person has known you as a child and is a part of the roots to your past. Chances are that he or she experienced you in unique and intimate ways. Some of these might have been quite pleasant, such as sharing family traditions and holidays. Some might have been unpleasant or situations in which you had little control: seeing you in embarrassing situations, participating in family jokes against you, being hurt by your childhood insensitivity, and so forth. This person knows the family scripts for you and the family myths about you.

You may not agree with your sibling's perceptions of all you have been through together. In fact, it is not uncommon if you don't. Most of us remember our childhood in ways that differ somewhat from our siblings. Also, our perceptions may be quite different now because of the people we have become. At times, those who have known us longest are the ones who least recognize our changes since then, precisely because they are operating with old information that is hard to alter. Nevertheless your sibling *was* there, and the unique co-history you two share can be an important bond between you. When death takes your brother or sister, it also takes away one of your connections to the past, someone who knew you in a very special way, totally unlike those who know you now as an adult.

When your brother or sister dies, you lose someone who has been in your life for a very long time. A constant in your life is gone. This itself may make you feel a little insecure, a little anxious. Although you may not have had frequent contact with your sibling, at least you knew that another member of the family was there. While your sibling may not have been a current real force in your life, he or she probably was a symbolic one, and certainly was one in reality in the past. This person's death can make you feel older. It points out to you that your family is dwindling.

If this person was your final connection to your family of origin, you are now the last one left out of those you started out with.

Because your brothers and sisters share your same genetic background, the death of one of them may increase your concerns about your own death. You may see implications about your own death, such as how you will die and at what age. This identification can cause you some stress later on when you reach the age at which an older sibling died.

Your Grief

Depending upon your relationship with your sibling and the manner of death, your grief probably will follow the typical responses to loss outlined elsewhere in this book (see chapters 2 and 3 for more on this). You may also, however, experience additional feelings of guilt. This often stems from the ambivalence of the sibling relationship and from any relief that you feel, understandably, that you are not the one who has died. If there had been increased stress in recent years, this too could cause guilt and regret after the death. Any type of stress may have affected your adult relationship with your brother or sister, either bringing you closer together or driving you farther apart. For example:

Developmental stress, as when one of you becomes widowed and temporarily becomes a little more dependent

Psychosocial stress, as when one of you receives a promotion and moves away

Emotional stress, as when one of you cannot have children and is jealous of the other who can

Physical stress, as when one of you develops a serious illness bringing pain and debilitation

Economic stress, such as when one of you loses your job and is in financial jeopardy

Guilt, as well as sadness, also can develop when you recall that in younger days you had been closer, but that as adults this had changed. This is normal; as adults you had fewer common experiences than when you were younger and shared more of your lives. But the recognition of this difference still can be uncomfortable.

Conversely, you can experience guilt, sadness, and regret because the relationship never was what you ideally would have wanted it to be. Perhaps you never had the closeness that you would have liked. If you feel this type of regret, you will grieve not only for what you had and lost but also for what you never had at all.

This grieving for what you never had can be intensified if you have been raised with unrealistic expectations about family relationships. Television sitcoms from the 1950s to the early 1970s wanted us to believe that siblings and their parents related to each other with uninterrupted warmth and concern that permitted little resentment or frustration. The sitcoms of the later 1970s and 1980s are much more real, some of them irritatingly so. However, they do us less of a disservice. Those of us who grew up with the earlier ones lack what the youth of today see portrayed on their television sets—the information that there always will be ambivalence in our closest relationships. Far too many of us suffer from the guilt and resentment that can develop in grief from unrealistic expectations. In few situations is this more apparent than following the death of a brother or sister.

Your survival itself can be another source of guilt. There were probably times when you wished that your sibling were not around, would disappear, or would drop dead. These feelings usually come back to haunt us. Also, since we do share the same biological backgrounds, we may wonder why death took our sibling first. Unanswered questions about this also can fuel survival guilt.

The adult who loses a sibling shares many similar issues with parents who lose adult children. While certainly the relationship is different, the concerns of the person left behind and the responses they receive may be very similar. For example, you may find that you do not have much part in decisions pertaining to your sibling's death and the funeral or other rituals. These decisions are usually made by your sibling's spouse and children. When this lack of control is combined with the failure of others to recognize that you are profoundly bereaved, it can be most difficult for you. For example, you may not be included in ceremonies honoring your deceased sibling with whom you have shared your last fifty years, while others in his life, who had known him for far less time, are recognized as legitimate mourners.

Also like bereaved parents of adult children, you may find it hard to accept that your brother or sister has really died if you have become accustomed to his or her living elsewhere. There is no acute absence to signal to you that he or she is permanently gone. Seeing the responsibilities left unfulfilled (especially regarding the children left behind), struggling with discomfort when your former in-law starts dating again, worrying about losing contact with your nieces and nephews, or fearing that your deceased sibling's children will not be brought up in the way he or she would have wanted—these are all issues that you can share with parents whose adult children die. (See chapter 12 for more discussion of these shared issues.)

If your sibling died from a long-term illness, the experience may have brought up old rivalries as attention, time, or financial resources of parents and other family members were directed toward your dying sibling. This and other experiences inherent in the terminal illness may have increased resentment on your part (see chapter 7 for more on this). After the death of your sibling, this resentment can come back to haunt you. You will need to put the normal issues of sibling ambivalence in perspective with the normal issues of losing a loved one after a long-term terminal illness in order to cope most effectively with this aspect of your grief.

Like any other death in the family, the death of your brother or sister will force you and the other surviving family members to reorganize your roles and relationships with one another (see chapter 8 for more on this). You may experience additional loss or stress as a consequence. The death may change your position in the family—you may now be the eldest child and be expected to care for an invalid parent, or you may have become an only child. The death also may give you a new status in the family. For example, you now may get some recognition for your achievements, since you are no longer being compared with your older sibling. As with younger children, your parents' responses to the death of your sibling will have a profound impact on you, your grief, and many aspects of your subsequent life. Subtly conveyed messages that the "wrong" child has died, impaired parent–child relationships stemming from parental grief, increased or inappropriate roles assigned to you, and abnormal parental grief responses such as expecting you to become like your deceased sibling—all are unhealthy for them and for you as well.

Time changes sibling relationships, as it does all others. As with your parents, you may find that you can sustain a much better relationship with your sibling when you are both independent adults and involved in your own families and lives. Sometimes this happens after your parents die and you are no longer embroiled in the same old sibling conflicts. When death robs you of a sibling to whom you only recently grew closer, it may seem particularly unfair, untimely, and cruel.

As society fails to validate this as an important loss for you, and many of the people who are close to you did not know your sibling or recognize his or her importance to you, you may very well fail to get the social support you need in order to grieve successfully. You may have to demand this support and assert your right to grieve for this loss.

The death of your sibling may receive little social acknowledgment, but the loss can affect you in many ways. This stems from the special roles siblings play in our development and the need to contend with the ambivalence that marks most sibling relationships at some point in their history.

12

Loss of a Child

I N her book *Marilyn*, on the life of Marilyn Monroe, Gloria Steinem offers a theory about why we pay so much attention to stars who have died young. She attempts to explain why celebrities such as Marilyn Monroe or James Dean have such intense cult followings, in contrast to many venerated, older actors who left much more behind. She cites Henry Fonda as the perfect example of a well-respected and seasoned actor whose death was mourned in a much more conventional way than the deaths of Monroe and Dean. Steinem writes: "When the past dies, there is mourning, but when the future dies our imaginations are compelled to carry it on."

This is also true when a child dies. No matter how old that child was—infant, adolescent, or adult—that child still represented the future to its parents. And we can expect the mourning, like that for Monroe and Dean as compared to Fonda, to be much more intense.

Parental grief is particularly intense. It is unusually complicated and has extraordinary up-and-down periods. It appears to be the most long-lasting grief of all.

When reading this chapter, it is important for you to remember that in most regards the age of your deceased child is irrelevant. Many of the same issues apply to parents who have lost a three-year-old child as to those whose child was seventy-three. Yet in some ways the age *will* influence your grief, because the age of your child relates to the developmental issues that were occurring at the time of death, which you must deal with afterwards. For example, if your child died in adolescence, at a time when she was being normally rebellious against you as a parent, you probably were left feeling that you had been in a struggle with her. In contrast, if your child died at twelve months, rebelliousness would not be an issue for you. However, you will have to cope with the loss of a child to whom you gave physical, hands-on care, someone you could "baby." The age of the child colors every parent's grief because it identifies the issues that were present in the parent–child relationship at the time of death.

There is a curious social phenomenon of denying the importance of death at the extremes of childhood—that is, the deaths of infants and of adult children. Most of the books and movies that have been made about dying or dead children pertain to children who are school-aged or teenagers. Yet parents who lose infants or adult children are bereaved just as much as those who lose children in between.

Finally, keep in mind that with the death of your child you not only have lost that particular child but also the specific hopes, dreams, expectations, fantasies, and wishes you had for that child. You have lost parts of yourself, parts of your partner, parts of your family, and parts of your future. While this is true for mourners who lose others besides children, the impact of it is especially difficult on bereaved parents.

Your child's death changes your life in many ways. In the following section we will talk about how it affects you both as a parent and as part of a couple and how it affects your family.

You as Parent

The parent–child relationship is unlike any other. It is closer and more involving, demanding much time and energy. Yet it is also more precious and harder to lose. By understanding more about this relationship, your grief, and its difficulties, you may develop some insights into what you feel and how to handle it.

Your Role

From the time of the first news of pregnancy, the prospective parents attach many feelings (both positive and negative) and hopes onto the child-to-be. For example, you may view the child as a symbolic extension of yourself, or as a sign that you are a worthwhile person. The child may represent love or proof of maturity to you, or may provide you with purpose and meaning.

Your relationship with your child is a combination of feelings and thoughts about yourself and others, as well as about that particular child. As a result, your feelings may range from delight in seeing her to feeling that she is the worst part of yourself. You may regard the child as the beloved product of the union between you and your partner. You may see her as someone who makes you feel good because you can give her love and security. She may prove to you that you are competent, or offer you the chance and hope to rectify past mistakes and "do it right this time." An infinite number of feelings, meanings, needs, expectations, and hopes characterize what this child signifies to you. And they are different for each child you have.

Whatever the child represents to you, she is also a unique person, connected to you in fundamental and lasting ways, yet separate as well. Your relationship to your child is determined by the distinctly original person that she is—her particular personality, characteristics, abilities, and roles—as well as the meanings, needs, and hopes that you have placed upon her.

In no other role are there so many personally assumed and socially assigned responsibilities as in the role of parent. The social expectations for you as a parent are enormous. You are expected to be all-loving, all-good, all-concerned, totally selfless, and motivated solely by your child and her welfare. In no other role are you subject to such unrealistic expectations. They do not allow for normal frustration, ambivalence, and anger—expectable feelings in all relationships with people we are close to. As a result, the role of parent sets you up to feel guilty whenever you do not meet these expectations. Just think about it. You hear many mother-in-law jokes and countless humorous stories about husbands and wives. In contrast, how many times are children made the butt of jokes? By and large, we don't laugh at our parental roles as much as at our other roles. We take this role more seriously. As parents, we take on more expectations and responsibilities, unrealistic though they are, than in any other relationship.

Parents have a number of roles with their children. You are expected to be both protector and provider, problem-solver and advisor. You are accustomed to being self-sufficient and in control of what happens to and with your children; you are used to "fixing" things. All of these roles help define your feelings about yourself as a person and as a parent. Typically, the death of your child will cause you extreme guilt for failing to meet all these various expectations, roles, and responsibilities, despite the fact that they were totally unrealistic to begin with.

Your Grief

We know that the relationship between parents and children is the most intense of all human relationships—physically, psychologically, and socially.

When your child dies, those aspects of the relationship that gave it its intimacy and uniqueness are the very aspects that will intensify your bereavement.

In all other relationships, you have an attachment to someone (for example, your spouse) in which you are separate but connected. Your children, however, have sprung from you. They are a part of you and, consequently, in some ways are the same as you. In this way, losing your child means losing parts of yourself. One bereaved mother described it this way: "When you lose your spouse, it is like losing a limb; when you lose your child, it is like losing your lung." Not only does this happen because of the emotional investment you have in your child and the needs, hopes, and dreams you have for her; it also happens because parental attachment to a child consists both of love for the child and self-love. This is why the loss of a child increases the losses to self usually felt after the death of anyone close.

Another way in which you lose part of yourself concerns your sense of immortality. Your children are not only a part of you in the present but also in the future. Part of yourself that would have been perpetuated is destroyed when your child dies. You may have felt comfort that death might claim you but not your genes, as represented physically in your children; and not your thoughts and values, as represented in what you had taught your children. When your child died, those parts of yourself that would have gone on living in your child also died. You are no longer immortal.

One of the major stumbling blocks in resolving parental grief is the unnaturalness of a child's dying before a parent. This is something that most parents cannot comprehend. You expect that, as the parent, you will die before your child. The death of your child, therefore, is a death out of turn. It violates the cycle of nature in which the young grow up and replace the old. The very order of the universe is shattered, and this is something that you might not be able to make sense of. You may experience "survival guilt," the guilt that people feel when the one they love has died and they continue to live. Therefore, the death of a child is one of the very most difficult to cope with because it does not make any sense, it violates all expectations—even nature itself—and leaves bereaved parents feeling guilty for being alive.

With the death of your child you have failed in the basic function of parenthood: taking care of the children and the family. You are supposed to protect and provide for your child. You are supposed to keep her from all harm. She should be the one who grows up healthy to bury you.

When you "fail" at this, when your child dies, you may feel that you have failed at your most basic function.

The death of any child is a monumental assault on your sense of identity. Because you cannot carry out your role of preserving your child, you may experience an oppressive sense of failure, a loss of power and ability, and a deep sense of being violated. Disillusionment, emptiness, and insecurity may follow, all of which stem from a diminished sense of self.

You will have to grieve and relinquish your former assumptions and beliefs about yourself and your capabilities as a parent. This may involve quite an identity shift for you. Whereas before you may have been able to carry out the roles of protector, provider, problem-solver, and advisor, now you cannot do this. You cannot protect your child from being dead. You cannot solve the problem that is your child's death, and your ability to give advice is useless. This is why you understandably may feel so strange and so powerless.

Along with the loss of the ability to carry out your basic function as a parent, there are multiple secondary losses you may feel when your child dies. This happens after the death of anyone close; however, because of your huge investment in your child, there are many more secondary losses to be dealt with. Also, with the death of your child you lose a very special love source—someone who needs, depends upon, admires, and appreciates you in a unique and gratifying way. All of these losses combine to burden you with a major loss overload, which is one of the things that contributes to your lowered self-esteem and the identity problems you may be having.

In addition to losing your child, you lose the family as you have known it. There is the irretrievable loss of the child's presence and the roles she fulfilled. While this is not uncommon when any family member dies, the absence of a child is particularly poignant because families usually are centered around children. The child who was the clown, or the mediator, or the scapegoat served a function in the family. With the absence of that child, the family is left with a void. The rest of the family will have to make significant changes. Additionally, you lose the part of yourself that was in relationship to that particular child. That special, interactive relationship unique to you and this particular child is gone forever. Although you may have other surviving children, that part of your parental role that existed because of the relationship with your deceased child is altered.

If your child's death was sudden or accidental, you may experience an even greater sense of helplessness and threat. Unexpected, dramatic, and untimely deaths are more likely to produce traumatic effects and more problematic bereavements. (See chapters 6 and 7 for more on this.) Deaths like these typically prompt enormous efforts to find meaning in the death, to determine who is to blame, and to regain some sense of control.

If your child's death occurred from genetic or unexplained medical illness, you also may have increased difficulty with guilt. Because of the biological link, parents often feel that they "gave" the illness to their child. One very bright man, who knew that cancer is not hereditary, never could relinquish the belief that he had passed on cancer to his daughter. Despite all the evidence to the contrary, he asssumed guilt for it, saying "The cancer was in her genes. I gave her her genes. Therefore, I killed her." Parents hold themselves responsible for not producing a healthy child who could survive longer, and often feel deficient and worthless as a result. Even when the cause of death is unexplained, parents blame themselves. Some search all the way back to the earliest prenatal experiences in attempts to find the reason for the medical condition: "Perhaps it was because I took aspirin when I was pregnant that she developed the beginnings of the illness that took her life at eleven." Some find even earlier reasons to take the blame: "I didn't take care of myself when I had the measles as a youngster and perhaps this did something to damage me which I, in turn, passed on to my son."

The final issue is one that you may be uncomfortable about admitting. In losing your child, you lose someone who could have cared for you later in life. This may be particularly important to you if you already are older and have been receiving emotional, physical, or financial assistance from your adult child who died. If you are like other parents who had hoped to see their grown children and their children's children, the broken expectation may serve to underscore the unnaturalness of your loss and make it more difficult for you to contend with.

Parental Grief: Different from All Others

What is normal in parental bereavement often would seem exaggerated or abnormal in other types of bereavement. This is because of the nature of this loss. It is also because there are a number of issues inherent in losing a child that in and of themselves make bereaved parents more susceptible to unresolved grief. In fact, most of the factors associated with the failure to properly grieve any loss are typically found in the loss of a child. Therefore, the death of your child leaves you in a situation where there is an extraordinarily high number of factors known to compromise your grief. This does not mean you cannot successfully resolve it, only that it will take a longer time and more work to do so as compared to other losses.

You can expect the general grief symptoms and issues to be more intense and to last longer than usual. (See chapters 2 and 3 for these.) This can cause problems if you and others expect your mourning to be the same as you might feel after the death of a spouse, parent, or sibling. It will not be. Parental grief is vastly different from all other griefs. You and others must realize this and never expect it to be the same. In addition, you may have particular problems with some of your grief reactions because of this kind of loss. These will be identified next. (See chapter 3 for general bereavement reactions as this discussion will focus on only some of the many possible grief responses.)

For many bereaved parents, guilt is the most prominent feature of their grief. In general, whenever you violate your expectations of yourself, you tend to feel guilty. Since, as a parent, you typically have unrealistic expectations and inappropriate standards for yourself about fulfilling parental responsibilities and roles, you are set up to experience a large amount of guilt after your child dies. The fact that these expectations were totally inappropriate to begin with may not stop you from holding yourself responsible for failure to meet them; as a parent you can be quite unreasonable with yourself. When this is combined with other normal reasons for guilt in grief, you may have problems with this emotion.

Another major problem may be your anger. Usually there is strong anger at the death of a child because it violates the very order of nature. Also, since it severs the parent–child bond, which is the most intense one in the world, it is only natural that the anger be quite intense. Your anger may be fueled even more when others start to avoid you because you make them uncomfortable, or they expect you to recover quickly, failing to realize that this loss is totally different from any other. Finally, because the death of a child creates so many secondary losses, and because it is such a tremendous assault on your parental identity, you can expect your anger to be quite profound.

There is separation pain following the death of anyone you love, but it can be particularly intense when it involves the death of your child. The pining and yearning for your child can be excruciating. You may miss the sight of her, the smell of her, the touch of her, the sound of her, and even the way she tasted when you would kiss her head or nuzzle her ears.

If you still were involved in hands-on caretaking, frustration of the desire to care for your child can be torturous.

Because this child was a part of yourself, the loss is even more difficult to bear. You may feel as if part of yourself has been ripped out. Parents of both sexes frequently express their loss in physical terms, saying that they feel "mutilated" or "disabled." Mothers often feel that their child has been snatched out of their arms. Sometimes these feelings are experienced physically as well as psychologically—a gut-wrenching, gnawing emptiness. These acute pangs of separation, deprivation, anguish, sadness, and longing are so intense that they can surprise and shock you. You may fear that you will be overwhelmed by this mental suffering.

Because of the unnaturalness of your child's dying before you, and because of your heightened feelings of guilt and failure, you most probably will embark consciously or unconsciously on a desperate search for meaning. You need to understand why this unnatural event has occurred. You may find that it makes no sense that children must suffer and die, and may wonder why you did not die instead. Like those of other mourners, some of your questions may be answered, while others will remain unanswered. Because of your anger and need to restore order, you may find yourself needing to assign someone the blame for your child's death. A major problem develops if it inappropriately gets assigned to your spouse because he or she is the closest and easiest to strike out at in your pain and grief.

One of the ways that you can relate appropriately to a loved one who has died is by identifying with some aspects of that individual's personality. (See chapter 14 for more on this.) However, this is easier to do if the person you loved was an adult, rather than a child. In these circumstances, identification is more difficult, since there are fewer behaviors that are appropriate for you to emulate as an adult. Nevertheless, identification is possible. Parents of a little child can, for example, identify with their dead toddler's courage and spunk. The tenacity of an infant's struggle for life may be inspiring to other parents. Problems can arise, however, if identification with your child occurs in these ways:

Too intensely, so that you lose your own sense of personal identity

Inappropriately for an adult—for instance, acting childishly

In areas in which you lack competence, as when you try to be the life of the party that your son was but are not that sociable a person

In ways that are incompatible with your other roles—for instance, becoming a dreamer like your teenaged daughter had been and functioning poorly at work because of it

"Growing up with the loss" is something that all grievers must do, but it is particularly difficult for bereaved parents. This is because as a parent you tend to mark your life by the events and accomplishments of your children. Consequently, times at which your child would have graduated, gotten married, or had children—times that would have reinforced your parental role—often can be marked by brief upsurges in grief. This is to be expected. It must be distinguished from chronic grief, which remains in an acute stage and never subsides.

Finally, the problems that you as a bereaved parent have in getting social support from others can intensify your difficulties. While society values the parent–child relationship above all others, it does little to assist you as bereaved parents. There is not even a word to identify you, such as the term *orphan* for a child who has lost its parents or the terms *widow* or *widower* for one who loses a spouse.

There are greater social problems in responding to the death of a child than to other deaths. This is because as a bereaved parent you represent the very worst fears of every parent. If it happened to your child, then it could happen to my child. As a result, bereaved parents are avoided more than most other mourners and are victims of social ostracism and unrealistic expectations. This is why so many report that they feel like social lepers.

The strange and callous response you may get from others can lead to a lack of important social validation about your child's death and also about ongoing reality. Like individuals who participated in sensory deprivation experiments, you will have difficulties with judging reality if you do not get feedback from others in your environment. When this lack of support and validation is coupled with the inappropriate expectations that society has for bereavement in general and specifically for the loss of a child, you actually can be hurt by society—it not only doesn't help you but can also make the situation worse for you.

As you are struggling to cope with intense reactions of grief following the loss of your child, it is particularly difficult to have to contend as well with these insensitive and hurtful responses of others. You may see this rejection by others as further evidence of the deficiency or lack of value you already may feel because of your inability to protect your child. This is not so. And this is why it is so important for you to associate with other bereaved parents, either informally or through such formal organizations at The Compassionate Friends or groups devoted to specific types of loss such as Mothers Against Drunk Driving (MADD) or those existing for support for parents who miscarry, have stillbirths, or lose their child to Sudden Infant Death Syndrome (SIDS), among others. (See chapter 20 for a full listing.) These groups have arisen to meet some of the psychosocial needs of bereaved parents and to fill in the gaps left by other members of society who are made anxious by you. Use these groups to help you in your grief over the loss of your child.

You as Part of a Couple

One of the things that makes the loss of your child so difficult to endure is that it strikes both you and your spouse at the same time and confronts each of you with the same overwhelming loss. As a result, both of you lose the person to whom you each would normally turn for support, as you both are deeply involved in grief. You experience a loss upon a loss.

Impacts of Grief on the Marital Unit

If your marriage was close before, that strength now may be a disadvantage. It makes both of you particularly vulnerable to the feelings of blame and anger that grievers often displace onto those nearest them. Such closeness also means that you must deal with the grief of your spouse as well as your own. If there is a tight marital bond, you may find little opportunity to get away from grief psychologically or physically. Your sadness may be increased as you see the grief and pain in the face of your spouse. Although one of you may desperately need a respite from the other, it is often hard to request and sometimes even harder to take. Guilt can abound. Feelings of failure in your marital role can develop. While it does not have to damage your relationship permanently, severe grief does not help it at the time. Grief attacks your feelings of security, strength, assertiveness, independence, and health—all necessary for keeping any relationship positive and growing.

Difficulties can arise in the best of marriages when normal ways of relating are disrupted by grief. You must watch out that normal marital friction not be blown out of proportion, as well as take care to minimize the strain put on the relationship because you both are grieving. Be aware that day-to-day problems may not get confronted due to your preoccupation with the death, trying to protect each other, lacking strength, or attempting to avoid a mutual downward spiral. However, when communication does not occur, problems tend to accumulate until there is an explosion. This can result in greater misunderstandings and feelings of helplessness for you both, and you are already overwrought. Communication problems often develop in reaction to the grief:

One of you asks the other unanswerable questions, such as why the death occurred.

One of you avoids communicating with the other out of fatigue or for fear it will upset that person.

One of you makes irrational demands, such as asking the other to take away the pain.

One of you makes rational but unrealistic demands, such as requesting that one of you assume all the duties of the other.

Such communication problems may fuel your fear that you will lose your marriage and your family, in addition to having lost your child. For this reason it will be essential to make a commitment to keeping the communication lines open, despite the tendency to close down in grief. It will be important to set specific time aside to discuss events that have taken place, to plan for what is necessary for other family members, as well as to share your thoughts and feelings with each other. Along with this, however, must come the recognition of the need for some personal solitary time for reflection, respite, and healing. You must balance both.

An often overlooked, but quite sensitive, issue that you might confront is that your spouse may remind you of your deceased child (this can happen with other surviving family members as well). To look into the face of a loved one and see the mannerisms of your deceased child or the twinkle that had been in his eye can be a very painful experience. Yet, on the other hand, you may be among the bereaved parents who are comforted by this, and who treasure it as a beautiful reminder of the child they loved and lost.

Differences in How Each of You Grieves

One of the major problems you may have as a couple is the failure to recognize that each of you has experienced a different loss and will have a unique grief experience. While you may say that you know people grieve in highly personal ways, if you forget this when it comes to your spouse, there will be problems. Be careful that you are not operating under the erroneous assumption that each of you has suffered the same loss and should deal with it the same way. In fact, each of you has suffered a *different* loss. This is because each of you had a separate and unique relationship with your child. Consequently, you will be grieving for different things, despite the fact that you both have had the same child die and perhaps lost some of the same hopes and dreams.

The different social roles and relationships you and your spouse assumed with regard to your child will influence the type of grief experience each of you has after the child's death. For example, if you are the mother in a traditionally oriented family, you may be accustomed to more intimate contact with the child on a daily basis. Therefore, you may have a more acute sense of loss over the lack of presence of your child: not being able to touch him, feed him, smell him, see him, or hear his voice. In contrast, in this example of a traditional family, if you are the father, your contact with your child will probably have been different because your responsibilities are centered outside of the home. For you, the inability to interact with your child through roughhousing, playing sports, or building things may be more painful. You may especially miss your child on weekends when you had shared time together. Your wife may have especially hard times in the afternoons when your child would have been returning home from school. Since each of you had a separate and individual relationship with your child, different things will constitute losses to each of you. You must recognize this and not expect your mate to be grieving the same losses as you are.

Not only will you always be somewhat dissimilar in what you grieve, but usually the two of you will not be synchronized in your grief experiences. It will be common for one of you to be up emotionally while the other is down. Differences also can be expected in other areas of grief:

How you express your feelings—one of you may want to talk about your child, while the other may want to avoid discussing him.

How you carry out your work or daily activities—one of you may find comfort in returning to work, which may provide a respite from your grief, while the other may be overwhelmed by responsibilities that only highlight the loss.

How you relate to things that trigger memories of your child—one of you may want all the photographs to be removed from the home, while the other will want to make sure they are all hanging up.

How you respond to your surviving children—one of you may withdraw from them in an attempt to protect them from your grief, while the other struggles to remain open to them, appropriately share grief, and remain as normal as possible with them.

How you deal with the support of others—one of you may want to attend self-help group meetings, while the other prefers not to discuss your deceased child and avoids all other bereaved parents.

How you cope with your sexual relationship—one of you may be interested in resuming sexual intimacy, while the other may feel uncomfortable or conflicted about having sex.

How you react to socializing and resuming your life—one of you may feel that if you ever enjoy life again you are betraying your child, while the other feels that life must go on, and some enjoyment is healthy.

How you search for the meaning of what has happened—one of you may find comfort in religion, while the other may give up former religious beliefs.

What problem areas you experience in grief—one of you may have difficulty in letting out feelings and asking for support, while the other may have difficulty in expressing anger.

The differences in sex-role socialization will become apparent here (see chapter 5 for more on this), contributing to the differences between how you and your spouse deal with your child's death and with each other's grief. Traditionally, the male has been conditioned to be self-sufficient and to exert emotional control. He runs into difficulties because precisely what is demanded in grief work is prohibited by his social role: expressing feelings, being preoccupied with memories, requiring support and validation from others. Conversely, women traditionally have been socialized to accept help from others and to express their emotions, although they have more difficulty accepting and expressing anger than do their husbands. Most of the tasks of grief work are compatible with their social roles and conditioning. You will have to look at the particular sex-role factors influencing each of your responses to grief. These stereotypes are changing and are accurate only in general, but they should be taken into account when trying to understand one another.

Too often, fathers receive insufficient support as bereaved parents. Concerned others may ask the father how the mother is doing but not inquire about the father himself. Although we know that many men still have problems sharing their grief, it is critically important that they be given the opportunities to do so. Perhaps such invitations to discuss their grief ultimately will help them give themselves the permission many of them need to process and communicate about their loss.

Mothers and fathers will tend to grieve differently over time. For fathers, grief seems to decline much more rapidly than for mothers. Grief tends to be particularly intense for mothers two years after the death, although this will diminish after more time has passed. This implies that the father's grief decreases while the mother's grief is either remaining the same or increasing. Thus parents who were once grieving in a similar way may come to a point where they are grieving quite differently. If you are in this situation, recognize that for a period of time this will be a normal course of events. It is upsetting, but it should be recognized and understood as a normal phenomenon.

The situation between you and your spouse will be ripe for conflict if one of you interprets the other's grief response as meaning that that person did not love the deceased child enough. It is critically important that you grant your spouse a very wide latitude for difference in grief expression. You must attempt to understand these differences in terms of your spouse's personality and past. There is no one correct way to grieve. You cannot expect your spouse to be just like you in grief, any more than you can expect such similarity in other areas of life. You will seldom be at the same place at the same time in your grief process, and this does not mean you do not still love one another. It is important for you to convey to each other that this love still exists, despite apparent differences. Overuse of behaviors that continually direct attention away from the marital relationship can seriously compromise it. Overinvolvement at work, too much time spent with others outside of the family, increased alcohol consumption—all can contribute to further marital strain and can impede the grief process.

There also must be the recognition on both your parts that the grief experience will change each of you. Neither of you can expect your mate to be exactly the same person as before. Major loss changes all of us. Some changes will be for the good; some will not. Nevertheless, your spouse will be changed in some fashion. Predictably, this will create a change in your marital relationship that must be recognized and adapted to.

Sexual Problems

A primary area of difficulty may be your sexual relationship. It is not unusual for sexual relations to be negatively affected for up to two years following the death of a child. There are many reasons for this: fear of having and possibly losing other children; guilt over any pleasure experienced; and interference caused by normal symptoms of grief and depression. While a close and intimate sexual relationship may be precisely what one of you may need at a given moment in your grief, it may be exactly what your spouse cannot endure at that same moment. Some of you may be worried that if you let down your barriers to feel intimacy and closeness, there is a chance that you also could feel pain, grief, and loss. In an effort to avoid these painful feelings, you may become like many bereaved individuals who back away from sexual contact for a while. This can become a problem when it is perceived as a rejection or as an additional loss by your mate. Bereaved couples often begin to fight over this area, especially when the one who desires sexual contact cannot understand the reasons behind the other's desire to avoid it. This is an exceptionally sensitive area, so you must exert the utmost patience and understanding with one another. Grief affects each of us in different ways, and this is no less true in the sexual area.

Traditional sex differences play a part in these problems as well as personal differences in grief style. For example, a bereaved couple may grow farther apart because the wife is perceived as unresponsive and totally wrapped up in her grief when she tells her husband she is not interested in sex. In contrast, he may be perceived as being insensitive when he expresses his desire to be close to his wife sexually. In fact, both are hurting individuals who are attempting to minimize their own pain. Again, sexual behavior must be viewed as but one area of grief response. It is an area where gentle exploration of underlying feelings, and communication about these feelings, can allow the couple to move closer together.

Divorce

There is a major myth that a higher than average number of divorces occur after the death of a child. Estimates have run as high as 90 percent. It is important for you to know that this is a misinterpretation of the situation. *It is positively untrue that parental bereavement must lead to divorce.* Previous studies in this area failed to take normal divorce rates into account. More recent studies indicate that while bereaved parents do suffer significant distress, there are no data from which to conclude that divorce is inevitable.

When divorce does follow the death of a child, it usually is the result of other problems that existed before the death. In many cases, these problems no longer seemed worth fighting after the child died. Certainly the death of a child may play a part, but it is not really the central factor in a divorce. In fact, some of the positive responses to bereavement—reordered priorities, a sense of strength and endurance, and assertiveness—may contribute to many bereaved parents' decisions to tolerate no longer the unsatisfactory marital relationship that had existed before the death.

It is very important that this myth of a high divorce rate following the death of a child not become a self-fulfilling prophecy for you. I have often heard parents say that they "know" they will get a divorce, since their child has died. This incorrect information is making it worse for bereaved parents. While certainly the stress of a child's death can put severe burdens on a relationship, we also know that there are positive responses to bereavement as well: deeper family commitment and unity, increased personal growth, closer relationships, increased sensitivity, new meaning to life, an increased awareness of life's preciousness and fragility, and an improved ability to express feelings. Important contributions have been made, for example, through such self-help groups as Mothers Against Drunk Driving, which has changed drunk driving legislation. Psychosocial support groups have been started, such as The Compassionate Friends and other bereavement support groups devoted to specific types of child loss. All of this illustrates how some of the pain of grief can be channeled into constructive responses that can be used fruitfully as parents continue to function in a world without their child.

Certainly, there could be few, if any, bigger stresses on any relationship than the death of a child. What is important to remember is that the high rate of divorce frequently assumed to be inevitable for bereaved parents is not true. Marriages and families can and do survive after the death of a child.

Your Family

Grieving for the death of your child will occur on a family level, just as it does on an individual and a couple level. As mentioned in chapter 8, your family will need to reorganize following the loss. This will bring up many issues in regard to the surviving children.

Replacement Children

Severe problems can develop when surviving children are expected to fill the void left by their deceased brother or sister. Depending on what role reassignments are made, and what expectations are placed on them, your children can be helped or hurt by the way you respond to them. If they are expected to "replace" the deceased child, serious psychological problems can develop. If they are made to feel that they should have been the one to die instead of the child who did, they can have significant problems with self-esteem, resentment, guilt, and impaired relationships with you. In some pathological cases, children have actually been conceived to take the place of a child who died, or existing children have been assigned the identities of deceased siblings. In these instances, parents are unwilling to relinquish the deceased child. Instead they force the surviving or new children into a sick world of recreating the lost child. All types of problems and symptoms can develop in situations like this.

Idealizing the Lost Child

It is quite common to hear bereaved parents talk of their deceased child as the one who had been the "most special," the "most loving," the "favorite" child, the "best" child, and so forth. You may find yourself doing this and tending to sanctify your deceased child. This means that you are focusing on all of her good points and failing to recall that she also had negative points and was a normal child. In most cases, this reflects your overfocus on the one who has been lost. You are paying increased attention to that which you are missing and for which you are longing.

In fact, you would also miss the special and unique qualities of your other children if they had died instead. Only in cases where there had been clear preferences before the death, and the child who died had been especially favored, would it not be expected that you would grieve about as much for another child. You may feel guilt over your longing for the deceased child. You need to recognize that, to a certain extent and for a certain length of time, this is quite normal. However, you must understand that it is your reaction to your child's absence which makes him the focus of your attention, surpassing that given to your present, surviving children.

At this time your surviving children may compare unfavorably in your eyes to your deceased child. This is because surviving children are real children: They make mistakes; they drive their parents wild. Deceased children don't do this; they are perfect, like saints. They also are frozen in time, which means that they don't get any older, don't develop increasingly more difficult problems like real children do. In contrast, your surviving children may look bad. You must be realistic when you make these comparisons and understand that a normal, ongoing relationship, with all of its ambivalences and imperfections, will always seem poor in comparison to an idealized and sanctified one.

Sometimes your children may be graphic reminders to you of your child who died. This can be either comforting or distressing. Siblings often resemble one another, and you may see the mannerisms of your deceased child in those who remain. Also, clothes, toys, and personal possessions often are passed on to surviving children. Seeing these children use such articles can bring up both positive or negative feelings in you.

Difficulties in Parenting

You may see all too well the deficiencies you temporarily have in dealing with your remaining children. Grief saps you of the energy and emotional investment you ideally want to have for your surviving children. Not being as good a parent as you would like may add to your feelings of failure and frustration.

Be realistic in what you expect of yourself. Just as you now recognize that some of your expectations of yourself as a parent of your deceased child were unrealistic, you may have to recognize that it is unrealistic to expect that you can act ideally with the surviving children. This does not mean that you do not put forth your best efforts to care for these children. Rather, it means you are realistic in what you expect of yourself. You are a grieving individual, which means you will not be functioning at an optimum level for some time. You may want to tap into other resources available to you and your children at this time, to assure them of getting as much of what they need as possible. (See chapter 13 for a further discussion of this topic.)

Your family's closeness will make all family members vulnerable to displacement of anger, frustration, and other negative feelings. If you catch yourself doing this—for example, being too short with your son or taking out your upset feelings on your daughter—you may feel quite guilty. Again, you must recognize that you are at a disadvantage because you yourself are so overwhelmed with your own grief. You may have little to give anyone else despite your desire to do so. With this recognition, you must balance your resources and energies to do the very best you can in taking care of your family as well as yourself. To focus exclusively on either will be unhealthy for everyone concerned.

You may be surprised to notice that you have some resentment that your other children are still living or that they appear not to have grieved enough or to have adjusted too quickly. This results from your natural preoccupation with and desire for your deceased child. However, it also reveals your anger that life goes on without your loved one.

You might fear that your relationships with your surviving children are less intense, or that you have lost your ability to love. In most cases, this is a common response to a major loss. Dealing with the loss, you are temporarily unable to invest yourself in other relationships to the same extent as before. Sometimes it reflects a desire not to invest in other children for fear that they will die too. Usually, with continued grief work, this will change over time. You will continue to heal, to take risks again, and to turn to others the emotional energy that was focused on your deceased child both during her life and in your grief over her death.

Out of your desire to avoid the pain of loss and to ensure that nothing will happen to them, you may overprotect your remaining children. The irony is that while you want to draw these children closer, such overprotection actually serves to push them farther away. Reactions such as hostility, resentment, anxiety, insecurity, angry misbehavior, and estrangement from parents can result when remaining children are overprotected. If your children are not allowed to be children, if they are not given age-appropriate responsibility and experiences, and if they are not allowed to develop normally, then serious problems can result for them and for you, despite the fact that you are acting with the best intentions.

Understanding Your Children's Grief

You as a parent must have an understanding of your surviving children's grief so that you are not misled by some of their behaviors. While children are in many respects similar to adults in their grief, they are quite different in the way that they show it. Often parents erroneously assume that children do not understand or that they have been unaffected by the loss of a sibling, when in fact this is not the case. In order for you to be most effective with your children, you will need to know how they process their grief. (See chapter 13 for more on this.)

You also must recognize that your child's surviving siblings are in a unique situation.

They will live longer with the death of their brother or sister than anyone else.

They have had it illustrated to them that they, too, can die.

They may be struggling with guilt over the sibling relationship and anger at your inability to have prevented the death.

They usually are experiencing emotional turmoil that is the result not only of their own response to the death of their sibling but also to your parental grief.

They may try to live up to unrealistic standards they set for themselves in their attempt to take away your pain, to be perfect, or to replace the deceased sibling for you. You will need to watch for such behaviors in order to help your children give them up, since they will not be helpful to either of you.

Problems will arise if you think that you can protect your family from the pain of grief over your child's death. Fathers are notorious for this, but they do not hold a monopoly on it. Mothers, and often surviving children, also try to rescue others from the pain of their grief. They may do this by ignoring their own needs and concentrating on the needs of others, or by creating distractions so that the family will not have to think about their grief. One adolescent decided to have trouble in school so that his parents would concentrate on him and get their minds off the pain of losing his sister. While it is admirable that family members want to rescue one another from the intense pain of loss, it is unrealistic to think that this can be done successfully. Families cannot be shielded from the pain following the death of the child. To attempt to do this will only interfere with the healthy mourning process that must be allowed to occur, both for the person trying to do the protecting and for other family members. Sometimes the person focusing on the rescue of others is doing so to avoid facing their own pain. This can be as counterproductive as any other escape.

Grandparents and Other Extended Family Members

A note must be made about grandparents and other extended family relatives who also are affected by a child's death. Too often these people are overlooked. When grandparents have been involved intimately in family life, they are like bereaved parents of a second order. Not only have they lost their grandchild but they have also "lost" their own child to bereaved parent status. Many times they wonder why they could not have died instead, to save the life of their grandchild and to take away the pain of their child. Many of the issues that are pertinent to you as a bereaved parent are pertinent to your parents as well.

This is not to say that all grandparents and extended family members are helpful to bereaved families. As in any other situation, they can either help families in grief or cause more problems. Grandparents and relatives who are not supportive, who place inappropriate expectations on bereaved parents and families, and who put their own concerns above those of the bereaved parents and siblings are often major problems for bereaved parents. Far too often, the loss of a child can start a process that ends in alienation of the bereaved parents and their own parents.

Special Death Situations

Some deaths of children are less recognized by society. For example, the deaths of unborn infants by miscarriage or stillbirth, and even the death of a newborn, often are not considered to be as serious as the loss of an older child. Conversely, the loss of an adult child is sometimes not seen as a meaningful loss to the child's parents because the child has left home and has his own spouse and family. However, in either case, parents still have much to grieve.

As families are changing, becoming smaller and more fragmented, some different kinds of family configurations are becoming more prevalent. There may be only a single parent who is head of the family, or the parents may be divorced at the time of the child's death. Parents may lose an only child. These situations create some special problems for the parents involved in them.

Miscarriage

Up to 25 percent of all pregnancies end in miscarriage. Despite these large numbers, usually little attention is paid to the grief that results. Frequently there is a lack of social support following a miscarriage. There may have been no external signs of the pregnancy, and there was no living person for others to know and develop memories of to share in the bereavement process. The child was not real to them, and so they have a more difficult time validating the parents' loss. Despite this, many parents are invested in the blood and tissue that would have become their child. The amount of parental grief is not related to the length of gestation but to the meanings, hopes, values, needs, feelings, and expectations that parents had placed upon this child-to-be.

The grief of the mother and the grief of the father often differ, reflecting the differences in the amount and types of involvement with the unborn child. Mothers tend to form a bond with the unborn child more quickly, since they carry the child and feel it develop within them. However, many fathers become involved in the image of their child from early in the pregnancy. For both parents, involvement and bonding increase as time goes on and as more bodily changes occur and more movements are felt.

You can expect to experience all of the normal symptoms of grief after a miscarriage. Their extent depends on when it occurs and what your feelings are about it. In addition, you may experience a profound sense of worthlessness, failure, and deficiency. Both of you, but especially you if you are the woman, may be concerned about your inability to produce a healthy child. You may feel especially anxious if you have no other children.

Guilt is relatively common, especially for women, because they feel responsible for the miscarriage. Many couples erroneously attribute miscarriage to something they have done, for example, having sexual relations or going for a long ride. For this reason, you should try to obtain factual information about the probable cause of your miscarriage. If it occurred early in the pregnancy, before your quite normal feelings of ambivalence about having the child had been resolved, you may need assistance in dealing with your guilt. Since unresolved loss can lead to pathological grief, it is important for you to share your fantasies, thoughts, feelings, hopes, and expectations about the unborn child in order to effectively complete the mourning process.

Many counselors feel that it is important for the parents to see the products of the miscarriage. This helps to reinforce reality and initiate the grieving process. Hopefully you were given the chance to do this, although you should not feel guilty if you did not want to see them. Some parents are given Polaroid pictures of the ultrasound tracing of their child. If you are offered this, you may want to seriously consider taking it. In the absence of a viable fetus you must mourn a dream, which is difficult to do without its somehow being made real for you. This is why it is so important to have some confirmation of what you have lost.

Anniversary reactions will occur for many of you. You may have many thoughts about what the child would or could have been. Anniversaries of the day when the child would have been born may bring brief upsurges in your grief. Within certain limitations, this is quite normal and may continue for many years.

A point must be made here about abortions. Whether they are elective or therapeutic, they still always involve the loss of a child. This loss needs to be grieved, even if it was an elective abortion. Unfortunately, society may give a message to the woman that if it was an elective abortion she should be pleased and relieved rather than sad. Society fails to recognize that the two different sets of feelings may exist together. This makes some women unable to address their distress and sadness, since they feel it is incompatible with the decision they have made. Such women need to understand that the decision in no way dismisses any ambivalence they might have had about the choice. Both sets of feelings will need to be processed in the grief period.

Stillbirth

Stillbirth occurs approximately once in every hundred births. In these cases, the mother has been able to keep the child for a longer period of time. There has been more opportunity for intensified bonding. You may have gone through the whole pregnancy only to have the child die right before its birth. This is an incredible shock to all. You may have had a sense of danger zones having been passed and everything having been made ready. In some situations, the mother has had to continue to carry the damaged or dead child until the natural onset of labor or until labor was induced. Viewing the child's body after such a situation is also difficult because of its deterioration.

Those of you who have experienced the death of your child at birth usually have been least prepared. Your family has been ready, the baby shower has been held, the birth announcements are at hand, brothers and sisters have been prepared, and babysitting arrangements have been made. Then the unthinkable occurs: The baby dies. The miracle of birth turns into a tragedy. This death happens without any warning, and you are the victim of unanticipated loss.

In contrast, some parents do have warning.

Movements have ceased, or parents have been told of the death. Some parents are glad they know before the birth that the child is dead, while others do not think they could have gone through the experience if they had known it ahead of time. Obviously a family's preparation for the loss will depend upon whether or not they knew of the baby's death prior to delivery. In those cases where there was knowledge only at the time of delivery or shortly beforehand, the mother probably was physically exhausted and/or sedated. Under these circumstances, the father may feel pressured to make decisions rapidly, excluding the mother. More enlightened hospitals now are changing this procedure, and decisions are delayed until the mother can participate in them.

Part of the problem with stillbirth is that it is quite difficult for others to validate your loss. Those outside of your family often do not understand it. They assume there will be no grief, for although the baby had been very much a part of the lives of you and your family, it had not existed for others. This isolates you and your family from support. When combined with the well-intentioned but harmful admonitions of others who urge you to "look ahead" and concentrate on having other children, this lack of social valida-tion can cause significant problems for you and your family.

Often, overprotective grandparents urge that autopsies be refused and funeral rituals be bypassed, and they try to make things easier for you by taking over your decision making. This robs you and your spouse of important experiences that can help confirm the death for you and give you a way to express your grief. You and your family need to be given permission to grieve. You have a right and a need to mourn your loss. Despite the fact that the baby was not real for anyone else, you had feel-ings, hopes, dreams, attachments, and plans for that baby and what he or she would contribute to your family. All of these now must be mourned regardless of what anyone else says.

As a parent, you may find yourself experiencing many of the grief reac-tions experienced with any other loss. As with a miscarriage, a stillborn baby raises the issue of your physical defectiveness in producing a baby that cannot survive. If you are the mother, you may believe that you have failed to prove your womanhood because of your inability to conceive and deliver a healthy baby. You might feel damaged. If you are the father of a stillborn child you, too, can feel guilt. This guilt may be over having impregnated your wife and contributed to the emotional turmoil you each experience now. Couples often believe that sexual activity during the preg-nancy caused the stillbirth. You will need to seek out accurate information to determine, if possible, the true cause of your child's death. Assuming inappropriate guilt will not help you.

As with parents of older children who die, you and your spouse may question your competency as parents and may feel guilt, inadequacy, and defectiveness. Fantasies about certain thoughts or feelings having caused the death only add to the normal parental guilt. Problems in the marital relationship or with the entire family can develop and future parenting may be affected if this loss is not appropriately grieved. You will probably feel anger and the need to blame someone, either yourself, medical personnel, clergy, or God.

If you are the mother, your bereavement can be made more complicated by your physical condition. Depression and lack of energy due to the normal hormonal changes that take place after delivery are common. Your physical condition also reminds you that you have given birth, but there is no child. Sometimes these changes add insult to injury. For example, it is particularly hard to have milk start coming in with no baby to nurse.

As a father, you may find you are ignored after the death of your stillborn child, even more so than following the death of an older child. As a result, you yourself may dismiss or underestimate your grief. You may frequently be asked how your wife is, with little regard for your own reactions. People's concerns tend to center on the physical and emotional health of the mother. Despite this, you, too, are significantly affected and must grieve. Resist making decisions alone about your wife's care and the disposition of your child's body. This should be done with your wife if it is to be therapeutic for you both. Trying to protect her by shielding her from the experience will only hurt her more.

When the child is dead at or shortly after birth, most parents need to have some validation and confirmation of the child's existence. You should have been given the option of seeing, holding, touching, and spending time with your dying or dead baby. Parents who did not see or touch their babies find it more difficult to believe they actually had had the child. Their grieving is affected by this uncertainty. One woman went around weighing vegetables to find one that had the identical weight and height of the child she had given birth to but had never been allowed to hold. Until her loss had been made real for her by holding such an object, she had been compelled to search for what she had lost.

For this reason you should give serious consideration to doing those things that will make your baby real to you, so that you can say good-bye to him or her. It is too hard to say good-bye to someone who is only a dream.

If acceptable to you, it is better to experience the baby rather than to delay the grief and later find it difficult to believe your child ever existed. If it is still possible, look at and hold your dead baby. Take an active part in certification of the stillbirth, and name the baby. Provide him or her with a memorable funeral. You must acknowledge that there had been a life and now is a death. Siblings and other family members should be involved in this too, not only because they also had anticipated the child but also because the dead baby needs to be made real in their minds and to be a part of the family so that they can then mourn it healthily.

With other bereavements there is much to remember, and memories to share and cry over. With stillbirth, there is little to talk about and few people to discuss, cry, and share the loss with. As a parent of a stillborn child, you frequently may find yourself isolated. You may avoid contact with others because of your feelings of shame, guilt, and discomfort. If you continue to act on this, you will be deprived of the opportunity to talk about your loss, which is critically important to you in your mourning. You need to allow people to ask you direct questions about the stillbirth so that the child becomes more real in your mind. Then you can mourn that child.

As with all other types of bereavement, you need to remember and review your thoughts and feelings about this child from the very beginning of the pregnancy to make him or her seem real. Indeed, it is precisely the absence of a sense of reality that makes this particular loss so difficult, since there is a lack of focus.

Involve your other children in mourning as well. They, too, had hopes and feelings about the child's coming to join their family. Young children will need sensitive and factual information about the loss. Too often they assume responsibility for the death because of their previous jealous and angry feelings toward the new child. Those feelings are completely normal; nevertheless, children often experience profound guilt. All children will require support in completing their grief because it will be exceptionally difficult for them to separate from a brother or sister they have never seen.

Newborn Death

A newborn death shares many of the characteristics of bereavement as stillbirth. However, in this case you have had a limited opportunity to know and experience the real, live child. You have something besides fantasy to relate to. Unfortunately, your experiences with your child may have been painful, as he or she may have been critically ill or attached to strange machinery, or you may have had to make treatment decisions that you regretted later on.

Your grief as parents of newborn children who die is similar to other types of parental grief, but it does have several unique aspects. Like stillbirth, the death is socially negated. The loss is discounted, and therefore your grief is minimized. People offer you clichés such as "You are lucky you didn't take him home," "You can have other children," or "It's lucky that you hadn't become attached yet." All of these statements indicate a lack of appreciation for the fact that your emotional bonding and involvement with this child had been taking place gradually since the beginning of the pregnancy.

You will have many of the same feelings of grief as other bereaved parents. There probably will be guilt and blame, much of it quite irrational. You may feel that you should have protected your child and, as in miscarriage and stillbirth, possibly could feel defective in having produced a child that could not survive. Usually parents in this situation have a strong desire to know and understand why their child died and a concern for the success of future pregnancies. Again, it is important for you to seek out the most accurate information as to what caused the death of your child and how it will affect you and future children.

Your mourning process will involve repeatedly going over the details of the pregnancy, the birth, and your child's short life. Your sense of helplessness at watching your child, your anger at hospital personnel, and all of the many other feelings that the experience creates will have to be worked through so that you successfully can mourn and relinquish your lost baby.

As in stillbirth, well-intentioned and concerned people may act in ways that can complicate your grief. For example, uninformed clergy, concerned grandparents, and sometimes fathers collaborate to get the funeral services over with as soon as possible, with the least amount of maternal, family, or social involvement allowable. Many times mothers are excluded from making arrangements for or attending the funeral, despite the fact that this usually brings intense anger at the exclusion. Some newspapers have a policy of not printing death notices for newborns or stillborns.

Friends and relatives may go into your home before you return and remove all preparations you had made for the baby. Mental health practitioners may not even relate the symptoms of grief to any of your responses, but may regard your responses as abnormal. Medical caregivers tend to overprotect parents and may not have wanted to offer you the options you have in relating to your dying or dead baby.

As with stillbirth, one of the major problems in this grief is that it lacks focus. That is, there is not a clear image. The baby has died before you have experienced the reality of his being alive. There can be many reasons for this. Perhaps you were still confined during his brief life, or perhaps the baby had been acutely ill and hospitalized in a regional newborn intensive care unit after the birth. You still may have been sedated, and this may have interfered with your experiencing your baby. Consequently, you may find it hard to identify who or what you are grieving. The pregnancy, labor, and delivery, and your child's life and death may seem as if they were all a dream. And dreams are difficult to grieve.

For this reason, caregivers are encouraged to provide parents with as much contact as possible. This makes the baby real to parents and gives them the experiences for memories and an image they can mourn. You should have been offered the opportunity to see, touch, hold, or talk to your sick, dying, or newly dead baby. Pictures, a lock of hair, the hospital bracelet, footprints, birth and death certificates, a name, a death notice, a burial—all are important, tangible items you need to help you focus and allow you to grieve.

Talk with others about your baby's brief life and death. Recall your memories of the pregnancy, labor, and delivery, and events in the nursery. Your fantasies about and expectations of your baby also will need to be reviewed. You will need to mourn this child just as if he were a child who had lived to be older.

If you did not have a chance to experience your child and now feel a need to do something symbolic because of it, explore what options you currently have in order to mark your baby's life and death. Chapter 16 will tell you more about developing personal bereavement rituals.

Sudden Infant Death Syndrome

One type of newborn death that is particularly stressful is Sudden Infant Death Syndrome (SIDS), the leading cause of deaths of infants between one week and one year of age in the United States. Between 8,000 and 10,000 deaths annually are attributed to SIDS. This type of loss is often a major crisis for the bereaved family. Very intense grief follows this loss, especially because the family is still centered around caring for the infant at the time the child dies. There is intensified searching for the baby and preoccupation with her image. Anger, frustration, and irritability are common. The strong and poignant grief of the mother often renders her unable to care for her family. It is not uncommon for her to feel that her heart has been ripped right out from her. Many of the grief reactions and issues discussed above for stillbirth and newborn death are applicable if your child died from SIDS.

The suddenness of the loss, with no opportunity to prepare for the death of a seemingly healthy child, leaves your family overwhelmed. You become victims of the unanticipated grief reaction. Guilt and blame may be especially high for you, because with SIDS there is often no medical explanation of why your baby died. This fuels feelings of guilt and responsibility, leaving you, your spouse, and any surviving children bewildered.

Because the death is sudden and of unknown cause, you may have to deal with the police, medical examiners, and hospital personnel who are designated to protect the interests of your child and the state by investigating deaths like this. It can be especially painful to have to cope with insinuations that your child's death was caused by neglect or actions on the parts of you or your family. This places an additional burden of guilt and pain on you all, despite the fact that in the majority of cases such blame is unwarranted.

The Question of Having Another Child

If you are like many couples who have lost a child, the question of whether or not to have another child will probably arise. This may be especially critical if you do not have an older child. You may question your ability to produce a normal, healthy child or to protect and care for one.

It is important that you not get pregnant too soon after the death of your child. You must first achieve some resolution of her loss. This means you should have successfully reviewed your fantasized and real relationship with that child and mourned her. You should not feel that you need to have another child to resolve your grief. The new child should be conceived because you want to have a child, not to prove you can produce a healthy baby or resolve your lingering guilt. Any pregnancy stemming from the desire to avoid dealing with grief over your older child's death will lead to serious psychological problems from the beginning, as will one designed to alleviate the stress between you and your spouse or among your family members.

Before having another child, you should consider all the pros and cons and be quite clear on the appropriateness of this decision. It will be important that both you and your spouse are ready together. Also, you both must understand that the new child will involve a new pregnancy, need a new name, and will be a unique person with her own needs and wants. The new child must not be seen as a replacement for the deceased child.

When the new baby does arrive, you and other family members should be prepared to experience a combination of both joy and pain. You must recognize that this is a totally different child who needs to be treated as an individual, and you must be alert to the dangers of being overprotective in an attempt to avoid what happened to your older child.

Death of an Adult Child

As with the death of an infant, parental grief over the death of an adult child is often overlooked. Attention is focused on the child's spouse and family. People seem to forget that the adult, despite his age, was still a child to his parents. I vividly recall sitting in the church at a funeral mass for a dear friend, a physician who died suddenly at the age of fifty-nine. The priest talked about the contributions this man had made to the community, and how he would be missed by his wife, his children, and his colleagues. There was never a mention of his mother, who sat in the front row and went totally unrecognized!

Because your relationship with your adult children is different from that with your younger children, or from when the older children themselves were younger, you can expect to see differences in your grief experience when your adult child dies. As your children mature, there is less physical, hands-on caretaking and more offering of advice and sharing of mutual interests. The relationship becomes more equal. Many describe it as one of being friends, of having a connection marked by reciprocity and equal access to power and resources. Depending on your age and that of your child, role reversals or dependency shifts may have already begun, with your child now caring for you. While your earlier parental nurturance is not forgotten, the maturing of your child adds new facets to the relationship that bring up specific bereavement issues if this child dies.

In the past, few parents lived long enough to see their children become adults. Parents would have been dead by the time their fifty-year-old son died suddenly from a massive heart attack. Now, with longer life spans and improved medical technology, there are an increasing number of parents whose adult children die.

It may be particularly difficult for you to see your child robbed of reaping the fruits of his labors. You have witnessed your child's struggle for education and job security, and now all of this has come to naught with his death. It can bring an acute and angry sense of unfairness.

It may be even harder on you to see the responsibilities left unattended with the death of your child. The children left fatherless, the company without its director, the projects that will remain incomplete—all illustrate your child's absence. You may particularly regret any unfinished business you had with him. You are likely to be deeply disturbed by all this. The incompleteness of your child's life can leave you with a gaping void.

You can expect that you and your spouse will grieve more similarly following the death of an adult child than you would following the death of a younger child. In one study, this type of loss was found to precipitate the most severe grief of all for fathers, while mothers remained at similarly high grief intensities for children of all ages. Your grief is profound; your sense of meaning crumbles. For many, the stability of life is gone completely after an adult child dies. The rest of this section examines the special issues confronting parents when an adult child dies, which are in addition to the general issues faced by all bereaved parents.

Acknowledging the Death

You may find that you are unable to believe the death has occurred. After all, your child has been reared successfully through more dangerous times. This is supposed to be the time in your life when you can let down your guard and relax. Your job has been accomplished successfully: You have protected your child, and now he can protect himself. However, the death of your adult child viciously points out the fallacy of any parents' ever being able to feel truly secure. It makes no sense: infants die of Sudden Infant Death Syndrome; young children succumb to cancer, adolescents drink, drive recklessly, and die in automobile accidents. Why should someone who has survived all of this die before his natural life expectancy is reached?

It also may be difficult for you to accept the reality of the loss if your child was living outside your home. There is no dramatic absence to signal to you that the death has occurred. For instance, if you have become accustomed to your child's living away in another state, it may be hard for you to grasp the fact that he is not still alive there. He left at other times, but he always returned. Consequently, the holidays may be particularly bad for you, as these are the times at which you may finally realize that your child is dead. He will not be coming home as he always did.

Because there is not the expectation of seeing your child on a daily basis, it may take a long time before you feel that your child's loss is permanent and know that he has, in fact, died. However, although your intellectual acceptance of your child's death may be hard, your emotional adjustment may be relatively easier than it would have been had he still been living with you. You don't have to live with daily reminders of his absence.

Effects of Age on Your Grief

The developmental issues that you confront as an aging parent of an adult child can complicate your bereavement. You may be experiencing personal losses, such as retirement, widowhood, failing health, or mid-life crises. These may lead you to feel that you have lost control, a feeling which is made worse by the death. Often, witnessing the pain of your child's family and being unable to do anything about it can exacerbate your own pain. How can you answer your grandchild's question "Why didn't you die instead of my daddy? You are so much older" when it is the precise question with which you yourself struggle?

Another problem is that, depending on your age and the opportunities available to you, you may have diminished strength, abilities, and options for reinvestment of your emotional energies following the death of your child. You probably are unable to have more children. You may be retired, without the diversion of work. Physical difficulties may restrict you; for instance, your eyesight may be so poor that you cannot read, or you may no longer be mobile enough to visit with others. You might not have enough energy to do something active to change the conditions that contributed to your child's death, such as raising money for cancer research.

You may be concerned about having to assume caretaking duties for your grandchildren at a time when you yourself are emotionally or physically depleted. While some bereaved parents are able to manage this successfully, others cannot. If you are unwilling or unable to do so, you may have to contend with your own guilt or others' reactions.

Depending on your circumstances, you may suffer from the absence of a support system to nurture you and help you with your grief. This is especially true in retirement communities and similar situations in which friends and neighbors never knew your child. They do not know how to react to your loss because they can see no observable changes in your life and did not know your child well, if at all. You also already may have lost a number of your friends and relatives through illness, relocation, or death.

On the other hand, you probably have had to cope with other traumas and bereavements in your life. If you successfully resolved these losses, you know that grief can be managed and survived. This is an important realization to have in your grief. In this regard, age and experience can be positive factors for parents who lose older children.

Social Exclusion

As mentioned earlier, a major problem for bereaved parents of adult children is that they tend to be excluded from the concern of others. Much of the focus of attention is on the child's spouse and children. Not only does this leave you with a lack of validation for your unique loss, but it may also mean that you are omitted from important activities following your child's death that could help you cope with the loss. For example, while your adult child's spouse and children would certainly be invited to a ceremony in which a scholarship is given in his name, it would not be uncommon for you to be overlooked and not included. The focus simply is not on you, as it would be if your child were a youngster.

There is also a curious social phenomenon in which older individuals are expected to be less grieved by death. Some people assume that previous loss has made you immune to grief, or that advancing age means that you are comfortable with death because you are closer to it. These assumptions are not necessarily valid, and frequently the opposite is true. The older bereaved parent can be in an extremely vulnerable position. Sometimes you may feel that you should suppress your own grief out of your concern for your spouse or your child's spouse and children; other times, others will place this expectation on you. In either case, it will not be helpful. Everyone has the right and need to grieve this loss.

Lack of Control

One of the major issues for any parent whose adult child dies is your significant lack of control. This stems from having less contact with and decision-making power over your children once they are adults. This is normal, but it can become a problem when you review your child's life, the events of his death, or funeral or memorial service decisions.

It is very probable that you were not actively involved in your child's last days or in his life in general. This may have been the result of emotional or geographical distance, or may have reflected your child's desire to keep you only peripherally involved for your or his own protection. You may feel more intense guilt if you fail to appreciate the fact that increased independence, with its resulting psychological and geographical distance, is a normal part of a relationship with any adult child. Sometimes you may regret the independence you granted your child, as if you magically could have protected him from harm. Although it is untrue, this can fuel your anger, depression, and marital stress. On the other hand, you may be grateful that your child had the opportunity to achieve independence and enjoy his adulthood before he died.

If you were not involved actively in your child's daily life, you may have been precluded from participating in your child's care if he died from an illness. Thus you lost out on the benefits that such participation could have brought. In addition, if your child had been maintaining a life-style or making medical treatment decisions of which you did not approve, you may be left with feelings of ambivalence, anger, disappointment, and guilt.

Decreased control and lack of everyday contact may mean that you must struggle with incomplete information as you attempt to understand the circumstances that preceded your child's death. Your questions may not all be answered, which will make it harder for you to resolve your grief. You may have to deal with your concerns about your child's emotional and physical state, your worries as to whether everything possible had been done to prevent his death, and your anxieties about whether all his needs had been met. If you feel that there were problems prior to the death with which you could have helped, you may have additional difficulties. You may be angry with your child's family if you think they failed to provide your child with the type of environment or care you would have wanted.

Another issue that may affect your bereavement is your limited control over the decisions regarding funerals and funerary rituals. Most often your child's spouse makes these decisions, frequently influenced by her own parents and friends. You may be forced to endure rituals that are distasteful to you or suffer the absence of those that would be helpful and meaningful to you. For example, one set of parents was exceptionally offended by the fact that their child did not have a religious ceremony and that his body was cremated. This was not only upsetting to them in terms of their values, but it also contradicted their image of their child. To them he was a ten-year-old altar boy who strictly practiced his Catholic faith. They did not know him as the adult who had fallen away from his former religion and who had on many occasions expressed a desire not to have a religious service at his funeral. Parents in this situation are quite distressed. They cry, "I can make no decisions, yet he was my flesh and blood!"

On the other hand, it is possible that instead of feeling a desire for control, you may be relieved that you are no longer responsible for your child. This does not signify a lack of love but rather a normal surrendering of parental duties.

Secondary Losses

In addition to losing your adult child, you may be suffering a number of secondary losses. If as a consequence of your own aging your social world was diminishing, the loss of a child who occupied numerous roles will be felt in many more ways. Where a role reversal or dependency shift had begun, you may have become dependent on your child in a number of ways—financially, psychologically, socially, or physically. If you feel anger over your unmet dependency needs stemming from your child's death, you may feel guilty. Practical problems such as social isolation, financial instability, and unmet responsibilities around your home or business may have developed.

Even if your child was not caring for you at the time of his death, you have lost someone who would have taken care of you in the future. You must deal with serious questions about your physical, emotional, and financial livelihood. You also may have been deprived of a source of comfort at a time in your life when you needed it.

You may feel that the death of your adult child has robbed you of a source of status and pride. If you were accorded particular respect because of your child's position or accomplishments—perhaps he was a star athlete, a rabbi, a lawyer—you may lose social status with his death. If this status was one of the main supports of your self-esteem, this symbolic loss also will have to be grieved.

Your relationship to your child's family may well change with the death. You may lose contact with them. Your child's spouse may date others, and you may have to cope with the fact that your grandchildren will be raised by another who has taken your own child's place. You may fear that the family will move away, taking away the last pieces of your child and a beloved in-law as well. The possibility of remarriage, the surviving spouse's renewed dependence on her own parents, and the family's increased reliance on others for physical, emotional, and financial support all poignantly highlight the absence of your child. You may fear that your grandchildren will forget their real parent or will not be reared in the way your child would have wanted. As you have little control in this situation, you may feel frustration and loss.

Other secondary losses develop for bereaved parents of adult children, such as the loss of the family business or the family name. Depending on your relationship with your child's family and/or the existence of other children, you may feel particularly deprived at not having someone to whom you can bequeath important and symbolic heirlooms. You may lose a sense of personal and family continuity and immortality. Or, if you have already given these heirlooms to your child and they are retained by his family, you may have to face the awkward situation of wanting to get them back.

In summary, the relationship between you and your adult child has a number of characteristics that can make that child's death particularly difficult to address. In addition, your life situation as an older parent frequently complicates your bereavement. The loss of an adult child brings unique issues, problems, and demands that both you and those who seek to help you must recognize. You will have to accept the limits of your control, realize that decreased contact and increased independence are both natural and normal in a relationship with an adult child, and search for the information you need in order to successfully cope with your child's death. Finally, although society downplays the importance of your feelings, you will have to make sure that you pay attention to your grief.

Special Family Configurations

When family configurations differ from the two-parent, several-children model, there can be additional difficulties for parents mourning the loss of a child. These are outlined quite briefly here in an attempt to bring out special areas of consideration.

Single Parent

If you are a single parent, you face the incredible burden of trying to take care of yourself and your surviving children alone following the death of your child. You often must make crucial decisions without input and support, and face major events by yourself. Usually there is no one to spell you from your responsibilities, share in your duties, or relieve you from your burdens. You alone are responsible for meeting parental, work, financial, social, and household obligations—and all while you are actively grieving. (See chapters 9, 13, and 18 for more on this).

Because you lack another adult with whom to share your grief, you often do not have a sufficient respite from it. Frequently there is a general lack of support for single parents. This is not to say that friends and family are not concerned. However, when you are alone in the middle of the night and need to be held or want to share the pain of grief, you may not have the options of a bereaved parent who is in a relationship with another adult who is available to her. Or you may not have the energy required to reach out. This particular isolation only increases the normal alienation felt by bereaved parents in general, and underscores the critically important need for special support systems.

As a single parent, you probably lack the person with whom you shared the pregnancy and at least some of the development of the child, as is the case in traditional marriages that survive. Consequently, you are at a relative deficit when it comes to sharing memories of your child. Also, because you are alone, if you are having difficulties coping it may be a while before you come to realize this, since there may not be others to provide you with sufficient feedback. For such reasons it is important for single bereaved parents to have the support of others and to avail themselves of self-help support groups for bereaved parents (see chapter 20 for a listing of these).

The Remarried Parent

When your child dies, as a remarried parent you may have to deal again with your ex-spouse. If there is bitterness and unfinished business between the two of you, the grief of each can be complicated. Feelings of guilt and blame that are a normal part of parental bereavement may be worsened in this situation when you two come together again. Some are able to negotiate this successfully for their own mental health, as well as that of their surviving children. However, this is a situation in which issues are complex. This is especially true if one of you needs to have the support of the other because of the experiences that were shared around that child, and this puts pressure on a current spouse.

As a remarried parent, you also may have to deal with a blended family, and this brings up issues which will need to be confronted. There may be additional stepsiblings or half-siblings and other blended family relatives who will be involved in the extended family mourning your child. When there are differences among these individuals, the grief experience can be full of problems. Our society is only just now trying to deal with the difficult task of negotiating blended families in rituals of life, such as weddings, baptisms, and funerals. Regardless of the types of issues presented, the fact that there are more individuals involved in blended families will affect the bereavement experience, for better or for worse.

Loss of an Only Child

When you lose an only child, your parental responsibilities end, as well as your parental gratifications. You must then contend with the total absence of your former identity as a parent. This is tremendously disorganizing, confusing, and demoralizing. There is intense damage to your sense of self. You may wonder whether or not you can still call yourself a parent.

In addition, you may wonder to whom you will pass on your name and your heirlooms. There is no biological continuation of yourself and your immortality has been taken away. You will never be a grandparent. There are no other children for whom you can make a pretense of the holidays, or for whom you can force yourself to go on. Questions arise about who will take care of you and who will come to you on the holidays.

As a parent who loses an only child, you face the same issues as any bereaved parent, but you must do so in a vacuum of the parental role that is taken away with the death of the one child you had.

The death of your child exposes you to the most intense, complicated, and long-lasting grief known to humans. The loss is unlike any other particularly because of the unique aspects of the parent–child relationship, the unrealistic social expectations that accompany it, and the fact that it often robs you of your most important source of support by affecting your spouse as well. Unfortunately, most people fail to see its critical differences from other losses and don't understand that what is abnormal in those cases may be quite typical in the parental loss of a child.

13

Helping Children Cope
with Death and Mourning

T HE main point and bottom line of this chapter is very simple: Children *do* grieve. They need the help of adults to cope with major loss. Most of what is true for adults in grief also holds true in age-appropriate ways for children. Like adults, they display a variety of reactions; they go through long and intense types of grief; they have many of the same needs; and they experience many of the same symptoms and issues. This chapter will look at how children grieve a death and how you best can help them cope.

The examples used in this chapter are of children who lose a parent. The loss of a sibling will be discussed briefly, but we know much more about reactions to the death of a child's parent than of her brother or sister. This relatively greater interest stems from the fact that the loss of a parent poses the child with critical survival issues (physical and psycho-social) usually not of concern after the death of a brother or sister. However, another important difference to keep in mind is that children whose parents die are acknowledged more often as mourners, and therefore are given relatively more assistance, than those whose siblings die. Nevertheless, from their reactions to parental death, we still can get important information about how children grieve in general.

What Can Happen If Children Don't
Resolve Their Grief

Like adults, a child who suffers a major loss that is unresolved can experience psychosomatic illness, psychological disturbance, adjustment disorders, and behavior problems. While this does not mean that childhood bereavement always must lead to trouble, a loss that is not resolved can influence all aspects of your child's emotional health and relationships with others. If the attachment to the deceased loved one cannot be changed—that is, if it cannot be withdrawn from that person and the emotional energy reinvested in others—the feelings that stay attached to the deceased parent or sibling will remain unavailable for growth and maturation. This means that your child can stay stuck at the stage of development when the loss occurred. This is one of the reasons that death in childhood can be so traumatic. If a loss happens to an adult, that adult at least has matured and developed already; if it happens in childhood, it can interfere with normal development.

How Children Are Disadvantaged as Grievers

There are other ways in which a child is disadvantaged as a griever compared to an adult. One very important one is that the child is immature in her thinking abilities. For example, she may not understand what death means or its implications. A very young child may not realize that death is permanent, and she may expect her parent to return. Also, because of their intellectual immaturity and lack of experience, children tend not to have the words to describe their feelings, thoughts, or memories, which is so important in grief resolution. This should not surprise you. You know how overwhelming and confusing grief is; it is sometimes difficult for you yourself to identify thoughts and words that can help you manage your own feelings of grief. This is even more the case for children.

Children also have problems because they tend to take things literally. This is why you must be careful in how you communicate to your children. If you say that someone has been "lost," your child may expect the person to be found again. If you say that mostly only "old" people die, your child may be very concerned: no matter what your age is, that is old to your child. Another problem stems from the manner in which you have conveyed the news of death. The dishonesty of adults can contribute to the problems of their children and can instill fears in them where none may have existed before.

Because your child is a child, she has little control over her life. Being dependent upon you, she does not necessarily have access to resources that could help her cope. You know yourself that there are times when you need to get away from your grief and perhaps you decide to hop in your car and go visit a friend. Children are limited in what they can do and when they can do it. You may have people and resources to turn to for help in sorting out the confusing feelings of grief. If such resources are not immediately present for the child in her environment, she cannot go out and look for them as you do. She is more stuck with her grief than you are. This is why it is so important that you provide avenues for your child that will allow her to cope with grief effectively.

A child also may not yet have the developmental experiences that tell her that the pain will subside and that life will go on. She doesn't have the reassurance that people can survive these types of events, and this can leave her without the strength to take future risks of loving other people.

Your child does not have the capacity to tolerate pain intensely over time as an adult can. This is the reason why your child might manifest grief on an intermittent basis for many years, and why she alternately approaches and avoids her feelings so that she will not be overwhelmed. Adults often misinterpret this behavior. When they see a child resume play, they erroneously believe that this means that the child does not understand what has happened, or that the death had no impact. This may not be true; the child simply may not be able to grieve intensely for too long a time. This does not mean that the child does not understand or cannot cope with death.

Another reason why children may grieve intermittently, or not at all for a while, is that they must be certain that their physical and emotional needs are going to be met before they can give in to their grief. Consequently, many children don't resolve their loss but mark time until more favorable circumstances arise and they can acknowledge the pain of loss and mourn their deceased loved one. For example, they may need to wait until the family is stable again or until they can form a strong relationship with an adult who can make them feel secure enough to express their feelings.

Another problem is that parents tend not to appreciate that a child's play is her work. Play is the natural means of communication for a child, offering safe avenues for self-expression. It enables her to experiment with different identities and to rehearse difficult or anxiety-provoking events. Very important, it is a way she works through her problems. Oftentimes when children play death games or act out funerals it is because they are trying to master their loss, as well as take a break from their grief. Again, this does not mean that they are not affected by the death; they are just dealing with it in their own way. A child's play is similar to an adult's discussion and processing of feelings. Each is an attempt to cope with and master what the person is undergoing.

Finally, a child can suffer the negative effects of your attempts at protecting her from death. You are moved by your child's helplessness and fragility and would like to rescue her from painful feelings. However, if you deny your child's ability to deal with the death and if you exclude her from the events of the death, you will only harm your child. Your child has a *right* and a *need* to be included. She must be allowed to share her grief with those she loves. Silence about the death and isolation from important others at this time deprive her of the opportunity to deal with her own emotions. If children are not included, they start to feel insecure and abandoned as they see the adults in their life reacting to and sharing in an experience that they cannot share. Additionally, the fantasies of children are often much worse than reality. If you do not explain what is going on, or help them to understand why you are responding as you are in your grief, children will start to draw their own conclusions, which may cause problems later on. When this is coupled by their being withdrawn from their own secure and familiar environment (for example, when the child is sent away to stay with others during the funeral), this only increases their fear, confusion, and sense of isolation and abandonment.

Factors that Can Inhibit Your Child's Grief

A number of factors can inhibit your child's grief. You need to be aware of them so that you can work to avoid or counteract them as much as possible. They include the following:

Your own inability to grieve

Your own inability to tolerate the pain of your child and to allow her to mourn—for example, denying her feelings and their expression

Your child's fear about your vulnerability and her desire to protect you

Your child's concern for her own security, which may not allow her to give in to her grief because it is too frightening

The lack of the security of a caring environment

The lack of a caring adult who can stimulate and support her grief

Confusion about the death and her part in it

Ambivalence towards the deceased

Unchallenged magical thinking (see section below)

The lack of opportunities to share her longing, feelings, and memories

Instability of family life after the loss

Inappropriate reassignment of roles or responsibilities

Secondary losses

Other major variables influencing your child's grief are like those that influence your grief as an adult (see chapter 4 for more on this). They can help or hinder your child's mourning. In addition there is the special impact of what you tell her and what opportunities you later give her to inquire further about what has happened and to deal with her feelings.

Not only the death affects your child; as in adult grief, there are secondary losses as well. They have a profound effect on your child's subsequent adjustment and development. The major ones concern your emotional capability to provide for her care and security after the death. Because your child lacks maturity and self-sufficiency, she is vulnerable not only to her own emotional responses to a major loss but also to the consequences of your grief and the interruption of normal care and interaction patterns necessary for her growth and well-being.

If a young child loses a parent and is not provided with a consistent surrogate of the same sex as the deceased parent to learn to relate to, the child may have some difficulties in learning what adults of that sex are like and how to deal with them. This doesn't mean the surviving parent should rush into remarriage—it only underscores the importance of giving young children the opportunity to identify and interact with adults of both sexes. There is a special need of young children to have both a male and female figure to respond to.

Role reorganizations and reassignments that occur in the family as a consequence of the death also will influence your child's bereavement. If there are changes in family rules for expressing feelings, obtaining gratification, or gaining support, they will have a profound influence on the child's experience. So, too, will any change in relationships among family members. Finally, the family's acceptance of the necessary tasks and processes of grief will be crucial. In families where discussion of death is taboo, children have a particularly difficult time.

Related to this, if your child feels that she needs to protect you from the additional pain of her grief, she may not allow you to have any access at all to her mourning. This can cause her to inhibit her grief indefinitely. She also may try to take on roles and responsibilities over her capacity or may try to replace the lost loved one in an attempt to take care of you. Beware of this, for it not only robs your child of her childhood but it also interferes with resolution of grief because of the additional stress it puts on her.

Bereavement at Different Ages

Your child will respond as a child first and foremost; for example, adolescents will be adolescents first and grievers second. Below you will find a summary of the writings of the Australian psychiatrist Beverley Raphael (1983) on bereavement in children at different ages. This will give you a framework for understanding the bereavement of your child.

Infant in the First Few Months of Life. This bereaved infant cries and shows distress if there is a withdrawal of nurturance. Good replacement nurturance will soothe this reaction quickly.

Four to Five Months to Two Years. From four or five months onward bereavement may be expressed by nonspecific ongoing distress in reaction to the absence of the mother. This is probably the earliest manifestation of grief as part of the infant responds to the specific absence of the parent as a particular person. The absence can be caused either by the death of the mother or by the mother's being involved in her own grief and not acting the same toward the infant.

The child from six months to two years of age shows the initial beginnings of grief and mourning in the way described by John Bowlby in 1980. At first there is shock, rapidly followed by protest which is designed to bring the mother back and "punish" her to prevent future repetitions. If the separation continues, the child manifests despair and sadness. Recollection, yearning, longing, and pain follow. Because the child cannot tolerate these reactions for prolonged periods, he eventually will give up looking for his mother, no longer expecting or hoping for her return. Despair and sadness become evident, and he loses interest in usually pleasurable objects and activities. If the separation persists, the child will become detached from everyone unless a constant and caring person takes over. In cases where the loss is of someone other than the mother, such as a father or sibling, it is difficult to tell if the child's reaction is truly a reaction to the loss itself or is a mirroring of the grief of the mother.

From the age of two and a half on, the processes and responses of grieving children differ little from their elders, although the children lack the capacity to put their thoughts, feelings, and memories into words.

Two to Five Years Old. Because this child's grief is only intermittently seen, parents often erroneously think the child is not affected by the loss. However, this lack of outward evidence does not mean grieving is not occurring. Initially, your child may not understand fully and may ask seemingly inappropriate questions. Later, younger children show a degree of bewilderment and may show some regressive behavior, such as clinging and demanding. They inquire repeatedly about the whereabouts of the deceased and demand to know why she has not returned and what she is doing. There is obvious yearning for the parent's return and angry protest when it does not happen. Often there is anger with the deceased for the desertion and for the resulting chaos in the family life. The anger can be directed towards the surviving parent, or the parent may elicit such anger by withdrawing in his or her own grief and being unable to give the child comfort.

The loss will be worse if your child is sent away to an unfamiliar environment for "protection" from adults' grief and from funeral activities. This often results in anxiety, since your child is deprived of the secure and predictable world of the family. This can totally disrupt her sense of security and bring about concerns for her own survival.

At this age, obsessive thinking about the deceased, longing, and sadness are common. A child of this age will be likely to review and remember her relationship with the deceased. Grief and withdrawal of emotional attachment may take her a long time, even if she feels secure enough to let it occur. She may have a tendency to overidealize the deceased. This can cause problems later on if she compares survivors to an idealized loved one.

At this age, you and other adults may find it intolerable to acknowledge your child's painful grieving. As a result, you may deny her feelings and try to inhibit their expression. This can be quite harmful to her. While adults may inhibit a child's mourning at any age, it is a greater problem for the child at this age, since she lacks the security and resources to address her grief in the absence of support from adults.

Five to Eight Years Old. At this age your child has a better understanding of death and its implications, although not at an adult level. He is particularly vulnerable since he understands much about death but has little coping capacity to deal with it. Denial is often the prime defense in the face of loss. For example, your child is particularly likely to act as if nothing has happened. He needs to hide his feelings out of concern about being babyish; he has a great fear of loss of control and of being dependent on adults as he was when he was younger.

Your child may have taken on adult demands for containing emotions, or he may have identified with adult restriction of feelings of grief. As a result, your child indeed may cry and express deep feelings, but only in private. Even those of you who are close to him may not be aware of this. Thus, while he is affected by the loss inside, it is not reflected in his outward behavior. As a consequence, you and others incorrectly may see him as being uncaring, unloving, or unaffected, and may not give him the support and comfort he desperately needs. This is particularly unfortunate because children of this age tend to shut out feelings and may end up not dealing with their grief unless they are given strong permission and support to do so. This is why you must clearly and repeatedly give him permission, through what you say and do, to deal with his feelings. You must actively help him to do so.

In an effort to cope, a child of this age may develop a strong fantasy life in an attempt to keep his relationship with the deceased loved one alive. When this happens, survivors, including yourself, may compare poorly with the fantasized, idealized person. Provide your child with more constructive ways to deal with his grief and to remember his loved one, such as giving him the opportunity to talk about his feelings in a trusting relationship. Make him feel safe enough to deal with his distress and sadness.

Other responses your bereaved child may have are guilt, which comes from his fear that his angry wishes may have caused the death; concern about being different from his friends, since a family member is gone; fear about your vulnerability and that of surviving family members; and a need to become self-reliant and helpful. For example, an eight-year-old girl may become a "little mother" to her younger brothers and sisters in an attempt to shut out her grief, overcompensate for the longing for her mother, and act out her own need to be cared for.

Eight to Twelve Years Old. Although the child of this age is not as dependent on you as before, her independence is still quite fragile. The loss of a parent or other family member can reawaken feelings of childishness and helplessness. Although she longs for the deceased loved one, she believes that these "childish" feelings must be controlled. As a result, she may be unable to share them with anyone and may put on a facade of independence and coping.

Anger is easier for your child to deal with, since it is more powerful than the "childish" feelings of longing and yearning. General irritability may be a symptom of this anger but often is not recognized as such by either the child or those around her. In fact, you may inappropriately label it as difficult behavior, and then your child either loses your support and that of other adults or receives punishment from you.

At this age your child is still unable to accept the finality of the specific death of her loved one, although she does recognize the finality and irreversibility of death in general. Added to the fact that her yearning and longing is often repressed, this puts your child at risk for unresolved grief. Just as younger children do, she may hold on to the relationship with the deceased in a fantasized, idealized way that can create further problems with you or other surviving family members. For example, negative feelings about the deceased parent now may be projected onto you.

A child of this age may choose to retreat into some symbolic behavior associated with the deceased parent, which is a way of identifying with the parent's behavior or style. She also may try to act "grown up" in an attempt to master the pain of her loss and deny her helplessness. She may start to compulsively care for others, or act in the reverse and become controlling or bossy. Both of these are attempts to deal with her feeling of helplessness. More than at any other time, there is a tendency for a child of this age to be fearful, to develop phobias, to be overly concerned with her body, and to become hypochondriacal.

Sudden death at this age will usually bring shock, denial, and possibly great anxiety and distress. Your child is frightened by what has happened. When the death is anticipated, there seems to be less need for the extreme denial that often comes into play following a sudden death; however, some denial is likely to occur.

Children of this age often lack opportunities to share their grief and are conflicted about inhibiting it. Your child needs to share her longing and begin the process of mourning. However, too often the grief and mourning of children in this age group goes unrecognized. This happens especially if they do not act out their bereavement but take it quietly and become withdrawn, marking time until they can acknowledge the pain of their loss and appropriately grieve. For some, grieving can only begin when the family becomes stable and secure again, or when a relationship is established with an adult who can make the child feel secure enough to express her yearning and sadness over the death. This will be important for you to do. Teachers also may provide such relationships, which can promote necessary mourning.

Adolescence. After a significant loss, your adolescent child will most probably feel helpless and frightened. She may want to retreat to childhood, where she had felt a sense of protection from death, but usually she is compelled by social expectations to act more as an adult. The conflict is painful when she is expected to comfort family members at the same time she is feeling childish and frightened herself. Additionally, the strong yearning and longing for the deceased may seem to her as if it is drawing her back into childhood, with its dependency and powerlessness. The normally rebellious adolescent finds this hard to accept. Consequently, her yearning is often repressed, and this makes her more susceptible to unresolved grief.

Anger is more easily expressed. This can give your adolescent a sense of power to counteract her helplessness. However, it also can fuel depression or can be used inappropriately to punish herself or others for the death. Denial, too, may be used as a defense, for the adolescent greatly fears losing control of her already strong emotions and is especially threatened by the idea of death. Like adults, this child now can conceive of the future effects of the death, such as the fact that her father will not be able to escort her down the aisle when she gets married.

Your adolescent will exhibit many adult responses to death, but they will be complicated by typical adolescent problems: resistance to communicating with adults; overconcern about whether others accept her responses; alienation from adults and sometimes friends; lack of knowledge of what is socially expected; and other developmental issues that can interfere with the processes of grieving, such as problems with separation and dependency, identity, heightened emotions, and sexual conflicts.

At times the ongoing tasks of adolescence can keep your child's grief from being completed successfully. The grief may be delayed, possibly until a secure relationship is present to help it come about, or it may occur intermittently. One of the issues that makes this grieving particularly difficult is that your child may be experiencing guilt as a result of her normal rebelliousness and withdrawal from the family that had been occurring prior to the death. This guilt can prompt conflicted mourning behaviors. When an adolescent's grief and mourning cannot proceed directly, it may be seen through exaggerated attempts to act like an adult, identification with the deceased, withdrawal and depression, sexual acting out, and behaviors designed to get others to care for her—not only to ger her some care, but also to release tension, self-punish, and sometimes replace the deceased.

Special Issues in the Death of a Sibling

There are some additional issues which arise when your child is mourning the death of a brother or sister. This section briefly outlines these issues, which you must keep in mind as you attempt to respond to your child's reactions to the death. They definitely will influence his grief.

Siblings have many things in common. They have had similar experiences; they share the same parents. For this reason, it is not uncommon for the death of a sibling to be particularly traumatic to your child. More so than any other loss, this type of death profoundly illustrates to your child that he can die, too. Your child also may feel intense guilt because of previous hostile and ambivalent feelings about his brother or sister and/or because he survived while his sibling didn't. There may be even stronger anger with you for being unable to protect his deceased sibling and for failing to prevent the death from happening, for, if it happened to that sibling, it could happen to the surviving child as well.

Often siblings have a changed role in the family after a death; for example, they may move from second to oldest child or become the only living child. These transitions require sensitive handling on your part. If you assign the child inappropriate new roles and responsibilities, or expect him to take over the identity of the deceased child, it may be particularly harmful. (See chapters 8 and 12 for more on this topic.)

Sibling bereavement can be made more difficult if you overprotect your child, if you compare him with the deceased child, or if you are unable to attend to the surviving family members' needs due to your own involvement in grief.

It can be particularly frightening for him when a surviving child reaches the age at which a sibling died. He will need an adequate explanation of the cause of death in order to confront this anxiety.

Siblings may have additional trouble dealing with their deceased sibling's effects. For some, inheriting these may be comforting; for others, it may be disturbing. Each child will feel differently, and you must use sensitivity in deciding what should be done with the deceased child's belongings and room.

Keeping the Right Perspective on Yourself

It is important for you to recognize that in most cases where your child is bereaved, you are bereaved too. This means that you will be acutely grieving your loved one at the same time you are attempting to assist your child with her mourning. How can you aid your child when you are overwhelmed yourself?

This is a very important question. It doesn't have a simple answer, only a simple perspective: You do the very best that you can under the circumstances. Be realistic about what you can expect of yourself, and tap into other resources to help you help your child and yourself.

Doing the best that you can under the circumstances means that you recognize the critical importance of helping your child to mourn, and that whenever possible you act in ways to further the successful resolution of her grief. Realize that your preoccupation with your own loss and your other grief responses may make you concerned about your love for your child, or worried that you are a failure or at least not as good as you "should be" as a parent. Such feelings, along with anxiety that you can't give enough to your child right now because of your own grief, can make you feel quite guilty. Avoid punishing yourself, do whatever you can to minimize the omissions or commissions that concern you, and work on having realistic expectations of yourself. If you are a bereaved parent who has lost a child, you may be vulnerable to other issues with regard to your surviving children. (See chapter 12 for more on this.)

Having realistic expectations of yourself means that you are aware of your own depletion from grief, understand how your own acute grief affects you, and therefore will be appropriately reasonable in what you demand of yourself and how you evaluate yourself regarding your helping your child. For example, this means that you recognize that in acute grief you do not function at your optimal level, nor have the patience and emotional resources to be as emotionally available to your child as usual. You won't let this be an excuse—you will still try your best—but you won't give yourself additional stress for not being "super parent" at this time.

Tapping into resources means that you seek to identify the deficits and limitations in your ability to help your child and find appropriate and concerned others who can temporarily help fill in the gaps. Don't try to do it all yourself. Enlist the help of your child's teacher, her favorite aunt, or a trusted friend of yours to watch out for her, encourage her healthy mourning, and so forth. Even if you cannot be all you would want to be right now, you can arrange things as much as possible to ensure that the basics are provided to your child in this situation.

It is important for you to be honest with your child, to tell her you're having a hard time too (this has the added benefit of legitimizing her pain), but that you are "in it for the long haul" with her; you will get through it together. Your response to your child over time usually will have a greater impact than any one particular event. Try to keep this perspective. Don't come down on yourself too hard unless it truly is warranted. Giving yourself extra stress now by being unreasonable and unrealistic with yourself will only complicate your mourning and make it more difficult than it already is to deal with your child's grief at the same time as your own. All you can do is your best, even if it isn't that good because of your pain. Don't let yourself off the hook too easily, but don't hang yourself either. If possible, be in touch with other parents in a similar situation to make sure you continue to be appropriate in your expectations and behavior, in addition to getting support for and information about coping in these most difficult and demanding circumstances. (See chapter 20 for a listing of parent organizations.)

Helping Children Cope

Your focus should be on three areas to help your child cope with death and grief. First, you must be very careful about how you communicate about death and grief to your child. Second, you need to include your children in the funeral or other mourning rituals. Third, you must support normal grief responses and try to prevent unhealthy ones.

Communicating with Your Child

Keep in mind two principles of communication when you talk with your child about death and grief. First, make sure that you are clear and honest. Information that is not truthful, realistic, or straightforward will be harmful to your child, despite your intent to protect or help her. Second, communicate in words and ways she can understand, given her age and abilities. Be careful to gear your words and concepts to precisely what she can comprehend. This is hard enough to do in general, but even more difficult when dealing with the issues of loss, death, and grief.

Children often are told myths or fairy tales about death instead of the truth. Rabbi Earl Grollman (1974) gives some examples and illustrates their unexpected negative effects.

Example 1:
   "Mother has gone on a long trip."

Child's reaction:

Anger and resentment ("Why didn't she take me?" "Why did she leave?")

Abandonment and guilt ("I must have done something bad to make her leave me.")

Illusion that mother will return

Wonder at why everyone else is sad and crying

Example 2:

"God took Daddy when he was so young because your father was so good that He wanted your father for Himself."

Child's reaction:

Resentment and anger against God ("*I* needed him.")

Fear of being good ("I might be taken.")

Example 3:

"Grandma died because she was so sick."

Child's reaction:

Associates all sickness with death

Example 4:

"Your aunt died. Now she is sleeping forever."

Child's reaction:

Associates sleep with death and becomes afraid to go to sleep

There are a number of important things you should remember when telling your child of the death of a loved one:

You should tell your child immediately in order to prevent her hearing it from someone else. Use a normal tone of voice, avoiding hushed, unnatural whispers that may convey an undesirable message of death being unreal or spooky. As appropriate, hug or touch the child to provide comfort and security.

You or someone close to the child should tell her, preferably in familiar surroundings that give her security. Don't let her hear it from someone else; this will only be more frightening and make her wonder why you did not inform her. She won't be able to count on your being honest with her, and that is very important.

You should give your child as honest an explanation as possible within her limits of understanding. Very young children are not able to understand that death is irreversible and permanent, but they can understand something like the analogy of death being like a broken toy: The deceased does not function any more, and although we would like to fix it, he or she will not work again. Be specific by telling your child that her loved one's body has stopped working and will not do the things that it used to do, such as talk, walk, move, breathe, or go to the bathroom. Tell your child that the deceased will not have any feelings. The deceased will not be sad, mad, happy, hurt, or cold. This is important, because sometimes your child may be alarmed thinking that her loved one will feel being put in a casket or cremated. Be as concrete and specific as possible in order not to leave your child with the impression that death is merely another form of living elsewhere. If she gets this impression, she may expect that the deceased can return. This is why you should be careful if you use explanations of an afterlife. Make sure the child understands that this living elsewhere (for example, in Heaven) does not mean the deceased can come back.

Avoid euphemisms. As adults, we know what it means when we say that someone has "lost" someone they love. However, your children may be confused by this because they tend to take things quite literally. For example, *lost* implies that the loved one can be found; *sleep* means that the person will wake up. It is important that you look at what you are saying from your child's perspective. In this way you can choose words that will not leave misconceptions but will help them understand that dead is forever. If you do not do this, you may be setting up your child for further problems later on.

Recognize that repeated questions, either at the time you inform your child or in the weeks and months afterwards, are not as much for factual information about the death as they are for reassurance that the story has not changed. Your child is checking to make sure that things are still the same and that what happened is still in effect. Like adults, children wish that they could undo the loss or find out that it isn't true. Their repeated questions are merely attempts to find out that the death is not true. Actually, this is not so different from what you, as an adult, may do when you continue for some time to hope and wish that somehow you will find out that it has all been a bad dream, that you will wake up and be reunited with your lost loved one.

When you inform the child of the death of her loved one, it is important to make sure that the child knows that she is loved and will continue to be taken care of even though a very sad thing has happened and adults are very upset. It is frightening for your child to see the adults in her world distressed, but this must not be hidden, since it is a natural reaction. Also, by allowing your child to see you express your grief, you provide a very important model to her. If you tell her to express her feelings, but then you hide your own, she soon learns that actions speak louder than words. She will do what you do, not what you say. Show her what appropriate grieving behavior is.

Don't be afraid to let your child see you cry or express feelings related to your grief. Of course, your grief expression should be somewhat tempered in order not to overwhelm her. There is a difference between letting her see your sadness and letting her see complete despair or collapse. However, children usually can contend with much stronger reactions than adults believe, and in general it is better to err in the direction of sharing the feelings than concealing them from your child. The most important thing is that you give your child an explanation of your feelings as a normal response to grief, and accompany this with an attempt to make your child feel secure even though there is a great deal of change occurring. Family changes should be kept to a minimum as much as possible, although of course there will be changes in routine at the time of death and family reorganization following the death.

Predict for your child that she may feel sad and even have strange or different feelings for a while. Let her know that this is natural and that she should talk about these feelings. Make sure that she knows that such feelings will not last forever and that they are not abnormal. For example: "This may make you sad and unhappy for some time. It is normal to feel this way. Come to me and we can talk about it and cry together. Someday it won't hurt as much."

Tell your child what to expect in terms of the activities of the funeral and grief in general. Children will need to know what will happen to them and who will care for them. They need to know what events will occur, when, and why. As with adults, this knowledge beforehand will reduce their anxiety. For example, you can let them know what you have to do, where you have to go, and when you will be back. Inform them about what will happen at the wake, funeral, or whatever leave-taking ritual will occur. Be specific about the activities and the details.

For example, tell them: "Grandpa's body will be in a casket, which is like a box, and people will go up and look at Grandpa and say 'good-bye' to him." Also, let them know what they can expect from other people in order that they not be frightened or confused. For example: "Cousin Steven may tell you that you shouldn't cry, but that is not true. Crying is okay to do because you are sad that Grandpa has died" or "Auntie Ruth will probably get very upset and may even throw herself on the casket. Don't let this frighten you; that is just the way she is."

As in other situations of stress, children, like adults, do better when they know what to expect. In explaining grief you can say something like: "We are all very upset that Daddy has died. It hurts us all very much, and we will cry and be sad at times. When we miss him we can talk to each other about him and the things we remember about him. Although our family is hurt and unhappy right now, we will keep on taking care of each other and someday it won't hurt like this anymore."

Let your child know that you are not going to hide anything from her and that she is a part of the family and that all of you will get through this together. This makes her feel secure that she will not be excluded, and it treats her with respect. It also allows her to let down her guard. She won't have to feel that she always has to be on the lookout for what's going on, since she knows she can count on you to tell her.

Including Your Child in Funerals and Other Mourning Rituals

In an effort to protect your child, you may feel that you should shelter her from your grief expressions and from the funeral or other rituals of mourning. However, your child has a *right* and a *need* to be included. If she is not allowed to share her grief, if she is separated from the family at this time of crisis, and if she is not provided with accurate information, she will have more difficulty resolving her loss. Consequently, you should give your child the opportunity to decide whether or not to attend the funeral or other rituals.

If she decides not to attend the rituals, that decision should be respected. You can tell her that she may visit the grave or the church when she wants to and that you will go with her if she desires. *Never force* a child to attend the rituals or do anything she truly does not want to do—for example, kiss the body. These forced actions cause many fears and problems later on. This does not mean, however, that you can't strongly encourage your child to attend or participate in the ritual; it only means that force is a harmful tactic to use.

If your child does decide to attend the rituals, the details should be explained completely in advance so that she will have some idea of what to expect. You should tell her what will happen, when it will happen, and what her role will be in the proceedings. Make sure she doesn't read anything inappropriate into the rituals. For example, if she chooses to do something such as give a gift to the deceased and put it in the casket, make sure she knows that the deceased can't use it because he or she is dead. Nevertheless, it is important to your child not only to participate but also to have an opportunity to make a good-bye gesture.

You may be concerned that your child will be devastated by the funeral. However, this is a displacement of your own fears and concerns onto your child. In and of themselves, the funeral rituals offer nothing for your child to fear. Of course they will be sad, but it is always sad to lose a loved one. Since you are trying to prepare your child for dealing with life in the real world, you also must try to prepare her for the losses and deaths that she inevitably will confront. It is best if you allow your child to face the sadness of grief while you are present to help her cope with it. The alternative is to try to hide her from the real world, perhaps leaving her to confront its grief at a time when you are no longer there to support her—for example, at your own funeral.

Actually, the acting out of ritual and the procession of funerals are very well suited to children. They are fascinated by these types of behaviors, and have them in their lives in a number of ways. Children will be afraid of them only if they pick up on your fears and anxieties.

Helping Your Child to Grieve

The following are specific suggestions to help you deal with your grieving child. They are designed to support normal grief responses and to prevent the development of unhealthy ones.

Specifically give your child permission to mourn. Sensitive inquiry will help you determine exactly how he feels. Sometimes a child just needs the catalyst of your interest or your invitation to talk, especially to discuss feelings he has been reluctant to express or that have been surprisingly intense. Like adults, children need permission to grieve. Make sure you make your child feel secure enough to let the process of grief occur. Do not deny his feelings or disallow his mourning, even if it is painful for you to see. Never censor his feelings. Like an adult, he must express the angry and negatives ones as well as the more positive ones.

Be there for the child. Give affection and security, and show support, concern, and acceptance by appropriately touching the child. Provide demonstrations of your support and affection by being present physically. Maintain eye contact and touch him. He will benefit from your physical comfort— he desperately needs the security and reassurance it conveys.

Look for ways to help your child express his emotions both verbally and nonverbally. Like adults, children express themselves in a variety of ways. However, because of their age they do tend to use more nonverbal means of communication than do adults. This is why their play is so important. You can be helpful to your child in his mourning by encouraging him to express his feelings through such activities as art, (for example, painting, building sculpture, drawing), physical activity, (for example, running, jumping, dancing), playing games, or building projects. Any behaviors through which he can act out his feelings can be used. For older children, encouraging creative writing and journaling is therapeutic. Reading books that deal with other children's responses to death and then discussing them together can be very helpful, as can having them react to vignettes about children dealing with loss and asking them how they think the children in the story feel. The same process can be used with movies, television shows, or songs that pertain to loss and death.

Watch out for your child's causal connection of his personal wishes or actions to the death of his loved one. This is called "magical thinking." It also occurs on the adult level, but it is especially prevalent in children. For example, your child may feel responsible and guilty for his father's death because he had argued with him or had said "Drop dead!" For this reason, you need to develop an understanding of what your child thinks and feels about the loss. He may have significant misconceptions. Since these can interfere with his grief resolution, you must correct them as soon as possible. This requires explaining to him the difference between expression of a thought or feeling and the causing of the actual physical event of death. Reassure him that it is normal at times to feel angry or upset with the people we love, and that it has nothing to do with the death of the person he loved.

Keep in mind the developmental capacities of your child and her age-related concerns at the time of death. Both of these will profoundly influence the grief experience. For example, the normal problems of adolescence only serve to intensify the usual conflicts of grief. Whatever the age of the child, help her to understand the full meaning and implications of the death as much as she can.

Also remember that the young child has a special need to have both a male and female figure to respond to, so it may be important for her development that she has some consistent experiences with an appropriate surrogate of the sex of the deceased parent. Aunts, uncles, grandparents, and very close friends who will be around for a while (you don't want to expose her to another loss too soon) can help out, as can organizations such as Big Brothers or Big Sisters. Just make sure they have the appropriate commitment and emotional qualifications.

Remember that, depending on the age, your child's ability to remember a loved one in her absence may be inadequate. Younger children may require assistance to remember the deceased. This is why photographs are useful, as they can help the child to recall that person so that feelings associated with him remain available for grief work resolution. Dates of important birthdays and anniversaries should be remembered and observed in order to help keep alive the memory of the deceased. You can remind the child of the love, concern, pride, and joy that had been felt by the deceased for the child and that had been part of their relationship. Share and reinforce the memories of the deceased, and offer the child possessions as keepsakes and cherished mementos.

Be prepared for your child to need continual explanation of and communication about the death over time. You will need to help the child integrate the loss in an ongoing way. As the child grows, she will require new information about the death. Her thinking capacity will increase, and she will become intellectually, emotionally, and verbally mature enough to ask questions about the death that she couldn't or wouldn't before. You will need to fill in pieces of the story that the child may have been unable to comprehend when younger. Sometimes it is only at later points that people realize that they lack important information regarding the death of a loved one. For example, one woman recognized forty-five years after the death of an infant brother that she did not know where that brother had been born. This is not unhealthy, chronic grief but an example of the working-through process that has to continue over time. New life situations and maturity can evoke for the growing child aspects of the lost relationship and questions and concerns that were insignificant at the original time of the loss.

Recognize that your child is expressing feelings not only about the actual death itself but also about the changes in you and your family following the death. Like you as an adult, she is reacting and grieving over the many secondary losses that can happen after the death of a loved one. Keep things as normal as possible for the child. Even if major changes must occur, try to provide as much consistency and security as you possibly can in the situation. Do not forget that appropriate discipline still must be maintained. For a child to suddenly have no limits is terrifying, especially when she has already been made so insecure by the loss.

Do not evaluate your child's grief solely in comparison with yours as an adult. There are more similarities than differences; however, those differences are very important. Sometimes your child will not react at all to the news that a loved one has died. It may seem to you that he is insensitive to the death or that he does not understand, but this conclusion may be quite incorrect. A child engages in denial just as an adult does, and his behaviors may be more primitive manifestations of adult denial processes.

Watch your child's behavior for indications of how he is coping. If you want to know how your child is doing, observe him. Being less verbal, a child tends to act out his feelings more than adults, especially in play. Watch your child's behavior. Frequently it will convey more about his feelings than words. However, interpret his behavior carefully. Use gentle inquiry to confirm your guesses on how he feels. When your child talks about death in a way that is contradictory to his behavior, try to understand the discrepancy. Check out whether you are subtly sending messages about how you want your child to react. Your child will be very sensitive to your cues and, if he feels that his expression of grief will upset you, he will hide and inhibit his responses in an attempt to protect you. Also, if the emotions of grief conflict with the child's age-appropriate or personal concerns, there may be further inhibition of his grief expression. For example, the adolescent who wants an adult image may be reluctant to express very normal feelings of helplessness.

Let your child know that loss and death bring about intense feelings that he must deal with and help him to do so. Take the position that grief is important, although difficult, work to which he must pay attention. As noted before, give him specific permission to mourn and help him discover ways to express his feelings. You need to make him aware that you are willing to discuss the death and his feelings when he is ready. Then you must act accordingly. Don't promise to help him and talk with him and then fail to follow through.

Make sure that the roles that are reassigned to your child after the death of a family member are appropriate. Inappropriate role responsibilities can do major harm to children. To expect a child to be "the man around the house" or "the little mother" is unfair to your child, will be quite harmful to his or her future development, and often interferes with the mourning process.

Help your child to have patience with herself and others. The period of grief is a tumultuous time, filled with much anxiety. Give your child opportunities to vent her feelings by doing art work, running, exercising, and taking part in other physical activities, as well as by talking. Tell your child not to expect too much of herself right now.

Encourage your child to talk with her friends. This helps stimulate conversation about the death, especially with older children who may be reluctant to talk to you out of their desire to protect you. If your child is an adolescent, her peers may be the only ones she will talk with about her grief. Children of this age often are unwilling to talk about their mourning with their parents, no matter how much you try to facilitate it. Keep the door open, however, because this unwillingness may change in time. Try to discourage inappropriate social withdrawal. Like adults, children need support from their social group, too.

Be aware that your child may feel odd or different from her peers because she has had a loved one die. Help her articulate and cope with this discomfort. It may be helpful to allow her to have contact with other bereaved children so she can see she is not completely abnormal.

Recognize that your child, like you, will need some solitude for healing. Allow and support quiet time (which is much different from withdrawal). Your child will need this calm to reestablish a sense of security, order, and predictability. She needs a respite from her grief, so that she can continue to cope with it. Also like you, your child will require hope and encouragement to get through the difficult process of grief. For example, it may be helpful for you to say "I know that it's hard right now. There are many changes in the family and it seems like things will never stop changing. But I can promise you that things will calm down and we will someday be free from this pain. We will keep working at it together."

See that your child is not overwhelmed by grief. Like you, your child will have to break down her grieving experience into small parts that she can deal with and accommodate over time. Help her to do this to make sure she does not overwhelm herself.

Notice if your child's defenses have continued for too long. At times, you may need to judiciously interpret the defenses of your child if they are interfering with acceptance of the death and with the mourning process. For example, when a child continues to talk about her father's returning and you know that she knows that this will not happen, it may be helpful to say something like "We both know Dad is not alive anymore. You perhaps want to pretend that it isn't so because it makes us so unhappy. But he really will not be coming back."

In cases of sudden death, give your child extra support. The child who experiences a sudden death, like an adult in a similar situation, will need extra support in coping with the unanticipated grief response. The child desperately will need to get some sense of security again.

Be careful when explaining religious concepts to your child. In communicating with your child, introduce religious concepts only after you are sure the child understands the meaning of death. If you give them as an explanation by themselves, they may interfere with the child's understanding of the finality and irreversibility of permanent physical death. Religious explanations may be helpful at a later point. You need to recognize that such concepts are so abstract that they are difficult for children to understand even in the absence of coping with death.

A Note about Death Education
before a Loved One Dies

Ideally, prior to the loss of any loved one, your children will have had some conversations with you about death and its natural part in the course of life. In this way they can be better prepared when death must be confronted in their own lives. As a parent, you should utilize the numerous "teachable moments" that occur in everyday life to instruct your children about death and grief. For example, the death of a pet or a famous person can provide you with a natural opportunity to discuss death and its ramifications with your children. Bereaved individuals usually wish that there had been more preparation for their loss through open and honest family communication about death, sharing of grief with their parents, and greater exposure to death earlier in life. For this reason, it is quite important for you to look for ways to introduce death education in your family life and to support it in your schools.

Helping children cope with death and mourning is a necessary and difficult, but enormously critical, task. It will be important to remember that they are children first, before they are mourners. They have many of the same feelings and needs as you; however, they also have far fewer resources and abilities to cope with them.

PART
IV

Resolving Your Grief

14

What Is Necessary
to "Resolve" Your Grief

T HERE are three sets of processes that must be completed successfully if you are ever to "resolve" your grief over the death of your loved one. Note that the word "resolve" is in quotation marks. Although they will be dropped for the rest of this book, they are used here to help you to see that in most cases the term is a relative one. If the person you lost was truly significant to you, grief is not usually resolved in the sense of being finished and completely settled forever. Certain aspects of the loss will be with you until you die, and there will be times when you experience brief upsurges of grief again. Rather, the term indicates that the processes of grief have been addressed and completed as much as possible at a given point (with an understanding that aspects of it are never gone permanently or totally in cases of major loss) and the loss has been accommodated and integrated appropriately into the rest of your life. (See chapter 17 for a more complete discussion of what recovery means.)

As you read in chapter 2, the ultimate purpose of grief and mourning is to help you recognize that your loved one has gone and ultimately to adapt to the reality of that loss and live healthily in the new world without the deceased. To achieve this purpose successfully, you must complete three sets of processes:

1. Acknowledging and understanding the loss.
2. Experiencing the pain and reacting to the separation.
3. Moving adaptively into the new life without forgetting the old.

Acknowledging and
Understanding the Loss

You are going to need to acknowledge and understand the death of your loved one if you wish to commence your grieving and have the world continue to maintain some order for you.

Acknowledging the Death

In order for grief to begin there must be recognition of loss. If you deny that the death occurred, or if you refuse to believe that it is permanent and irreversible and continue to expect that the deceased will return to life, then you do not have to grieve the death; there is no permanent loss in your eyes, only a separation.

If the necessary grief process is to commence, the reality of death must be acknowledged. This is why in so many cases it is important to view the dead body. This is the ultimate proof that your loved one is dead. It confronts your very normal urge to deny that the person you have loved is now dead. Of course, you do not want this reality to be true. You want it to be a horrible mistake. Yet, until you recognize in your mind that the person is dead, you have no reason to start grieving. This is why confirmation of the death is so important, and why we spend so much time, money, and effort trying to recover bodies after airplane crashes, boating accidents, earthquakes, and so forth. Human beings frequently require evidence of the death before they can or will start to grieve it. In the absence of such proof, they may postpone their grief in the hope that the person still is alive, or may feel that it is unnecessary because they can see no reason for it, that is, no dead body.

Not knowing the status of a loved one leaves you in a type of limbo because you do not know how to proceed with your life: Is my loved one alive or dead? Is he out there somewhere wanting, but unable, to come home? Did the accident leave him with amnesia so that he cannot find his way back to us? Does he need my help? Should I still be looking for him? These and other difficulties are seen in families where a loved one's death cannot be confirmed. They also are witnessed in families of missing children and of men who are "missing in action" (MIAs) in Southeast Asia.

Understanding the Death

In addition to an acknowledgment that the death has occurred, you will need to come to an understanding of how it happened. You will have to develop an explanation of the death that makes some sense to you intellectually and that answers whatever questions you have about it. This does not mean that you like the cause of death, or that you can fit this death into your system of meaning or your philosophy of life. It only means that you understand the reasons for the events which led to the death. You have your own account which explains for you how and why the death happened like it did. It may or may not be the same as anyone else's, but that is unimportant as long as it satisfies you, for example, the wife who refuses to believe that her husband committed suicide and insists that he was an accident victim.

Those who are unable to fit a loved one's death into a context or some sort of rationale have trouble with their grief. They tend to become confused and anxious in their general lives, wondering about what happened to their loved one and what potentially could happen to them. Without the world making sense to them, including the death of the person they loved, it is difficult to recover from such a major loss. This is why, for example, parents whose babies die from Sudden Infant Death Syndrome frequently have such a difficult time when no cause of death is found.

Experiencing the Pain and
Reacting to the Separation

This set of processes has four operations that must be completed. They involve:

1. Experiencing the pain.
2. Reacting to the separation.
3. Readjusting to the new world without your loved one.
4. Changing your emotional attachment to and investment in him.

Experiencing the Pain

Put very simply, there is no way around it. There is no way around the pain that you naturally feel when someone you love dies. You can try to go over it, under it, or around it. For example, you can try to delay it, or you can try to deny it. You can avoid thinking about the loss, or you can cut yourself off from your feelings when you do think about it. You can try to minimize your loss, or you can overfocus on other family members' grief and not pay attention to your own. You can say that grief is unnecessary because you will be reunited with your loved one in an afterlife, or you can keep yourself so busy that you never perceive the separation or feel the grief. All of these things will cost you. True, they may work in some fashion for a period of time. Yet, if you want to resolve your grief, if you want to leave the pain behind, if you want to be healthy and symptom-free, if you want someday to have as fulfilled a life as possible, sooner or later you must go *through* the pain. Going through it is what will help you heal.

You cannot be blamed for wanting to avoid the pain of grief. Unless you are a masochist, no one would ask for the type of pain that comes after the loss of someone loved. However, despite its being natural to want to avoid the pain, to do so will only bring more pain in the future. You have to yield to it in order to move through it. You have two choices: You can pay now or you can pay later. As in any other situation of payment, if you choose to pay later you must recognize that the bill will be much higher because of the interest. In this case, the "interest" which increases the bill comes from such things as the additional defenses that you have constructed to deal with the grief and that will need to be worked through; the accumulated buildup of additional fears and symptoms over a longer time period; and the diminished presence of a support system which may have been available at the time of loss.

Notwithstanding this, at times you will need to take "breaks" in your grief; times when you need to get some distance from the pain in order to replenish yourself so you can cope with it more next time. Continued, unremitting, acute pain will debilitate anyone. We all need some relief from the intense pain of grief. Consequently, there will be times when you find that you are directing your attention away from your grief. Backing off from your pain is normal and healthy. It does not mean you are not grieving properly. It merely means that you need to do something besides grieve, oftentimes something that will give you a sense of control and accomplishment, such as cleaning the house or going to a movie. In both cases, you are doing something to take your mind off your pain and give it a rest from the necessary review processes of grief. These diversions give you a way to channel your restless energy. They are necessary to avoid being exhausted by the pain. We all need to turn away sometimes in order to reconnect with the living, growing parts of ourselves, to get reenergized and replenished. Problems occur only when we overfocus on taking breaks and pay insufficient attention to grieving.

Reacting to the Separation

Besides experiencing the pain, you also will have to deal with separation from the person you loved. You must become accustomed to the absence of an integral part of your life, someone who has contributed to your world and life being what it is. You will have to learn to be in the world without the person who was a partner with you in the unique relationship the two of you had, a special relationship that helped make you be you. You will have to learn not to need from this person all the different types of interaction, validation, and reinforcement that he gave you (both positive and negative) based on your particular relationship with him. You will have to change your hopes, dreams, expectations, feelings, thoughts, and needs that involved his physical presence in your life.

Of course, dealing with this separation from your loved one is not something you will be eager to do. You will want to resist it. However, in healthy grief the reality of the separation from your loved one will sink in despite your resistance and will prompt the two additional processes in this area: readjusting to the new world without your loved one in it and changing your emotional attachment and investment in him to reflect the fact that he is dead.

Readjusting to the New World

Readjustment to the new world without your loved one takes great patience and much practice. It is achieved painfully, step-by-step, as you gradually come to grips with that person not being in your life as he was before.

After a person dies, it may take a while to learn completely all of the roles he played for you. Some will be apparent immediately. For example, you will know at once that he was a companion, since the loss of his presence so painfully signals to you that you do not have that companionship. However, other losses only become apparent with time. You may not realize how much you depended on your loved one to evaluate your work until he is no longer there for you to give you his opinion or to critique the job you did. It is this learning to be in the world without the deceased that will point out to you exactly what you now are missing.

Each time you start to do something and your loved one is not there to do or say the things you need or want, you will (1) learn again that he is really dead and (2) have to readjust to his not being there and find some other ways of getting these needs and wants met. Usually the readjustment means that you will have to broaden your roles and your skills. For instance, this would mean that the widow has to take an auto repair course, since her husband is no longer around to fix the car, or that she will have to become more assertive, since he is not available to speak on her behalf.

When you lose someone with whom you have shared parts of your life, you will have to find some way to make up for what is taken away through the death. You either compensate in some way for what you have lost (for example, you take it over, you find a substitute person, or you find other ways of getting it) or you change your desire for what you had wanted or needed that now is unfulfilled. This is necessary if you are to adapt healthily to this loss, integrating into your existence the absence of this person and all he meant to and did for you. To be healthy, over the long term you cannot continue to behave in the ways you did when your loved one was alive. You must get used to the new world without him, and move into it in ways that reflect the fact that he is no longer in your life as he was before.

Changing Your Emotional Attachment and Investment

You also have to change your emotional attachment to and investment in your loved one to reflect the reality that, despite your intense wishes to the contrary, he is dead and will no longer be able to interact with you as he did in the past. No matter how much you need him, nor how much you are determined that things in your life will not change, the fact of the matter is that your loved one no longer can give you what he did previously. He will no longer be able to return your emotional investment in him. As a result, over time you are going to have to change your emotional investment in him to accommodate this fact.

This is not a betrayal. It does not mean that you no longer love the deceased or that you will forget him. The relationship is altered, to be sure, but it always will exist in a special place in your heart and in your mind. What it does mean is that you modify your ongoing emotional investment in and attachment to him as a living person who can return your investment—you must let go of being connected to him as if he were still alive. The emotional energy that went into your relationship with him gradually must be detached from him, since he can no longer return it, and in time it must be channeled elsewhere where it can be returned for your emotional satisfaction.

Picture your two hands clasped together with intertwined fingers, almost as if they were folded in prayer. Let one hand represent you and the other hand represent the person you loved who has died. When two people love each other and are invested in each other, they are intertwined emotionally, they are bonded together as represented by your two hands. When one of the people dies, the remaining person has to withdraw the emotional energy that was invested in the person who is no longer alive. That person has to relinquish the old attachments to the deceased and develop new ones based on the altered status of the loved one.

The most crucial task in grief is this change in relationship with the person who died. It is the untying of the ties that bind you to your lost loved one. Again, it must be stressed that this *does not* mean that the deceased is forgotten or not loved. Rather, it means that the emotional energy that you had invested in the deceased is readjusted to allow you to direct it towards others who can reciprocate it in an ongoing fashion for your emotional satisfaction.

In the analogy given above, this would be portrayed by disentangling and unclasping your hands and fingers. The hand which represented you will then be free someday to clasp another hand, or to do something else. To keep your hand positioned as if you were intertwined with another's, but to have no other hand there, renders your hand useless, and it will interfere with your normal functioning. This is what happens psychologically to grievers if they inappropriately hang on to past attachments. (Note the use of the word *inappropriately*. This means that there *are* some healthy ways to be connected to your loved one who has died. See section below for a full discussion of this.)

It is not an easy task to withdraw emotional energy and investment from someone you love. It takes a great deal of time and effort. It means that all of your ties to that person—your needs for and your feelings, thoughts, memories, hopes, expectations, and dreams about that person and your relationship with him—all must be brought up and revived. Then each one must be reviewed and felt. In this way the emotional charge is loosened or defused. You may still have the thought and memory of each one, but the emotional feeling accompanying it lessens in intensity. Gradually, over time, you do not feel the accompanying feelings any more, or at least not the way you did when they were intense and vibrant, kept alive by the ongoing, reciprocal relationship you had with your loved one before death.

There are many examples of grievers who have successfully resolved their loved one's loss in this regard. They are, for instance, those who can:

Remember their loved one without pain.

Mention him or tell stories about him without falling apart.

Express regrets without undue guilt.

Love others without feeling they are betraying the deceased.

Write the word *widow* without feeling abandoned.

Certainly they may have brief upsurges in grief at different times and for different reasons, but in general they have reached the point where they can remember what used to be and what they used to need, want, and wish from their deceased loved one and not feel the same way now, nor be overwhelmed with emotion because it is no longer the way it was. This does not mean they are happy about this, only that they have learned to live without constantly grieving because of it. As will be seen below, this now unattached emotional energy someday will be able to be invested elsewhere as a result of not being tied up in the deceased as before.

Moving Adaptively into the New Life without Forgetting the Old

The third series of processes necessary for successful accommodation and resolution of grief focuses on your moving into your new life, that is, life without your deceased loved one, without forgetting your old life. This involves:

1. Developing a new relationship with the deceased.
2. Keeping your loved one "alive" appropriately.
3. Forming a new identity based on your being without this person and encompassing the changes you have made to adjust to his death.
4. Taking the freed-up emotional energy that used to be invested in your loved one and reinvesting it in other relationships, objects, activities, roles, and hopes that can offer emotional satisfaction back to you.

Developing a New Relationship with
Your Deceased Loved One

Although death ends the life of the person you loved, it does not necessarily end your relationship with him. You can have an appropriate, sustained, loving, and symbolic relationship with the person who has died. Contrary to popular opinion, this does not have to be stagnating or morbid. As noted by the philosopher Thomas Attig, this can be a healthy, life-affirming, and life-promoting relationship in which you have relinquished the concrete loving of a person who is physically present and replaced it with the abstract loving of your absent loved one.

One of the problems in our society is that people fail to recognize the importance of a continued relationship with the person we have loved and lost. Many think that to deal with the loss you have to forget the person who has died. Usually grievers are devastated to hear this, with many refusing to grieve as a result.

For proof that continued relationship with the dead need not be abnormal, we need only turn to American society. Note the continued infatuation Americans have with John F. Kennedy, Marilyn Monroe, and James Dean, among others. These people are long dead, and yet we continue to keep them alive with our interest, our review of their lives, our conjecture and curiosity, our books, museums, and movies. Our conversation keeps them alive in the American consciousness. We wonder what they would think about today and how they would act. Sometimes we try to take instruction from their lives and apply it to our own. Not infrequently, many of us take what we know about how they thought and what they felt and use it to evaluate ourselves or make our decisions.

How much more so is this the case in situations of intense, personal involvement? Yet, this tendency is often seen as abnormal. Why is it considered appropriate to go to the writings of Saint Augustine to get a perspective on how to cope with a particular moral issue, but considered "unresolved grief" if you reflect about how your deceased father would deal with the same issue?

You *can* have healthy relationships with the deceased. The important issue is that there be appropriate recognition of the fact that the person is dead and that your expectations and abstract interactions with him reflect knowledge of this fact. For example, there is nothing wrong with a widow reflecting on what her deceased husband would do in a particular situation and then using this as one of the alternatives she considers when deciding how she will act. It would be different, however, if she felt she *had* to do things her husband's way. In this case, she is giving him ongoing control over her in death. Since this behavior and attitude on her part fails to recognize sufficiently that her husband no longer has power over her because he is dead, she is not having a healthy relationship with him. She has failed to withdraw her former emotional investment in him as a person who once did have this power. And, to the degree that she feels she must do what he wants, she continues to act as if he were still alive.

To have a healthy new relationship with your deceased loved one, you must have a clear and realistic image of him. You must remember him with all of his positive and negative aspects. In the beginning, it is quite normal to remember only the positive ones. As time goes on, however, you will need to remember him in a more realistic fashion, integrating all the different aspects of his personality and all the experiences you had with him. To maintain an unrealistically positive image requires enormous energy and does not permit you to review and process those thoughts, memories, and feelings which must be recognized and felt in order to be worked through.

The same review process which helps you change your emotional investment in your loved one also will assist you to develop an accurate image of him. The good and bad, the happy and sad, the fulfilling and the unfulfilling—all aspects of the person and your relationship and experiences with him—must be reviewed and felt. Then, based on all of this, you develop a composite memory image of him which you can retain, one which accurately reflects all you have known and experienced with this person. It will be with this image that you will interact in your new relationship with the deceased.

Along with the image come your feelings about it and the accompanying recognition that your loved one is dead. These will aid you in deciding which parts of your old life with him you can keep and which you must give up. In some ways it is appropriate for you to hold on to your loved one, but in others you must let him go. For example, you still may talk with him, as long as you recognize that any "talking" back is actually your interpretation of what you think he would say. You still may derive comfort and wisdom in taking the perspective you know he would have, and using this to help you consider your options: "Now, I know I have to think carefully about how to respond to Sally. George always said I tend to fly off the handle. I must review all of my alternatives and then decide how I want to deal with her." In this manner, talking with your deceased loved one can be appropriate, realistic, and healthy. However, in contrast, it would be inappropriate, unrealistic, and unhealthy for you to continue to *live* as if your loved one will return to you. This is an expectation you must give up. Part of developing a new relationship with your deceased loved one is learning what you can keep and what you must relinquish now that he is physically dead.

Keeping Your Loved One "Alive" Appropriately

There are many healthy ways in which you can "hold on" to your deceased loved one. It is not true that you have to sever all connection with that person who has been so much a part of your life. The previous section has illustrated the fallacy of this type of thought. Now we will look more closely at some of the ways you can have appropriate and healthy interactions with the deceased that can keep that person "alive" for you in your life.

If you dearly loved the person who has died, you will not want your life to be bare of indications that this person once existed. For many of us, it is important to indicate to ourselves and others that we have not forgotten those we have loved and lost. To forget, to live life without a recollection of that person's having been a part of it, is like a betrayal, and to many people this is tantamount to the deceased's dying again. As a result, you may find yourself doing, saying, thinking, or feeling things that illustrate to you and others just how much that person's influence continues to be present for you.

There are countless ways to interact with and relate to your deceased loved one and to keep her alive to yourself and others. As long as this is done properly there need be no problems. *Properly* means that you have a true recognition of the new relationship with the deceased, that is, that she is dead and you continue to live. It means that you do not let it interfere with the necessary emotional letting go of your old relationship with the deceased and your subsequent reinvestment in life. It requires that your actions in keeping your loved one "alive" are healthy and life-promoting, rather than unhealthy and death-denying.

To accomplish this, you will need to decide which parts of your old life and relationship with the deceased can and should be retained. For example, this could include your deciding to:

Keep certain routines you shared with your loved one (for example, taking a walk each Sunday morning).

Continue to reserve the special times you had put aside for each other (for example, taking quiet time for a snack each night before bedtime).

Display particular mementos of the relationship (for example, keeping up on the wall the artwork you purchased together in Canada).

You also must decide which parts of your old life and relationship with your loved one should be relinquished. For example, unless you want to see how bereaved you can feel, it would probably not make sense to go alone to the place you used to go ballroom dancing as a couple. These decisions can help you to see what you can continue to do from your past to allow you to feel close to your deceased loved one in a healthy way, thereby keeping that person alive to you without interfering in your healthy grief and ongoing life.

There are numerous healthy ways you can relate to your lost loved one, keeping her alive in your life. One of the primary ways is through your identification with her. As noted in chapter 3, this is a process through which you both hold on to the deceased and expand your own identity. It can be experienced in many ways:

Acting like that person (for example, deciding to order her favorite dessert and making it your favorite, too)

Reminding yourself of the way she used to be (for example, telling her special jokes and stories to bring back memories of her)

Learning more about her (for example, acting on some of her concerns, such as donating to her favorite charity, may help you to see how committed she was to try to improve things)

Making sure that others do not forget her (for example, quoting her sayings ensures that others will be reminded that she existed)

Rituals are another important way through which you can keep your loved one alive. (See chapter 16 for more on this.) A ritual is a specific behavior or activity that gives symbolic expression to your feelings and thoughts. It can be habitually repeated or a one-time occurrence. In grief, a ritual can provide you a structured way to recall your lost loved one and to make some statement about your feelings. Participating in rituals gives you a chance to interact intensely with the memory of your loved one for a limited period of time in a healthy way.

Your rituals may be formal (for example, an anniversary mass, or a Memorial Day celebration) or informal (for example, going to visit your old home town to talk with friends who used to know you both, or watching the movie that was designated as "your" movie). They may occur all the time (for example, mentioning her in daily prayers or at grace before dinner), on an infrequent basis (for example, visiting the cemetery twice a year or continuing the tradition of starting your Christmas shopping on the day after Thanksgiving), or only once (for example, going to your loved one's school to dedicate a plaque in her memory).

Concrete, tangible objects also can help keep your loved one alive. Photographs, mementos, pieces of jewelry, and other objects can be reminders of the one you lost and can symbolize her for you. Not only can these stimulate your recollection of her, but their presence in your life can be symbolic of her abstract presence in your life.

Perhaps the most effective way of keeping your loved one alive is through your own life and actions. There are countless ways in which you can do this. For example:

Talking about your loved one

Acting on the values and concerns you took from her

Thinking about memories you have of her

Enjoying and appreciating life because of having known, loved, and been influenced by the deceased

Being and acting who you are because of what you were given by your relationship with this person

All of these are ways of keeping your loved one alive through you. Since she was a special part of you and vice versa, you actually are a part of her that continues to exist in the world despite her death.

The ways you choose to relate to your deceased loved one do not have to be fixed and stagnant. In too many cases, however, they do become too rigid. They, and the images of your loved one, can become frozen in time and space. To keep your loved one alive healthily, you must relate to her in age-appropriate ways and in fashions that are suitable for you now. While relating to your loved one can give you a link to the past, it should not bind you to it nor keep you from growth in the present. For instance, if you were a little girl when your mother died, it will not be healthy to continue to perceive yourself, and to relate to your mother, as that little girl for the rest of your life. It *would* be appropriate, however, to wonder about and try to learn about your mother as the adult you never got to know. It would not be unusual for you to grow in understanding of her as you reinterpret things she said or did once you become old enough to see them in a different light. If you are open to it, you can learn about and from your loved one even after she dies: "Now I realize how she must have felt when I fought with my baby brother. Since I've become a mother of three I know what it's like when you have to play referee so often. This is what she must have meant. Perhaps if I try to do what she did I can handle this whole situation better."

This is only one of the ways in which your loved one can be a continuing influence upon you. If that influence is continuing, then it suggests some dimension of life, and by definition this is another way you can appropriately keep your loved one alive. As you mature, get older, and have new experiences, you can grow in appreciation for the person who has died, as well as for her influence upon you and through you on others. It is not uncommon for events later in your life to illustrate to you just how very much you have taken from your loved one. For example, after a particularly awkward social situation, you may be surprised at just how well you have learned to be gracious and put people at ease socially through observation of your parents. You may not have realized how much of them rubbed off on you in this regard. All of these types of experiences can affirm the "alive-ness" and ongoing meaning of your loved one to you and in your life.

In summary, the basic issue involved in this part of your grieving is to find healthy ways to relate to your deceased loved one. These can allow you both to remember her and to continue to benefit from her and your mutual relationship, as long as you maintain the proper realistic perspective on both.

Forming a New Identity

If the person you loved was a very important part of your life, his death inevitably changes you, too. This is because your interactions with him helped to define your sense of self and reality. For example, that part of you that was the wife to your husband or the daughter to your father contributes to your identity as the unique person you are. When he dies, the piece of your self that was the daughter or the wife also dies. Even if you one day marry a new husband, it will be a new relationship. The part of you that was created by or validated in your interaction in the old relationship with your first husband no longer exists in reality, although it can continue on in your memory. In external reality, without him there to interrelate with you in the unique relationship the two of you had, that part of you dies when he does.

There are several sets of transitions you must undergo to accommodate to the new world without the presence of your loved one. Each ultimately helps you to form a new identity. First, you have to adjust to the new world that exists. This means that you will develop different expectations, beliefs, assumptions, and knowledge about the world that reflect the fact that your loved one is no longer a part of it. This takes a long time, and quite naturally you will want to resist it. You want the world back the way it was before, when the person you loved was alive. You do not want to alter your thoughts about the world, the way it works, and the people in it, including yourself.

For this reason, time and again you may catch yourself expecting your loved one to come home at the regular time, find yourself planning for two before realizing you need only plan for one, or being shocked to find that no one is as concerned as he was about your job project. With a stab of pain, each of these types of experiences teaches you again that your loved one is gone. And, as you start to see and experience the world in a new way, you will eventually see and experience yourself in a new way as well. This results in a changed identity for you.

Your identity changes as you slowly make the change from a "we" to an "I." This is caused by the necessity of responding to the new world without the deceased, which demands that you take on new ways of being, thinking, and feeling in the world to reflect the reality that he is dead. You will have to give up or modify certain hopes, expectations, and experiences you had with your loved one, and you must develop new ones. To compensate for his absence, you must adopt new roles, skills, behaviors, and relationships. You will change in different ways. You may gain new aspects to yourself (for example, feel more competent because you have mastered new skills); lose old ones (for example, give up your passivity); or modify the ones you retain (for example, recognize that you can have a career and be a good mother simultaneously). Whatever you do, as your new self comes into being, it will affect your sense of identity. While this is happening, your identity can be augmented further by any identifying you do with your deceased loved one.

You will need to develop a perspective on what has been lost or gained in your self. That which has been changed (positively or negatively) must be recognized and grieved; that which continues must be affirmed; that which is new must be incorporated. You then will need to integrate your new and old selves together.

Reinvesting Your Emotional Energy

The emotional energy that you withdraw from your former relationship with your loved one must be reinvested elsewhere so that it once again can return you satisfaction and gratify your needs. Your relationship with your loved one can no longer do this. It is unhealthy for you to have no appropriate investment in anything or anyone. Therefore, the emotional energy that had been used to keep your previous relationship alive must be redirected towards establishing and maintaining rewarding investments in other people, objects, and pursuits. This will not be a replacement for your lost loved one: No one can take his special place. However, your new attachments and investments of emotional energy once again will provide you with the emotional gratification you lost when your loved one died.

This emotional energy need not be reinvested exclusively in another person. It can be reinvested in objects, activities, roles, hopes, beliefs, causes and so forth—anything that you can care about or have an attachment to. It may be tangible (for example, another person, your house, a car) or psychosocial (for example, a relationship, your dream of being a doctor, being president of the Chamber of Commerce). It does not have to be reinvested in the same type of person or thing from which it was withdrawn. For instance, a widow does not have to remarry to reinvest her emotional energy. She can do this by undertaking volunteer work with handicapped children or by going back to school. The only requirement is that she has a place into which to put her emotional energy and involvement.

These three sets of processes are essential to undergo if you want to resolve your grief and mourning. The following chapter will outline specific suggestions to assist you in completing them successfully.

15

Specific Suggestions
for Resolving Your Grief

I N the last chapter, we looked at the processes you had to complete in order to accommodate and resolve your grief. In this chapter we will identify the specific actions you must take to ensure that you successfully complete your grief work, learn to accommodate and live with your loss, and adjust to your new life accordingly, ultimately recovering optimally from your loved one's death.

Give Yourself Permission to Feel Your Loss
and to Grieve over It

In order for you to work on your grief, you have to feel that it is acceptable for you to do so. If you do not acknowledge or understand the death, or if you believe that you must be "strong" and should not express emotions or can have only positive feelings, then you will not be able to allow yourself to grieve. If you want to work through your grief, you will need to give yourself the permission—the license and the time, opportunities, and acceptance—necessary to complete the process.

Recognize and accept your loss. You must come to an intellectual acceptance of the fact that, despite all your wishes to the contrary, the loss has actually occurred, your loved one is indeed dead, and he will not return, at least not in this life. If the loss is not real to you, you will not have to grapple with its implications or your feelings about it. You will not have to grieve it.

Work toward understanding the death. You need to understand the reasons for the events that led to the death. This does not mean that you are unmoved by the death, that you like it, or even that you can fit it into your system of meaning. It only means that you recognize that the death occurred and have your own account explaining how and why it happened. Not having this explanation of the event would make it quite difficult for you to go on, not only with your grief but with your life as well.

Feel and deal with all *of your emotions and thoughts about the death.* Some of these may be upsetting or unacceptable to you, or they appear to be uncharacteristic of the way you usually are. Nevertheless, you must give yourself permission to experience all of them—the good and the bad, the happy and the unhappy—or else your grief can never be resolved. Grieving means allowing yourself to feel your feelings, think your thoughts, lament your loss, and protest your pain. Your focus must be on working through the unpleasant and negative parts of the lost relationship, as well as the more positive ones.

Make a conscious decision to get through this grief. You can decide whether you will triumph over your grief or whether it will vanquish you. Successful mourners often report that often in the early stages of grief and intermittently thereafter, they made a decision to survive their grief and not to let death destroy their lives. Typically they went from "I don't care about anything" to "Sometimes I care" to "I care." This does not mean that grief wasn't as hard on them as everybody else. It means that they made a commitment to themselves (and often to loved ones) to continue to work it through and to make life meaningful again, even if it took a very long time and much pain before this could happen.

Accept Social Support and Tell Others What You Need

Mourners desperately need the support and assistance of others—their presence, nonjudgmental listening, compassion, and concern—to help them cope with their grief. This is one of the most crucial requirements in grief. Ensure that you have people around to aid you, and permit yourself to accept their assistance when it is given. Many people will not know how to help you, so you must educate them. If you are not being offered what you require, ask for what you need or go after what you want.

Do not isolate yourself. Social support is vital throughout the entire grief process. It helps you better tolerate the pain of your loss, and it provides you with the acceptance and assistance necessary to complete your grief work and ultimately move back into the new world without your loved one. The presence of accepting and nonjudgmental others can be very helpful to you, especially early after the death, when you need to feel grounded in the midst of all the chaos. They can help give some security, order, and a sense of reality to your world, which has been shaken by the death of the person you love. Although they cannot give you what you most desire—that is, the return of your deceased loved one—they can help you with their genuine care and compassion. It is well known that when grievers are socially isolated they tend to do more poorly in resolving their grief.

Accept the help and support of others. Let others reach out to you in all ways—physically, socially, emotionally, and behaviorally. In the early period of grief, it is perfectly acceptable for you to give up some control and let others assist and nurture you. They may keep you company, make meals, run some errands, help you make funeral decisions, or babysit your children. This does not mean that you are weak, immature, or dependent. It also does not mean that they can do your grief work for you. It only means that you permit yourself to take the comfort and aid you need in order to meet the heavy demands of grief. Allowing yourself to accept support now will make you stronger later.

Be assertive; tell others what you need, and go after what you want. You must be assertive in your grief. You must ask for what you need and want. You may or may not get it, but you should try, and you ought to feel comfortable about doing so. Often this is difficult to do, as you have little energy to reach out. However, many people who would like to help you do not know how. If you want their assistance, you must educate them about grief. For example, you might tell your extended family that when they visit at the holidays you do not want them to avoid mentioning your deceased loved one. Or you may tell a friend that you want her to ask how you are doing even though you cry, or that your anger is a normal reaction. It is unfortunate that at this time when you are so depleted you have to teach others how to help you. However, not to do this means you may suffer from the inappropriate expectations of others or a lack of the assistance you do need.

If what you want is not available from those around you, go and seek it out. If you do not have people to talk with about your loss, determine who can help and reach out. This is why self-help groups are so popular. Go after what you need to help you resolve this loss.

Be Realistic in Your Expectations of
Yourself as a Griever

You must have realistic expectations of yourself. These will influence how you allow yourself to experience your grief and what you will let yourself do about it. To be realistic about yourself as a griever, you must have accurate information about grief in general and your loss in particular; be well aware of the uniqueness of your own grief experience and how to keep others from interfering with it, despite their often good intentions; know that you can take time to fit it into your religious or philosophical framework; and realize that, if you are doing your grief work, your pain *will* subside at some point.

Make sure you have accurate information about grief in general and a proper perspective on what is realistic. You will need this so that your expectations of yourself are appropriate and realistic and so that you can evaluate yourself fairly. This includes having all the facts about grief: its nature; its purpose; how it proceeds and how long it takes; and the manner and extent to which it affects you in all areas of your life. Unrealistic expectations or negative feelings about essentially normal reactions cause the majority of problems in grief. You need to understand what is normal and react accordingly. For example, you must recognize that grief normally involves reactions that would signify mental illness in other circumstances, or that may be contrary to the way you usually are. You have to give yourself room to experience many unusual reactions without feeling that you are crazy.

Be realistic about the amount of time the process of grief will require. Grief is a choppy "two steps forward, one step backward" experience that will continue for much longer than you had anticipated and will expose you to more feelings then you ever knew you could have. For this reason, initially you should adopt a "one day at a time" approach to avoid being overwhelmed.

Make sure you have accurate information about this death in particular and what problems it presents to a griever. Besides knowing about grief in general, you must have an understanding of the specific consequences of this type of death. You should know how they influence your grief and what issues they will bring up to you.

Expect to have some negative feelings and volatile reactions. You are not a bad person. Anger, protest, upset, or lack of concern for others are all natural, normal, and expectable in grief. No matter what type of person you usually are, you can expect that you will have some measure of less-than-positive feelings somewhere along in your grief.

Recognize that your grief will be unique. Despite the fact that you will share some similarities with other grievers, your grief is unique to you and your particular loss. It is shaped by the unique group of factors that describe your particular loss: what you have lost, how you have lost it, your personal characteristics, and the social and physical factors influencing your response. You must be careful about comparing yourself to others. For example, even though two sisters each lose their brother, they will grieve differently according to their special, individual relationship with him and the other factors that influence their particular grief responses.

It doesn't make any difference what others think. This is your loss. Do not be talked out of it. You will need to define and decide for yourself what are the biggest problems for you, prioritize your concerns, and deal with these concerns as well as you can. Do not let others' personal judgments about the meaning of your loss rob you of your grief or determine how you should feel or what you should do. For example, just because others do not think you should be grieved over the death of your grandparent does not mean that there is anything wrong with you if you feel grieved. The seriousness of your loss and what you need to do about it can only be understood in the context of what this loss means to you. It cannot be compared to other losses for other people.

There is no one correct way to grieve, so you must find the best way for yourself. As long as you are attending to the tasks of grief, and are not causing yourself any additional stress by your coping behaviors, you should go through the grief process in your own way. There are many different ways of reaching the same destination; you can choose your own style and do things in ways that are comfortable for you. Be careful about following all the advice of well-meaning others. Critically evaluate the advice and determine if it is right for you in terms of your own personal ways of dealing with stress, crisis, and grief. This does not mean you shouldn't listen to feedback from others. This is important, especially when you might be too close to the situation to think clearly. It merely means making sure of its suitability and usefulness for you.

Keep in mind that the death of your loved one will affect your family as well as yourself. Different family members will have different reactions, and you all may stimulate each other's grief at times. Remember that a death in the family means that your family will have to reorganize itself and that new roles and responsibilities must be assigned. With the death of your loved one, you also lose the family as you had known it, despite the fact that it continues on without the person who died.

Maintain a realistic perspective on what you can expect from others in your grief. Recognize that despite their desire to be of help, no one can take away your pain, they only can help you to deal with it. You also must realize that others may feel helpless around you. However, this does not mean you should not continue to reach out for their support and ask them for what you need.

Do not feel that you must accept the statements of others who seek to comfort you by telling you that you should feel better because you have other loved ones still alive. Do not allow anyone to rob you of your legitimate grief. Do not let anyone make you feel guilty for being sad despite the fact that you still have good things in your life. You can appreciate what you do have, but this does not minimize your grief over what you have lost. These statements are well-meaning attempts to console you, but you do not have to accept them.

Do not think that you need to fit this loss into your religious or philosophical framework immediately. It is perfectly all right if it does not fit right now. For many grievers, this kind of integration takes time. You can work it out gradually. However, do not let this rob you of your grief. Recognize that God can deal with any cold, angry, and upset feelings or questions you have. It is up to you to deal with them now and to recognize that for a long time they may be quite hostile or resentful. Over time, if you are concerned about how the death of your loved one fits into the scheme of things, you can follow up on trying to get answers that make sense to you. Just don't expect this of yourself too soon, before you are ready to let go of some of your normal negative feelings.

Do not let others' needs determine your grief experience. Ask for what you want or need. Do not let others determine what you will and will not do. Of course, you don't want to alienate those who are supporting you, but if these people love you they will *have* to understand that there are things you need to do to help yourself resolve your grief. For instance, there will be times when you will need to cry despite the fact that it makes them uncomfortable. Essentially you must recognize that you have rights as a mourner and that you need to exercise them.

Do not let anyone minimize your loss, but do not give up realistic hope either. Sometimes people try to "pretty up" your situation. You are right in maintaining that grief is exceptionally difficult. There are times when it will be quite painful and times when it will not make any sense. You will have to deal with many unpleasant feelings. However, you must not give up hope: hope that someday the pain will decrease; hope that someday you will have a reunion with your loved one; hope that someday life will have some meaning again; and so forth. These are not unrealistic hopes that would deny or invalidate your current intense experience of grief or the permanent changes that result from the death of your loved one. Rather, these are realistic aspirations that you need to have to get you through the painful experience of responding to the death of someone you have loved.

Try not to respond in ways that are contrary to appropriate grief. Your behavior should be aimed at reaching the goals of grief work and promoting the resolution of your loss. Behaviors that are opposed to this will not be helpful. For example, do not try to censor your anger or guilt, unnecessarily take a tranquilizer merely to avoid some distress, or in other ways avoid or delay the grief work you must accomplish. It is important for you to take breaks from your grief from time to time, but this must be done with the recognition that you have to come back to it and deal with it. In an effort to help alleviate your pain, others may make suggestions that are contrary to appropriate grief; for instance, they may tell you not to cry. While you may want to follow these suggestions, you must realize that they will not help your grief work.

Recognize that, despite your being unable to feel that it's true, your pain will subside at some point if you continue to do your grief work. It is understandable to have many doubts. This is only normal, especially when you are in the middle of acute grief and cannot see any light at the end of the tunnel. However, you must keep in mind that there is a purpose to your grief and that at some point your pain will diminish, you will experience more peace, and you will be somewhat more like your old self than you are now.

Give Some Form of Expression to All of Your Feelings

Feeling and expressing your emotions is one of the most critical requirements in grief. It is absolutely necessary in order for grief resolution to occur. If you can find avenues of expression that are personally comfortable, can differentiate among all of your various feelings, and can find people who will listen to you about them, you will be in a very good position as a mourner.

Identify, accept, and express all your various feelings over the loss and its consequences. This is the *most* important task in grief. If you do not find an acceptable way to express all your feelings of grief, you will not be able to resolve it. Dealing with only some of them will not do. You first may have to give yourself permission to violate previous social, cultural, ethnic, religious, or personal resistances to accepting certain feelings of grief as tolerable or normal. These then must be identified. For example, "This is anger that I'm feeling" or "This must be the guilt they say is so common." Finally, you will have to express them in some fashion in order to resolve your grief.

You will need to find ways to express your feelings that are comfortable for you. For some people, talking about their anger is sufficient; others need ways to act it out, such as running, hitting a punching bag, or pounding on a bed. Some people find that it is helpful to write about their feelings. Others use art, dance, or other avenues of expression to release their emotions. It does not make any difference which manner you choose.

You may surprise yourself at how you express your feelings—some grievers cannot believe they could swear so much or scream so loudly—but this doesn't mean you are losing control, only that you have many emotions that cannot be handled by your usual modes of expression. As long as you are releasing them healthily, and you are not causing yourself any additional problems with your choice of expression, it is all right.

You will have to give expression to *all* of your feelings, the negative ones as well as the positive ones. Intellectualizing them, that is, dealing with them in your head but not in your heart, will do you little good.

You repeatedly must allow yourself to cry and cry, talk and talk, review and review without the interruption of anyone else's sanity. This is a necessary part of the process, especially in the early period of acute grief. Do not close it down in any way, shape, or form; it will enable you to complete your grief work. You will have to go through the procedure again and again. Each story told, each memory relived, each feeling expressed represents a tie to your loved one that you must process by remembering, feeling the emotions generated by it, and then letting it go. If you are dealing appropriately with your grief work, each time you do this you are getting more resolution of your grief.

Differentiate clearly among your various feelings of grief so that each one can be fully processed and your grief can be better managed. You need to separate your different feelings so that they are more manageable and don't burden you under one huge, confusing mass of mixed painful emotions that is too hard to deal with. This requires that you recognize and label each one. For example, sorrow is different from depression, although they sometimes can feel all mixed up together. Separating them gives you more of a sense of control. By breaking the pain of grief down into its component parts, you can address each one individually and do what is necessary to cope with it. It is much easier to cope with specific feelings than with global, undifferentiated (and thus more terrifying) pain.

You then need to identify the specific sources for each feeling. For example, your anger may come from the sense of desertion you feel; your helplessness may be a result of your inability to reverse the loss; and your anxiety may develop over your concerns about being alone. Also, you probably have to learn the difference between issues and feelings pertaining to this loss and those that have been resurrected from previous losses and old unfinished business in your past. This, too, will lessen the emotional confusion you may feel now.

Look for those who can listen to you nonjudgmentally and with permissiveness and acceptance. You need repeated opportunities to express your emotions without fear of rejection. This is critical, since so many feelings of grief are unacceptable and guilt-provoking to any mourner. It is important for you to talk about your grief and sorrow. As Shakespeare wrote: "Give sorrow words; the grief that does not speak whispers the o'er-fraught heart and bids it break" (*Macbeth*, Act IV, Scene 3). If you do not feel accepted, this very necessary therapeutic process will be stymied.

If you appear to be resisting the grief process, ask yourself why and try to change it. Many people are afraid to express their emotions of grief, fearing they will lose control or break down. Some are afraid to deal with their feelings out of concern that they will lose a connection to their loved one. For others, there may be excessive dependency, anger, or guilt that interferes with the normal grief process. If you discover that a concern in one of these areas or some other resistance of yours is interfering with your grief, review the information about normal grief. If you still are concerned that something is interfering with your grief, seek professional assistance to work it through.

Remember the Deceased and Review Your Mutual Relationship

Realistically remembering the deceased and your relationship, plus obsessively reviewing your memories and the feelings associated with them, will be necessary processes in your grief. Only in this way can you withdraw your emotional investment in your lost loved one, form a new relationship with him that reflects the reality of his death, and build new relationships in the new world without him.

You will have to realistically review and talk about the deceased and your mutual relationship. You will have to repeatedly review the entire relationship, back to its earliest beginnings and all the hopes and fantasies that formed it. You will need to discuss its ups and downs, its course and development, its crises and joys—all aspects of it through the years. As these events are gently unfolded in your memory, you relive them and examine the feelings associated with them. Only by obsessively reviewing this unique relationship will you be able to experience and identify the feelings you have that must be processed. You do this gradually over time by feeling them and then letting go of their emotional charge, which had kept you connected to the deceased in the way you were when he was alive and could return your investment. This is how you slowly begin to withdraw your emotional energy from your loved one and reestablish a new relationship with him that is not based on the give-and-take of real life.

To do this completely, you must address both the positive and negative aspects of the deceased and your relationship with him. Initially the review may tend to be overly positive and you may idealize your loved one. In time, you will be able to remember him in a more accurate way that recalls the good and the bad. You will have a more realistic image of the deceased and see him as having both positive and negative traits, as we all do. Unless you can remember what he wasn't, as well as what he was, you have not fully grieved. To reach this point, repeated discussion of all aspects of the person and your relationship with him is necessary. This means you not only review the happy times but also the times that were not as happy.

Expect to talk about many of the same things repeatedly. You will need to review again and again your attachments and relationship to your deceased loved one and the circumstances of his death. Not only the dramatic memories need to be remembered, the ones that bring tears—they all do. This repetition is part of the critical process of withdrawing your former emotional investment so that you can develop a different relationship with the person that reflects the reality of his death. It also will free you to have new investments and form new relationships in the future. The process of review allows you to see repeatedly that your needs, feelings, hopes, desires, and expectations for being with your loved one are continually being frustrated. You can no longer be with the deceased as you used to be. This helps you to start to accept the finality of the death and to detach from him. Reviewing the situation of the death, the events that surrounded it, and its meanings and implications will allow you to understand how things occurred, put them into perspective, and find some meaning and sense in them. Each time the story is told, each time you experience the feelings associated with a thought or memory of what you lost, you get more of a handle on them and a little more control over them.

You have to review not only the deceased and your mutual relationship but also all of the hopes, dreams, expectations, wishes, and needs that accompanied it. These are major secondary losses that must be reviewed, felt, and processed in order to accomplish your grief work.

Identify and Work to Resolve Your Secondary Losses and Unfinished Business

When your loved one dies, you must grieve not only for his physical death but also for the secondary losses that are occurring now and will occur in the future as a consequence of his death. Also, you must try to finish any unfinished emotional business you had with him so that it does not interfere with your grief resolution.

Identify and grieve for the current and potential secondary losses (both physical and symbolic) that result from the death. These losses will require their own grief responses. Too often they are overlooked and not identified as legitimate losses. Simply because they are secondary does not mean they are insignificant; frequently they are harder to resolve than the initial loss. Examples of such secondary losses are loss of the hopes and expectations for the relationship; loss of a sexual partner; loss of time with children because of the necessity of working; partial loss of the person you used to be; loss of social life as it had previously been experienced; and loss of the home to pay for medical expenses. Don't overwhelm yourself with attempting to deal with these secondary losses all at once. They can be addressed gradually. The important thing is that at some point they do get worked through and you can come to some resolution of them.

Identify any unfinished business you had with the deceased and look for appropriate ways to have closure. Unfinished business can prevent you from resolving your grief. As mentioned previously, unfinished business refers to those emotional issues that were never addressed or resolved in the relationship between you and the deceased. For example, were you able to express the things you needed or wanted to express to one another? Did you come to some resolution about your mutual relationship? Were there any loose ends in the relationship that were not addressed? Unfinished business remains just that—unfinished. This lack of completion provokes anxiety and may cause you to search restlessly for an opportunity to come to closure with your lost loved one. You may need to find some way to say the never-said "I love you," "I needed you," or "I'm sorry."

Although you cannot have the actual interaction with your loved one that you would like, there are ways that you can deal with unfinished business. Fancy techniques are not needed. Frequently, a discussion with caring others about what you would have wanted to say or do can help. Sometimes writing a letter to your lost loved one can be therapeutic. You may want to create a particular ritual or do something symbolic to finish the unfinished business (see chapter 16 for more on creating personal rituals). Whatever the unfinished business is, you need to determine what you must do in order to achieve a satisfactory sense of completion in your relationship with the deceased. If this cannot happen, you may need to seek professional assistance in finding ways to do this.

Yield Productively to the Grief Process, Taking Care of Yourself as You Do It

In your grief, you must balance between actively feeling and dealing with the pain and work of grief and taking care of yourself while you are doing it in order not to wear yourself out in the process.

Recognize that you must yield to the painful process of grief. As stated earlier, there is no way to go over, around, or under grief—you must go through it. Grief cannot be delayed indefinitely; it will erupt in some way, directly or indirectly. The inescapable fact is that you have sustained a major loss requiring a painful period of readjustment that demands excruciatingly hard work and causes more pain and trouble if you do not attend to it. If you want to get done with your grief, you must go through the pain. Although the pain is distressing, the experience and release of it is a healing part of the process.

Know that it is understandable that you would wish to avoid the pain of grief. There is nothing wrong with you if you wish there was some way you could avoid the pain. You would have to be a masochist to have any other feelings. It is common to want to avoid the pain and just as common to wish that you did not have to change your emotional attachment to the person who has died. You wish that the world would go back to the way it used to be, when your loved one was alive. Although it is only natural to want to escape grief and its painful emotions, you must continue with your grief work in order to be able to go on with your life in a healthy fashion.

You must be patient with yourself and not expect too much. Don't impose any "shoulds" on yourself about the grief process unless you are quite sure that they are appropriate. Even if they are, you must give yourself the time to deal with them. Grief takes much time and energy. It will progress at an uneven pace. You will make progress and then backslide again, but you will never go back as far as you were when you initially confronted the death. Make sure that your expectations are appropriate, and do not additionally stress yourself by unrealistic standards.

Give yourself quiet time alone. As important as talking about your loss and receiving social support is in your grief, you will need some amount of tranquility and solitude. If you do not save some of this kind of time for yourself you will not have sufficient opportunity to reflect on your loss, review the relationship, process your feelings, and so forth. Avoid constantly being with others or always being on the go—this can be a way to postpone or repress your grief. Find a happy medium between tending to your own personal needs and those of others.

Understand that grief involves not only dealing with emotional responses but coping with practical problems as well. Worries about finances, a lack of education that precludes a better job, and other practical, day-to-day concerns are significant stressors to many bereaved individuals. So, too, are the grief-re-lated practical concerns with which you must contend, for example, not knowing what to do with your loved one's clothes and personal effects. Unfortunately, many others in society will not recognize their importance to you, and often fail to offer adequate understanding and support in these areas. Try your best to avoid being overcome by these problems. Recognize that grief is an overwhelming experience, and take your problems one at a time, responding to demands when necessary but accepting help and support with them when possible. (See chapter 18 for a discussion of practical problems.)

Give yourself breaks from your grief. You cannot focus on your grief exclusively all the time. Every so often you need to take a respite from it, just as you would if you were engaged in heavy physical labor. This will allow you to get the energy to continue with your grief work. For example, you will need some solitude so you can replenish yourself, but also should allow yourself to enjoy other people and other aspects of life. This is not a betrayal of your lost loved one. It is an important aspect of caring for yourself so that you can resolve your grief at some point in time.

Find a variety of ways to replenish yourself following the severe depletion that results from the loss of your loved one. The ongoing strain of grief, in which you are continually giving out and giving up, makes it essential for you to replenish yourself in a number of ways. Such things as adequate rest and nutrition are important, as your grief work requires enormous energy. You also will need social support in order to face the painful processes of grief and all they entail, and will benefit from any other appropriate sources of emotional nurturance that can help you to recover from the pain. Intellectually, religion or philosophy, literature, art, and the media can give you ways to find meaning in the loss or simply allow you to escape reality for a while. If you fail to replenish yourself, you will "burn out" in your grief and not be any good to anyone, including yourself.

Avoid making precipitous changes or engaging in flight. Some grievers attempt to cope by moving, taking an extended vacation, or making significant changes. If you do this too early, you will find that you are stripped of your roots and the security of your familiar surroundings. In the future these changes may be helpful to you as you attempt to relinquish some of the past and integrate new roles into your life and personality. However, changes that happen too soon will result in more loss for you at a time when you are already overwhelmed with many losses. For this reason, if at all possible, don't make important decisions and major changes during the first year of bereavement. If these changes must be made, discuss them with trusted friends and advisors who can lend an objective perspective to the situation in the event that your decision-making still is affected by your grief. Sometimes actions may appear viable and productive to you but will only cause further disorganization, stress, or secondary losses.

Engage in some form of physical activity to release your pent-up emotions. Grief often can make you feel angry, frustrated, victimized, guilty, anxious, and depressed. These types of feelings are difficult to talk about and can easily become channeled into physical symptoms. Physical activity can reduce tension and anxiety, release aggression, and relieve depression and other unpleasant feelings—all components of the grief reaction. Physical activity also helps prevent further physical and psychological problems due to the grief process.

Work to maintain good physical health. If you are to endure the difficult grief process and avoid physical complications, it is important for you to have good physical health. As mentioned earlier, you must make sure you get sufficient exercise and rest. Drugs must be avoided, unless medically prescribed. A balanced diet is important, and you should give special attention to calcium, vitamin D, and phosphorus, all of which are depleted by the stress of grief. It is important for you to remember to eat even at times when you are not hungry. You will have to keep up your energy in order to do your grief work.

It is inadvisable to resort to medication too soon in an attempt to avoid the pain of the loss. However, it is equally inadvisable to fail to recognize when medical treatment is necessary. Physical symptoms of psychological distress can interfere with the grief process—for example, not sleeping or not eating for a long period of time. Don't ignore the physical aspects of grief in favor of focusing exclusively on the psychosocial ones. Get appropriate medical evaluation and treatment when your symptoms warrant it. Grief is a time of high physical risk, and therefore you need to act to minimize adverse physical consequences. A number of them may be normal in grief, but at times they persist for too long or are too acute and you will require professional assistance.

Seek professional assistance if necessary. Many people need professional assistance either to help them experience the natural grief processes or to work through conflicts impeding normal mourning. (See chapter 19 for a thorough discussion of this issue.) If you need this type of support or intervention, make sure you get it or else you will not be able to resolve your grief.

Accommodate to the Loss of Your Loved One

Major changes must occur in your life when someone you love dies. As you meet the new world without your loved one, you are required to develop a new identity, altered roles, and additional skills. You need to determine how to make the death meaningful to you and in what ways you will want to continue to relate to your loved one. Finally, at the proper time you need to reinvest emotionally in other people, objects, activities, or beliefs in your new life and to recognize whatever gain has been derived from your loss. Many of these changes have been discussed in depth in chapter 14 and are referred to only briefly here. Review that chapter for more comprehensive information.

You will need to develop the proper perspective on what resolution of your grief will mean. You will never forget the loss, but the pain can diminish. You will survive, but you will not be exactly the same. There will always be reminders of your loss. One purpose of grief is to help you to recognize this fact and continue living, without inappropriate clinging to your deceased loved one. (See chapter 17 for a discussion of what recovery will and will not mean.)

Recognize that a major loss will always change you to some extent. Again, you will never be exactly the same as you were before your loved one died. Very simply, this is because adapting to a loved one's loss makes it necessary for you to make numerous changes in yourself.

You will have to form a new identity. For all who lose a loved one, where once there was a "we," now there is an "I." This is a highly significant and painful transition which you must make. It involves developing new expectations and beliefs about the world without your loved one, along with new roles and skills for you in that world. As you develop your new identity, you will need new friends to validate it. This does not mean you will not need the support and continuity provided by old friends, but new relationships with people who share important elements of your new identity can prevent your feeling alienated and isolated. For example, if you are a newly widowed woman, you may be interested in associating with other widows because they have coped with similar problems and may understand what it is like to feel like a "fifth wheel" in social situations. The same is true for other types of mourners—there is great benefit in some association with others who can support us in our new identities. This is why mutual self-help groups are so important.

Determine which roles you must take on or give up as a consequence of the death and which skills you must develop; then incorporate these into your life. This will not only ensure replacement of necessary functions and fulfillment of certain needs, but also give you a sense of control and help you develop your new identity in the world without your loved one. For example, in terms of roles, a widower may need to learn how to "mother" his children and, in terms of skills, may benefit from some cooking classes. A widow might learn to relate to the neighborhood as the family spokesperson, and might have to be taught how to handle the time management problems of being a single parent.

Changes from your past identity must be noted and grieved, both the losses and gains. Understand that such changes are stressful. Ask for help and support in making them and in problem-solving the concerns and dealing with the feelings they bring up in you. Related to this, you need to recognize what aspects of yourself have remained constant despite the trauma of your loss, since this will provide you with a much needed sense of security and continuity. For example, it might be helpful for you to see that in spite of all you have been through, you still have a sense of humor.

You will need to form a healthy new relationship with your deceased loved one. Although death has separated you from your loved one, it has not ended your relationship. It simply means that the relationship has changed from one based on her presence to one relating to memories of the past. Your new relationship with her will have to reflect this fact.

Decide in what appropriate ways you can keep the deceased's memory alive and continue to relate to her. Find new ways to relate to your deceased loved one while maintaining the proper perspective on the new relationship. This can be done through identification and through ritual behaviors—for example, anniversary celebrations, prayers, commemorative donations, and grace over dinner. You can foster the deceased's memory through concrete symbols such as a photograph or memento or through your own life and actions—for instance, talking about her or taking on her concerns.

Do not equate the length and amount of your suffering with some kind of testimony to your love for the deceased. This will only promote unresolved grief. You must understand that healthy grief does not mean abandoning the loved one but rather developing a new relationship based on loving memory. This change eventually should free you to have other relationships, which should not be seen as betrayals of your loved one. Suffering should not be seen as a bond to the deceased or as proof of the value of the relationship.

Find some way to make this death meaningful to you. A major loss often begins a search for meaning, not only meaning regarding the loss but also for the griever's life. Since the continuity of your life has been disrupted, you must develop a new set of assumptions about the world that will account for the death of your loved one and your situation of being without her. For example, if you previously assumed that the good will be protected by God, you probably will have to reexamine this idea if your young child has been senselessly killed. When trying to understand why your loss occurred, you may need guidance in answering the questions that can be answered and accepting the fact that some cannot. You may have to arrive at a point where you realize that you may never understand why the loss happened, but that there may be a reason that cannot be understood. This is particularly important for those who have had an untimely loss, such as the death of a child or the murder of a loved one.

Everyone needs a reason to live. Therefore, you will need to identify beliefs and actions that will provide you with a renewed sense of purpose in your life. At first you probably will feel that there is no reason to go on, and you may have to go forth solely on the hope that in time meaning will be restored. If the death has provoked a crisis of faith in beliefs you previously held, perhaps new or renewed religious and philosophical ideals can supply reason and order to you. You may find it helpful to decide that something meaningful will come out of the death of your loved one. This is what has been done by those who have campaigned for stiffer drunk-driving legislation after the death of a loved one in an accident caused by a drunk driver. Essentially, you need to find a reason to go on. It can be based on the need that others have for you, on spiritual goals, or on humanistic concerns. If you can find a "why" to live, you will be able to find a "how" to survive.

Think small—goals, pleasures, progress. Grief resolution will not happen fast. Reconcile yourself to this. Therefore, when you set goals or seek pleasures to keep yourself going, make sure they are small. For example, instead of trying to plan a week's vacation, start by making plans for one night out at the movies. Instead of trying to feel immense joy, just try to allow yourself to appreciate a sunset without having pain. The enjoyment of these things initially will not be what you expect, but it will increase as you cope better with your loss. Be patient. Over time you gradually can work on bigger goals and larger pleasures. Take it slowly, one day at a time, but take it. You need to have some goals and pleasure in your life in order to keep you going, pull you forward, give your life a little meaning, and provide you with some purpose, direction, and focus.

Lastly, evaluate your progress in small bits and pieces. Twenty minutes without pain may be quite an improvement. Don't expect immediate or dramatic results. Be realistic. It may be hard to see any progress on a day-to-day basis, so you may have to reconcile yourself to evaluating it over a longer period of time (for example, "I'm better this fall than I was in the spring.")

At the appropriate time, find rewarding new things to do and people, objects, activities, beliefs, or causes to invest in. If you have appropriately withdrawn your emotional energy from your deceased loved one, there will be energy to reinvest in other people, activities, objects, beliefs, and causes—anyone or anything that can gratify your needs. This is difficult, but necessary after any major loss. It can be particularly problematic if you have been involved with caring for a loved one with a long-term illness prior to death. In this case, much of your time had been focused around the care of the dying loved one, and now this time may weigh all too heavily on your hands.

Additionally, you will need to find the support you require to adapt to your loss and to form new relationships with others. It may come through family, friends, job, or self-help or other organized helping groups. If you choose new tasks to accomplish and new causes to invest in, you may find support from people in social, educational, religious, or political groups.

Identify the gain that has come from your loss. In every loss there is a gain. This is not to dismiss the intensity of your grief, nor to minimize its tragedy.

However, whenever a loss takes place, there is a gain that comes about. For example, although a husband may lose his wife, the situation may force him to spend more time with his children. In this case, the "gain" that has occurred is that the husband may now be more closely involved with his children than he was previously. This does not mean that he is glad that the loss occurred or that he would have wished for his wife's death. The point is that at times it is helpful for you to recognize gains and to capitalize on them in your recovery process. They may help you cope with the pain of your loss by putting it into the perspective of the gains and losses that continually ebb and flow throughout life, and may give it some positive meaning.

Obviously all of these suggestions to promote appropriate grief resolution hold true only within certain limits. Grief that is absent, delayed, excessive, distorted, or too prolonged will require more in-depth treatment. If this is the case, you should seek professional assistance. (See chapter 19 for a fuller discussion of this.) The following chapter looks at the use of rituals in facilitating your grief work.

16

Personal Bereavement Rituals and Funerals

B EREAVEMENT rituals can be very helpful to you in your grief. Funerals are but one example of these rituals. They have remarkable therapeutic properties to assist you in confronting the death of your loved one and coping with the loss.

Personal Bereavement Rituals

Rituals give form, structure, and meaning to our feelings. They are unique opportunities for communication, ventilation, and appropriate acting out.

In times past, ritual celebration of significant events was a public display that promoted security, control, and predictability. It expressed the beliefs of the people involved and symbolized their values. Participants could communicate through symbolic activity. This is what is seen, for instance, in religious services and public ceremonies. Ritual served as a rite of passage and provided direction and formal patterns of behavior to guide and sustain people during confusing and chaotic periods of transition. It provided meaning at a time of inconsistency. This is why, in all cultures, major changes and transitions such as birth, puberty, marriage, and death all have rituals to help individuals and society adapt to the changed state and cope with the confusion that occurs during the transition.

Today, because of the changes in American life, there is a decrease in formal ritual behavior. We have fewer social ties and less stable roles than ever before. We are more mobile and more alienated from each other, and lack a feeling of belonging to a community. Decrease in ritual is seen in such trends as the decline in numbers of people attending religious services, the increasing number of individuals who live together without marriage, and the decreasing percentage of funerals and memorial services.

As a result, people are left without support and direction during times of change. The rituals that had sustained them and had given them prescriptions for what to do are no longer available. In the case of grief, those bereaved by a death sometimes find they have no idea what to do next. This leaves Americans in the ironic situation of using funeral and bereavement rituals less than ever before, but needing them now more than ever since other traditional supports are lacking.

You can create rituals that will function in your grief work as they function in other parts of your life. As noted in chapter 14, rituals provide a way through which you can keep your loved one "alive" appropriately. However, they also do much more to assist you in your grief. Here is an example:

> Al's teenaged brother committed suicide by shooting himself in the head with a shotgun in a field near their house. Now that Al can finally admit to the feelings of anger and betrayal that had complicated his grief, and has worked them through to a large extent, he is able to return to the place of his brother's demise and plant a tree to mark his brother's life and to offer something living in place of death.

What a Personal Bereavement Ritual Can Do for You

A ritual is a specific behavior or activity that gives symbolic expression to certain feelings and thoughts. You may do it repeatedly or only once. Rituals can provide a structured way for you to recall your lost loved one and to make some statement about your feelings. Since they acknowledge the physical loss of your loved one while allowing memory to continue, they can serve to encourage your necessary formation of a new relationship with the deceased.

Rituals have many specific therapeutic properties that can help you in your grief:

The power of acting out. Acting out enables you to do something constructive to overcome the feelings of emptiness and powerlessness that may accompany your bereavement. It gives you a sense of control and provides a here-and-now focus for your grief. Acting out cuts through intellectualization and other resistances to mourning to directly reach your emotions;

the physical reality of ritual behavior touches upon your unconscious feelings far more effectively than any words can. In this way, rituals allow you to express and display your feelings without overly intellectualizing and distancing yourself from them.

The legitimization of emotional and physical expression. Rituals give you permission to outwardly express your feelings. They provide acceptable outlets for your feelings and give you symbols to focus upon.

During her psychotherapy session Gina is given a rose on her wedding anniversary; her husband has been dead for three years. A candle is lit while she pores over wedding pictures and talks about their life together. She takes the candle home and will light it on special occasions when she wants to mark a special communication between her and her deceased husband.

The delimitation of grief. Grief can seem overwhelming when you experience it as a diffuse, global reaction. Ritual can channel your feelings into an activity having a distinct beginning and ending with a clear purpose. In this way it can make your feelings more manageable, especially during holidays and at other anniversary times.

The Morrison family plants a special tree in memory of their deceased toddler, Andrew, on his birthday. This provides them with an activity through which they can demonstrate their love for the child and illustrate to themselves and others that they have not forgotten him. Consequently, the Morrisons find it less painful and not a betrayal of Andrew if they do not feel constant pain throughout the anniversary date. They find it easier to give themselves permission to experience whatever joy is available to them on this day without as much guilt.

Michaela, a seventeen-year-old girl, was killed in an automobile accident. Her family was told they needed to commemorate her at Christmas, a day they were dreading. They decided to burn a candle throughout the holiday to symbolize that she was still an important part of their lives, although in a radically different fashion. At dinner her chair was occupied by a senior citizen who otherwise would not have had a holiday feast.

The opportunity to "hold on" to your deceased loved one without doing so inappropriately or interfering with your grief work. Participation in rituals gives you the chance to interact intensely with the memory of your deceased loved one for a limited period of time in a healthy fashion. Ritual legitimizes such emotional exchanges.

The provision of assistance in grieving and in confronting unresolved grief. Rituals allow you the opportunity to make a statement, consciously and unconsciously, implicitly and explicitly, that a loss has occurred. Through symbolic behaviors you can channel your feelings of grief or you can finish unfinished business. Participation in ritual behaviors can aid you in the necessary process of withdrawing your emotional attachment to your loved one.

> Rita was accompanied by her therapist as she visited the grave of her daughter who died nineteen years ago. She laid a bouquet of flowers on the grave, spoke of what she had lost in the intervening years and about when she would be reunited with her child. She then divided the bouquet in half, taking one half home with her and leaving the remaining flowers on the grave. She had told herself symbolically that while she had lost the physical presence of her daughter forever, her relationship continued based on loving memory. She had been fearful that if she acknowledged the death and grieved her loss, she would lose her daughter permanently. However, the ritual enabled her to acknowledge the death, grieve her loss, and still keep her daughter's memory.

The learning gained through doing and experiencing. Participation in rituals "teaches" you that your deceased loved one is gone. It provides the experience necessary to recognize and confirm your loss, and helps you to make adjustments to the environment in which your loved one is missing.

The provision of structure for ambivalent or poorly defined emotions and thoughts. Rituals give you a focus that is especially helpful in managing the confusing disorganization and loss of control commonly experienced in grief. They reduce the stress of grief and transition by prescribing specific actions to help you get through the social and emotional chaos. They provide both the conditions and the structure you need in order to feel grounded and safe while experiencing the intense reactions of grief.

The provision of experiences that allow the participation of friends and family. Collective rituals promote the social interaction that is necessary both for your own successful grief resolution and for your ultimate reintegration back into your social group. A religious service—for instance, a mass— would be an example of this.

The structuring of celebrations of anniversaries and holidays. Participating in ritual activities commemorating a special date provides an unusually effective way of tapping into or confronting your anniversary reactions, which you may not always easily recognize or accept.

How to Design Your Own Ritual

Rituals may be formal or informal, and can occur all the time, infrequently, or only once. Their basic purpose is to provide a structured way to recall the deceased and express your feelings and thoughts about him.

Consequently, an infinite number of behaviors could function as rituals for you in your grief work. You need to decide what you want to express and find a behavior that can convey this. You can create a ritual to help yourself with the normal process of grief work (as exemplified by Michaela's family) or with grief that has become more difficult (as seen in the example of Rita).

Once you know the impediments to your successful grief resolution, you can design an appropriate ritual to overcome them. For instance, in the case of Al, he needed something to symbolize that he could forgive his brother for committing suicide. He chose to plant a tree in his brother's place of death to illustrate that even though his brother had died, Al had a living attachment to him as represented by the tree.

Your ritual need not be overly dramatic to be useful. It only has to be tailored to your individual needs and pertain to the specific loss you have experienced. If it is, and it assists you in your grief work, then by definition it will be meaningful and therapeutic for you. If your ritual is too overwhelming, or does not have enough emotional meaning to you, it will not be helpful.

Rituals can be as effective in dealing with the terminally ill as they are with the bereaved following a death. The same therapeutic properties exist, since grief work is being addressed by both groups.

Sam was the patriarch of a large Italian family. As he was succumbing to a long-term illness, both Sam and his family had difficulties with his relinquishing his control and authority over the family. However, when Sam had come to the point where he had worked this issue through in his mind, he called his family together and gave his ring to his eldest son to signify the investiture of authority. Through this ritual behavior, he communicated to his family that he was letting go of the family reins, but that he did not want to be forgotten. All the family now knew that the eldest son had authority that had been legitimized by Sam. They also would remember Sam whenever they saw the ring.

Funerals and Other Leave-taking Rituals*

Funerals are not to benefit the dead, but the living. They have a number of unparalleled therapeutic benefits. As a rite of passage, the funeral assists you in recognizing the passing of your loved one, supporting you as you start your life without the deceased, and reintegrating you back into the social group as a person whose loved one is no longer alive. A funeral can mark the beginning of your new social identity.

Research confirms the value of funerals much more than the critics of the funeral industry would have us believe. Certainly there are instances in which funeral rituals have not properly addressed grievers' needs, and this has given some people a negative image of funerals. There also have been a relatively few unscrupulous funeral directors whose practices have contributed to the overindictment of funerals. But in reality, it is clear that funerals have a great potential to facilitate resolution of grief. In most cases they reach this potential.

The funeral ritual is unsurpassed in providing a good beginning for the healthy grieving process. For this reason, the often-heard criticism that funerals are "barbaric" is actually the opposite of the case: Funerals are most civilized. They are compassionate, social, and therapeutic.

The Therapeutic Benefits of Funerals

Knowing what you now know about grief, imagine what you would want a ritual to include if you were asked to design one that would help a griever at the time of a loved one's death. You would probably want it to have the following properties, all of which are aspects of the traditional funeral.

Funerals confirm and reinforce the reality of the death. Your natural urge to deny the death is confronted by the ceremony of leave-taking. Viewing the body is often quite helpful, as it challenges your normal desire to deny the loss while promoting acceptance of the death. Participation in the funeral ritual—standing at a wake and repeatedly looking at your loved one in the casket, attending the funeral service, accepting the condolences of others, seeing the casket at the grave—graphically illustrates to you that

---

*For some of you, this information will be an after-the-fact discussion of what you have already been through. In this case, you may get a perspective on it in retrospect. For others, this information before the fact may help you to make better decisions.

the death has indeed occurred. Even if you cannot accept it emotionally at the time, the memories of these experiences will later help to confirm to you the reality of the loss of your loved one.

Funerals assist in the acknowledgment and expression of feelings of loss.   Your emotional responses to the loss are stimulated when you focus on it specifically in a socially legitimized situation where catharsis and expression are supported. You can confront the pain of separation that must be dealt with and can accommodate it much better if you are aided by the presence and acceptance of concerned others. The presence of the body of your loved one during the funeral can be a meaningful symbol that you can focus upon to remind you of the emotions and memories that you need to express. What better symbol is there to stimulate memories about your loved one?

Funerals offer you an opportunity to express your feelings.   Funerals provide a public and socially legitimized opportunity to display certain feelings about your lost loved one. You can appropriately act out emotions necessary for resolving your grief—for example, demonstrate your love, expiate your guilt, or finish unfinished business.

Funerals stimulate the recollection of your deceased loved one, which is a necessary part of grief.   You can begin to review your relationship with the deceased, which will be necessary to complete your grief work effectively. Each story told, each incident remembered, each emotion shared with others, which usually happens at funerals, assists you in the gradual process of changing your emotional relationship with the deceased.

Funerals assist you in beginning to accommodate to the changed relationship between yourself and your deceased loved one.   In the process of mourning you will have to develop a new relationship with the deceased based on recollection, memory, and past experience, in contrast to the former interactive relationship. Funerals help you get a clear and realistic picture of the deceased as someone who lived and died. They do this by promoting your review of the relationship and your processing of all of the feelings that accompany it. By supporting remembrance of the deceased, and confirming and underlining the reality of the loss, the funeral helps you to remember your loved one in a context of finality. This is not the end of the relationship, but it signals the separation and the switch from a relationship of presence to one of memory.

Funerals validate the life of the deceased. They are a testimony to the fact that a life has been lived and that the person will be remembered. Funerals provide an occasion to fittingly mark the end of the life of your loved one. A lack of recognition for the ending of your loved one's life is depersonalizing and invalidating. It is tantamount to dismissing the importance of the person who had died.

Funerals allow for input from your family and friends that serves as a living memorial and helps you form an integrated image of your loved one. Tributes paid to your lost loved one emphasize the worth of that person and establish that he is worthy of the pain you currently feel. This not only legitimizes your discomfort but also puts it in a meaningful perspective that will help you to tolerate it better. You may find that you are bolstered by comments, feelings, and thoughts from others about your deceased loved one. Such comments also may help you to develop a more well-rounded, realistic composite memory of your loved one. You may hear stories about the deceased that you never knew before and learn many things about the person that you can cherish for the rest of your life.

Funerals allow your friends and family to give you vital social support. Through the funeral, society demonstrates that it recognizes your new relationship with the deceased and that it wants to help you maintain this new relationship through memory, commemoration, and ritual. As expressions of support and shared loss, these rituals strengthen the relations among the living as well as remembering the dead. The consolation of those who care gives acceptance to your feelings, nurtures you at a time of crisis, helps you bear your pain, encourages you to grieve, and affirms that you are not alone in your grief.

Funerals begin the process of reintegrating you back into society with a new identity. There is still a relationship with your deceased loved one, but now it is based on memory and identification. You are going to have to assume new roles and responsibilities as a consequence of the loss, and this will require a change in identity. Through the funeral, this change begins to be validated by those around you. Ideally, your path back into society as a person with a new identity and without the deceased will be smoothed by the support gained from others during the funeral through their presence, thoughtful gestures, and expressions of feelings of sadness and loss over the death of your loved one.

Funerals provide meaningful, structured activities to counter the loss of predictability and order that frequently accompanies the death of a loved one. They prescribe and define social roles and provide things to do at a time when self-directed actions and purposeful behavior are not easily attainable. This is especially true given the recent changes in American society which have left Americans without prescribed roles and norms and often with unrealistic expectations about how to act after the death of a loved one. There are no guidelines on how to be a mourner, and few models to emulate. Therefore, the funeral can provide structure to you at a time when direction is sorely lacking.

Funerals with a religious orientation can give you a context of meaning as you attempt to fit the death of your loved one into a religious/philosophical framework. Funerals can offer you meaning that transcends the death of your loved one, bearing witness to the hope for a new life beyond death. You may be able to comprehend suffering and accept it with the help of religious resources, which can keep the suffering from becoming overwhelming. You may be able to confront the meaning of your own life and death, come to terms with it, and rededicate yourself to worthy purposes. The services may provide a chance to praise God and offer thanks for life, and to pronounce a benediction on your deceased loved one and the life he lived.

The Value of Funerals

By design, funerals should catalyze acute grief responses, prescribe structured behaviors in a time of confusion and flux, and encourage both recognition of the loss and development of new relationships with both the deceased and society. If there are problems with funerals it is owing to their implementation rather than their design. There have been many criticisms of funerals in the last several decades, yet there are no suitable alternatives for the funeral in providing a way of coping with the highly emotional and upsetting experience of death. Additionally, there is striking evidence that suggests that the absence of such rituals robs the mourners of the therapeutic value that funerals can provide.

What You Should Know about Arranging Funerals

Basically, the funeral is for you. Make it meaningful for yourself. Unless you are carrying out the prearranged funeral of the deceased, you should recognize that you have the right to tailor it to your personal needs. You have many options of which you may not even be aware. Tell your funeral director about your specific needs and request that they be incorporated into the funeral ritual. For instance, you should be allowed to perform those personal behaviors that are important to you in terms of saying good-bye and finishing unfinished business—for example, allowing a child to put a favorite toy into the casket of his brother. You should feel that the funeral is as adaptive and personally meaningful as possible, and that it reflects your emotions and your image of your deceased loved one.

You also should make sure you have adequate private time to be with, touch, caress, and hold the body of your loved one. This may occur prior to public viewing or before the body is taken to the funeral home. If you have questions, ask the funeral director.

In certain cases of death, such as stillbirth, infant deaths, and suicides, it is critically important that you follow through with funeral rituals. Bereaved individuals frequently have been talked out of having rituals in such cases. This is quite unfortunate, since these types of deaths cry out for the confirmation of death and expression of mourning that funerals provide.

In 1984 the Federal Trade Commission adopted a trade rule that enables consumers to easily obtain information about funeral arrangements. As a result, there are certain things you can count on.* First, the funeral director is required to provide you with a list showing the total cost of the funeral goods and services you have selected. Along with this, the statement must disclose any legal, cemetery, or crematory requirements that compel you to purchase specific funeral goods or services. This statement will show the cost of each item or service so that you can decide whether to add or subtract items. Unless they are required by state law, you do not have to purchase unwanted goods or services as a condition of obtaining those that you do want.

Funeral directors are forbidden to tell you that a particular funeral item or service can preserve the body of your loved one in the grave, since this is not possible. They also must give you information about embalming that can help you decide whether to purchase this service. They cannot state that it is required by law when it is not, or charge a fee for unauthorized embalming unless it is required by state law. In addition, they must tell you in writing that you have the right to choose another form of body disposition, such as direct cremation or immediate burial, if you do not want embalming.

---

*The rule will be reviewed again in 1988 and may have changed by the time you read this.

Many people understandably are concerned about funeral expenses. However, few are aware of all of the costs and services that are included in wakes and funerals. Funeral costs generally will include the following:

1. Professional and staff services:

   Removal of the body from place of death
   Consultation with the family and clergy regarding the ceremony
   Preparation and filing of legal documents and death notices
   Care and preparation of the body
   Coordinating with others who provide other aspects of funeral service
   Supervising and directing the funeral service

2. Facilities and equipment:

   Use of the funeral home's facilities for care and shelter of the body
   Use of the facilities for the visitation, wake, or funeral
   Use of vehicles
   Use of other equipment provided by the funeral home

3. Funeral goods for use in connection with the funeral services:
   Caskets
   Burial containers, such as grave liners or burial vaults
   Register books
   Acknowledgment cards
   Burial clothing

4. Miscellaneous costs:
   Honoraria for clergy
   Obituary notices
   Certified copies of death certificates
   Additional transportation

In addition to all of this, there will be fees that will go directly to the place of final disposition, the cemetery or crematory.

How to Cope when Making Funeral Arrangements

Especially if the death of your loved one was sudden, you may be overwhelmed by having to arrange the funeral and tend to immediate practical matters such as notifying other family members, choosing a casket, making arrangements for other family members to come in from out of town, and so forth. Keep the following in mind:

Recognize that you will have many feelings and that this is a time of confusion for you. If something is not clear, ask for clarification. It is perfectly all right if you need to have something explained to you several times.

Restate the information you have received from people with whom you are making arrangements, in order to make sure that you have understood it correctly.

Whenever possible, write things down to keep from forgetting them and being confused later on.

Have someone accompany you who is not as emotionally distressed as you are at this point. This person can help you keep things straight later on.

Keep in mind the purpose of funerary rituals. This will help you to capitalize on what they can help you with and to make the most appropriate decisions.

Be sensitive to the fact that some decisions you make at the time of the death may be regretted later on. For example, you may feel that you want your deceased's wedding band to be buried with her, but later on you may wish that you had saved this as a memento. If you are not at the point where you can easily determine the consequences of certain courses of action, speak with your funeral director and ask him or her if there are other possibilities you have not considered.

Make sure the arrangements are what you want and that they are adaptive and meaningful to you. Many grievers welcome the opportunity to do "one last thing" for their loved one and spend hours arranging details ranging from the wording of the obituary to selection of the music. Make the ritual yours and your family's. Participate in the ritual as much as you can.

Don't be rushed. Within reasonable limits, take the time you need to ensure that this ritual is one with which you feel comfortable. Choose items and services that are appropriate from your perspective.

Do not be pushed into decisions that don't feel right to you, either by family or friends or your funeral director.

Your Funeral Director

If you have additional questions, even after the funeral, feel free to contact your funeral director for additional clarification and assistance. Your funeral director is trained to secure the information for your loved one's death certificate and to help you complete necessary paperwork (such as paid death notices, obituaries, and claim forms for Social Security, veterans' and union benefits, and insurance). He or she is also trained to answer questions about coping with death, to recognize when a person is having difficulty accepting the loss of a loved one, and to recommend sources of professional help for those who need it. Some even sponsor bereavement follow-up programs and self-help groups to support you after the death. If you have questions but are uncertain where to turn, your funeral director may be able to point you in the right direction.

If you are like most bereaved individuals, you will find that your funeral director is a professional with personal integrity, a caring person with a desire to serve other people at a time of great need. He or she is charged with attending to the legal matters surrounding the death and is responsible for arranging the details of the funeral and helping families make arrangements in accordance with law, custom, and the family's wishes. This person is an important source of information, support, and advice to you in creating the type of service that will be a fitting end to the life of your loved one and a suitable beginning for you in living without that person and coping with your grief. From the hour of death until final disposition, and through the bereavement process, the funeral director is prepared to help you.

Options for Funeral Rituals

For the reasons described earlier in this chapter, it is important psychologically that there be some type of ceremony or memorial service after the death of your loved one. You have a number of options when choosing funeral rituals. You may choose a ritual that is religious or one that is humanist—that is, a nonreligious ceremony in which families and friends gather to acknowledge the death, offer support to each other, and express their grief. It is just like a religious ceremony without the religion. Whatever rituals you choose to adopt, the important issue is that they be personally meaningful to you. Rituals that are not personally meaningful will have no therapeutic value, whereas those that are meaningful can be one of the most therapeutic parts of the grief process.

You can reap therapeutic benefits from these types of rituals despite whatever body disposition you choose. All of the forms of body disposition allow for some type of ceremony, whether with the body present or absent. The most important thing is that there be some type of ceremony, ritual, or rite—some type of symbolic behavior—that acknowledges the death and helps you with your grief.

In this regard, no matter how you handle the disposition of your loved one's body, it will be important to choose some form of marker or monument to memorialize your deceased. This may be a large marker placed at the site of earth burial or a small bronze plaque placed in a mausoleum; a name written in a Book of Remembrance; or a personalized memorial such as a marble bench in a park or a tree dedicated to the deceased's memory. Whatever the symbol is, it is critical to have one to memorialize your lost loved one.

There are a number of options for final disposition. The majority of people in the United States have a funeral with a body present; however, there are several alternatives for final disposition:

Earth burial. This is known also as interment. The body is buried in the dedicated ground of a cemetery or memorial park. This is the most common form of disposition in the United States. Many people prefer the idea of a final resting place and of a gravesite where they can go to remember the deceased. Also, this offers the opportunity for families to be buried together in a family plot.

Entombment. This is a fixed resting place where the body is entombed in a casket placed in a mausoleum, an aboveground structure usually made of marble or stone. Some people are reluctant to have their bodies put into the earth and prefer to have the casket stored above ground.

Cremation. Cremation can take place in several ways. It may occur immediately after death, with no ritual of any kind. This is called direct disposition. It may be used in conjunction with a memorial service (discussed later in this chapter) held at a later date. Finally, it may take place following all of the rituals of the wake and funeral, but the family accompanies the body to the crematory and deposits it there instead of at the cemetery.

In cremation the deceased's body is placed in an appropriate container and taken to a crematory. There it is placed in a retort, a specially designed furnace, where intense heat or fire reduces the body to a few pounds of bone fragments and ashes in about two hours.

Following this, there are several available modes of disposition for the remains. They may be placed in a small metallic or stone container called an urn or canister. This is called *inurnment*. The urn then may be buried in the ground as an earth burial, which allows the remains to be in the family plot, or may be placed in a type of mausoleum that is designed for holding cremated remains, called a *columbarium*. A third option is strewing or scattering the remains in places of sentimental attachment, in areas specifically designated in cemeteries, or into a stream or over an ocean. The process of scattering the remains is subject to legal prohibition in some areas, and you must investigate the legal requirements in advance. It also requires pulverization of the remains into ashes, since sometimes bone fragments are left after cremation. When remains are scattered, a focused memorial is important so that there will be a particular site the survivors can turn to as a final resting place. Memorial plaques, trees, or inscriptions in Books of Remembrance are frequently used so that there will be a specific place to visit when family members wish to remember the deceased. It is helpful to give them a focus. Finally, some survivors may choose to retain the remains themselves.

Cremation can have helpful psychological benefits. It can facilitate mourning by effectively symbolizing the finality of the relationship you had with the deceased and suggesting that life must go on without that person. The dissolution of the body in cremation makes it quite clear that the relationship cannot continue as before. Some survivors prefer cremation because they see it as a quick and clean incineration of the body that avoids the slow process of decomposition in the earth. Others feel comfortable that the body is reduced to its natural elements and then mixed with the elements of the earth, since for them it symbolizes oneness with Nature.

However, cremation also can have disadvantages for the survivor. It should never be done as a way to escape the grief process as rapidly as possible. Through direct disposition, some people think they can avoid the pain if they don't have a ritual. Actually, in most cases this only causes more problems because they lose the therapeutic benefits of funeral rites and ceremonies. Cremation should not be done if survivors have strong reservations against being cremated themselves. For example, it is not wise for you to arrange the cremation of another if you yourself do not want to be cremated (although it does not have to be your preferred mode of body disposition). For this reason, those who plan to be cremated should permit their closest survivors to alter that plan if the survivors have deep personal reservations about it. Still another problem may result from cremation if there has been a strong negative relationship between the deceased and the mourner. It can become a symbol of hostility, an acting out of negative feelings toward the deceased.

Scientific Donation. When the body is donated to medical science, often the organs can be removed immediately and then the funeral director still can prepare the body for a viewing and appropriate disposition. Where the entire body is given to medical science, this may not be possible if the body must be prepared and then delivered to a medical institution. As noted before, however, this still does not preclude some kind of ceremony or ritual.

Burial at Sea. This is another form of body disposition that occurs relatively rarely. In this case, all of the traditional rites and rituals are available, but the body is disposed of at sea rather than at the cemetery or crematory. In some cases, there are rituals that take place on the boat immediately prior to committing the body to the water.

Memorial Services

A memorial service is a ritual, a service that is held after the body has been buried or cremated. It differs in this respect from the funeral service, which is conducted in the presence of the body. Programs are varied and can be arranged according to the desires of the survivors. Music, prayer, reflection, and sharing of remembrances and feelings about the deceased may be included. In practice, the features of memorial services are sometimes incorporated into funeral services. If significant events that the deceased shared with the community are recalled, and people are allowed to express the meaning of their relationship to the deceased, the funeral will have achieved the same goals as a memorial service.

Prearranging Funerals

In recent times, prearrangement and prefunding of funerals have become increasingly popular. Prearrangement (also known as preplanning) means making funeral arrangements prior to need. It means specifying orally or in writing the details of what is desired. Often it includes naming a particular funeral director and delineating what is wanted in terms of the ritual, the funeral merchandise, and the method and place of final disposition.

Prearrangement allows individuals to have the assurance that the ceremonies and body disposition they receive will fit their personal beliefs, standards, and life-style. They can ensure that their special instructions and personal desires will be incorporated into all aspects of the process. Prearranging can help survivors by providing approximate cost guidelines. Finally, it allows those who have moved numerous times or maintained several residences to be certain that they will be buried at that location of their choice. In essence, preplanning allows people to exert some control over their final connection with society.

By accepting in advance the reality of death, and by talking about it with survivors, the planner and the family will be better able to meet it when it comes. Also, arranging the funeral ahead of time can remove some of the emotional burden from the family, eliminating some of the stress of making arrangements in an atmosphere charged with grief and trauma. It gives the family great comfort to know that the funeral reflects the wishes of the deceased. Instead of having to make decisions that can be quite challenging and guilt-provoking, they will know what is desired, how to get it, and what it will cost, and will not have to debate over whether selection of a particular casket reflects that they are spending enough on the deceased.

Recognize that funeral rituals are for the living, not for the dead. Consequently, if you are prearranging your funeral you really should review the possible effects of your plans on the survivors, or should make your arrangements with the option that they could have some say after the death. Discuss your funeral and burial preferences with your potential survivors to ensure that decisions will not be made that could be difficult or upsetting for them to carry out. One man had wanted his remains to be flushed down the toilet following his death, and this put his family in a terrible situation because they were not able to do this but then felt guilty that they did not follow his wishes.

Prefunding of funerals offers the advantage of paying for the funeral when it can be afforded and relieving the family of any possible financial burden at a time when finances might be tight. There are several ways to prefund a funeral, and these are regulated by legal guidelines. You can enter into a trust fund agreement in which you deposit money in a lump sum or in installments that will be managed by a trustee and used to pay for funeral services and merchandise. Or you can purchase a specially designed insurance policy that will provide benefits for funeral expenses. There are a number of laws covering these financial arrangements, and they vary from state to state. According to the National Funeral Directors Association 1986 Pamphlet "Easing The Burden—Prearranging Your Funeral," you should ask the following questions if you decide to prefund your funeral:

Is the prepayment refundable in part or in full?

What happens if the funeral home goes out of business?

Does the prepayment cover any cost increases later?

Who receives the interest on the account, and who must pay taxes on that interest?

Personal bereavement rituals, funerals, memorial services, and other leave-taking rituals are powerful individual and social behaviors that can be most helpful to you in your mourning. Determine the way they can be of assistance to you in your grief work and incorporate them in your attempts to resolve and live with the loss of your loved one.

17

What "Recovery" Will and Will Not Mean

K NOWING now what is necessary to resolve grief, and being armed with specific suggestions on how to achieve its resolution, you may be wondering precisely what "recovery" will and will not mean to you in your mourning. This chapter looks at the goal of recovery and what it entails. It ends by looking at the signs indicating whether you are reaching this goal.

You will notice that the word "recovery" has been placed in quotation marks. Like resolution, the term is a relative one. Recovery does not mean a once-and-for-all type of closure. It means to regain your abilities to function at your previous levels, and to have successfully resolved and integrated your loss as discussed in chapter 14. In some ways, however, you technically can never recover totally, because you will never be exactly the way you were before. The loss of your loved one will change you in numerous ways. What can be recovered, however, are your attributes and your capabilities, despite the fact that other aspects of you necessarily are different. You now have a slightly different self, arising from the changes in you and your world as a consequence of your loved one's death. For the rest of this chapter, recovery will not be enclosed in quotation marks.

The Goal of Recovery

The goal of your recovery should be to learn to live with your loss and to adjust to your new life accordingly. The adjustments must take place in yourself (through your new identity), in your relationship with the deceased (through the development of a new relationship with her), and in the new world (readjusting to it without the deceased and, at the appropriate time, reinvesting emotional energy in new people, objects, goals, ideals, and other pursuits). This does not mean that you would have chosen your loss or that you ever wanted it. It merely means that you no longer have to fight it. You "accept" it in the sense of learning to live with it as an inescapable fact of your life.

Recovery means that you can integrate the past with the new present that exists. You will never forget, but you will not always be acutely bereaved. Recovery from your loss will leave a psychic scar, like a scar that remains after a physical operation. This does not necessarily interfere with your present functioning, but there are certain days and particular conditions when the scar will ache or throb. It will remind you of what you have been through, and you will have to do something to tolerate the pain until it passes.

What Recovery Will Mean

Grief will bring many changes to you. As noted in previous chapters, you can expect to have a changed identity and redefined roles, relationships, and skills. These changes can be either positive or negative. As someone who has loved and lost, you either can be the richer for it or be diminished because of the parts of yourself that are irretrievably gone. Again, like the physical scars, our psychic scars can give us character or be sources of vulnerability. It will be up to you to determine your response to your scar. This means that you will need to choose how to respond to the rest of your life after you have worked through your grief.

While you may have had no control or choice over your loved one's dying, you do have a choice over how you will let the loss affect you. I am not speaking now about the acute period of grief in which you will be subject to many varying psychological, social, and physical effects in all realms of your life. I am speaking here about what type of perspective or attitude you will take toward the rest of your life as your mourning brings you to a recovered state. For example, will you make the most out of the rest of your life, or will you be bitter? Will you incorporate your loss and have it be a catalyst for growth, or will you stay stuck and mired in it, never to take risks again? Will the death of your loved one cause you to make sure you will never have any unfinished business with others you care about, or will it give you the sense that "the world owes me"?

Countless bereaved individuals demonstrate the positive benefits that can come from a major loss. This does not mean that you would have chosen to have lost your loved one, but that you have chosen to recover from it and capitalize on whatever good can come from this bad. This is not a sappy or unrealistic, overly positive view that denies the pain of grief and the price of the loss of your loved one. Rather, it recognizes that even in undergoing the pain of separation through death you can decide that it will have some positive meaning for the remainder of your life.

The positive responses can be many and varied. Those who have loved and lost have reported that their eyes have been opened to new experiences and priorities that were formerly overlooked. For instance, they were made more aware of those loved ones they still had. Many have found a commitment to living life more fully and meaningfully because of the death. The increased awareness of life's preciousness, fragility, and brevity has become a positive, life-enhancing force, pushing them to avoid putting off until tomorrow the things they can say and do today. They live their lives in such a way as to have the smallest amount of unfinished business possible with their loved ones.

Other mourners have reordered their priorities toward increased family commitment and unity. They no longer take for granted those they love. Bereaved individuals have become more compassionate and caring towards others, closer in relationships, and more sensitive. The pain of their loss has led many of them to fuller expression of feeling and more open discussion of sensitive emotional issues. Many have experienced greater personal growth and increased religiousness and spirituality. Losing a loved one has heightened perceptions and raised states of consciousness in many grievers. Like dying patients, many now can open themselves up without fear of vulnerability, since they have faced the ultimate loss of death. They truly can "take time to smell the roses." Such people often report increased productivity in their lives, and many have used their loss experience creatively, transforming their pain through art, literature, music, writing, and other creative efforts.

In their determination that some good should come from their loss, others have channeled their pain and rage into meaningful endeavors assisting both themselves and society. Bereavement support groups have been established to assist others, with some of them having a political focus such as Parents of Murdered Children, in which political changes are urged to ensure that no others suffer the same bereavement.

Many bereaved persons have discovered and developed new aspects of their identity that were previously unknown. They have realized new interests, found new relationships, or started living in ways that in some cases are more satisfactory and fulfilling than before. This does not mean that they were not grieved by the loss of their loved one. It only means that they responded to that loss, after the period of grief and mourning, in ways that made them become enriched by the pain. Successfully enduring the pain and suffering of grief and mourning have allowed these people to have a deeper sense of self-worth and to have become stronger persons. The strength gained in facing and surviving the adversity has made them better, more concerned, and more compassionate people. Many become capable of more intimacy than ever before. Many of them recognize that they have been through the worst, and now that they have survived, they want to get on with the business of living in as healthy a fashion as possible, focusing on their priorities and not suffering fools gladly. Many now no longer tolerate those people and things they put up with in the past. They are appropriately more assertive, and set more limits.

On the other hand, you may not want to use your loss constructively to have a better life. All of the aforementioned possible responses could be flipped and the reverse could be the outcome. You may become hardened, cold, closed, and unwilling to reach out for yourself or to others. This is your prerogative; it is your choice. Just recognize that you are making it and take responsibility for it. Do not blame it on the death. And do not think that if you *do* do something constructive with your loss and what you have learned from it, that this means you are unmoved by the death or that you are betraying your loved one.

What Recovery Will Not Mean

There are certain things that recovery does not mean. It does not mean that you forget, either your loved one or the old world. It does not mean that you have no relationship at all with your deceased loved one. And it does not mean you are always happy, never to have any more pain. Just as you can decide what recovery *will* mean, you can decide what it *won't* mean. Recovery will not mean that you are not touched by certain reminders, such as that certain song, that particular smell, or that special location. It will not mean that you do not experience the bittersweet combination of feelings that holidays can bring, as you rejoice with those who are still present and mourn for those no longer here. It will not mean that in certain events in your life you do not painfully wish for your loved one to be alive to be present with you, share in your joy, or be proud of you.

Recovery will not mean that you don't mourn any longer; it means that you learn to live with the mourning in ways that do not interfere with your ongoing healthy functioning in the new life without your loved one. For those who have lost someone they loved a great deal, the mourning will never cease entirely. This is described below in a passage written by psychiatrist Gerald Caplan, discussing widows. It can be applied equally to other bereaved people.

> In our earlier formulations we had thought that a [bereaved person] "recovers" at the end of the four to six weeks of her bereavement crisis on condition that she manages to accomplish her "grief work" adequately. We believed that thereafter she would be psychologically competent to carry on with the tasks of ordinary living, subject only to the practical readjustments demanded by her new social roles. We now realize that most [bereaved persons] continue the psychological work of mourning for their [loved ones] for the rest of their lives. During the turmoil and struggles of the first one to three years most [bereaved persons] generally learn how to circumscribe and segregate this mourning within their mental economy and how to continue living despite its burden. After this time they are no longer actively mourning, but their loss remains a part of them and now and again they are caught up in a resurgence of feelings of grief. This happens with decreasing frequency as time goes on, but never ceases entirely. (Caplan 1974, viii)

Most bereaved individuals eventually come to terms with their grief and carry on with their lives in healthy and productive fashions. However, total resolution of mourning, in the sense of completely and permanently finishing it and never being touched again by some element of the loss, usually never truly occurs.

Signs of Learning to Live Healthily with Your Loss

How do you know if you are recovering from your loss? What signs can you look for to see if you are resolving your grief? Below is a list of signs for changes in self, relationship with the deceased, and relationships with the new world and others in it. They are only some of the possible indications that you are learning to live with your loss and are adjusting to your new life accordingly. Rate yourself on each one as to whether or not "I am here now," "I am having a little difficulty with this," or "I can't do this yet."

Learning to Live with the Loss in Terms of Yourself

You have returned to your normal levels of psychological, social, and physical functioning in all realms of your life.

There is a general decline in all of your symptoms of grief.

You are not overwhelmed by emotions in general or whenever the loss is mentioned.

You are back to your normal level of self-esteem.

You can enjoy yourself without feeling guilty, and you don't feel guilty for living.

Your hatred and anger, if any, doesn't consume you and is not directed inappropriately at others.

You do not have to restrict your emotions and thoughts to avoid confronting something painful.

It is not that you don't hurt, but the hurt now is limited, manageable, and understood.

You appreciate how you are similar to and different from other bereaved persons.

You do not have to obsess about nor think solely of the deceased and the death.

You feel that you have done what you needed to do, either to atone for your guilt or to learn to live with it.

You lead the pain, it doesn't lead you.

You can appreciate the bittersweet quality of certain experiences, such as holidays and special events in which you feel the sweetness of those who are around you as well as the sadness of not being with your deceased loved one.

You are able to meet and cope with secondary losses in a healthy fashion.

You don't become unduly anxious when you have nothing to do. You don't have to be occupied all the time to be without tension.

You can remember without pain, and can talk about the deceased and the death without crying.

You no longer feel exhausted, burdened, or wound up all the time.

You can find some meaning in life.

You do not have to hold time, or yourself, back.

You have "accepted" the loss in the sense of not fighting the fact that it happened.

You are comfortable with your new identity and the new adjustments you have made to accommodate being without your loved one in the world. While you wouldn't have chosen to have to change, you are not fighting it now.

You are comfortable with the emotions that temporarily are aroused when you occasionally bump the scar from your loss (for example, at anniversaries or special events). You know how to deal with the grief and you understand that it is normal.

You know how and when to take time to mourn.

You can look forward to and make plans for the future.

You have a healthy perspective on what your grief resolution will and will not mean for you.

Learning to Live with the Loss in Terms
of Your Relationship with the Deceased

You can realistically remember the good and the bad, the happy and sad of both the deceased and your relationship.

Any identification you have with the deceased is healthy and appropriate.

You can forget the loss for a while without feeling like you are betraying your loved one.

You have a comfortable and healthy new relationship with the deceased, with appropriate withdrawal of emotional energy but also appropriate ways to keep that person "alive."

You are able to stop "searching" for your lost loved one.

You do not have to hold on to the pain to have a connection with your deceased loved one.

The rituals that keep you connected to your loved one are acceptable to you and healthy.

You can concentrate on something besides your deceased loved one.

In your relationship with your deceased loved one, you have achieved healthy amounts of holding on and letting go.

Learning to Live with the Loss in Terms of Adjusting to the New World

You have integrated this loss into your ongoing life. You are able to relate to others in a healthy fashion and to work and function at the same level as before.

You can accept the help, support, and condolences of others.

You are not inappropriately closed down in your feelings, relationships, or approaches to life. For example, you do not overprotect yourself or fail to take any risks.

You can let the world go on now without feeling it has to stop because your loved one has died.

You can deal with others' insensitivity to your loss without becoming unduly distressed or overemotional.

You are regaining interest in people and things outside of yourself or which don't pertain to your lost loved one.

You can put the death in some perspective.

There may be other signs that would indicate to you that you now are learning to live with your loss in as healthy a fashion as possible. The ones listed here will give you some examples of the ways in which resolution and recovery can be shown. You will note that none of them suggest that you not have some connection with your deceased loved one, or that you forget that person. They all center around learning to live with the fact of your loved one's absence, moving forward in the world despite the fact that the scar will remain and, on occasion, bring pain.

A Final Perspective

And, in the end, this moving forward with that scar is the very best that we could hope for. You would not want to forget your loved one, as if she had never existed or not been an important part of your life. Those things that are important to you in your life are remembered and kept in the very special places of your heart and mind. This is no less true with regard to the loss of a beloved person. Keep this loss, treasure what you have learned from it, take the memories that you have from the person and the relationship and, in a healthy fashion, remember what should be remembered, hold on to what should be retained, and let go of that which must be relinquished. And then, as you continue on to invest emotionally in other people, goals, and pursuits, appropriately take your loved one with you, along with your new sense of self and new way of relating to the world, to enrich your present and future life without forgetting your important past.

18

Solving Practical Problems

I N addition to the numerous psychological, social, and physical problems that grief can bring to you, it also can confront you with some
very practical problems. This chapter looks briefly at several of the key
practical problems and offers some suggestions for courses of action.

Handling the Holidays

One of the most painful issues for you to deal with is how to survive
the holidays after the death of the person you loved. Because holidays
are supposed to be family times, and because of the extraordinary (although
unrealistic) expectation that you should feel close to everyone, this time
of year can underscore the absence of your deceased loved one more than
any other time. The important thing to remember is that you and your
family do have options about how to cope with the holidays. These are
a few things to keep in mind:

As much as you'd like to skip from November to January 2nd, this
is impossible. Therefore, it will be wise for you to take control of the
situation by facing it squarely and planning for what you do and do
not want to do to get through this time.

Realize that the anticipation of pain at the holidays is always worse than
the actual day.

Recognize that what you decide for this year can be changed next year;
you can move to something new or back to the old way. Decide what
is right for you and your family *now*. Don't worry about all the other
holidays to come in years ahead. You will be at different places in your
mourning and in your life then.

Recognize, also, that your distress about the holidays is normal. It doesn't make you a bad person. Countless other bereaved people have felt, and do feel, as you do right now.

Ask yourself and your loved ones to decide what is important for you to make your holidays meaningful and bearable. Then, through compromise and negotiation, see if everyone can get a little of what he or she wants and needs. Give-and-take is important here.

Do something symbolic. Think about including rituals that can appropriately symbolize your memory of your loved one. For example, a candle burning at Thanksgiving dinner, the hanging of a special Christmas ornament, or the planting of a tree on New Year's Day may help you to mark the continued abstract presence of your deceased loved one while still celebrating the holiday with those you love who still survive. Remembering your deceased loved one in this fashion can make an important statement to yourself and others. (See chapter 16 for more on personal bereavement rituals.)

Recognize that the holidays are filled with unrealistic expectations for intimacy, closeness, relaxation, and joy for all people—not just for the bereaved. Try not to buy into this for yourself—you already have enough to contend with.

Be aware of the pressures, demands, depression, increased alcohol intake, and fatigue that come with holidays. As a bereaved person you may feel these more than others. Take time out to take care for yourself during this time. You will need it even more.

Reevaluate family traditions. Ask yourself and your surviving loved ones whether you need to carry them on this year or whether you should begin to develop some new ones. Perhaps you can alter your traditions slightly so that you can still have them to a certain extent but don't have to highlight your loved one's absence more than it already is. For example, you may want to have Thanksgiving dinner at your children's house instead of yours. Or you might open presents on Christmas Eve instead of Christmas morning.

Recognize that your loved one's absence will cause pain no matter what you do. This is only natural and right. After all, you are mourning because you love and miss this person. Try to mix this with your love for those you still have and your positive memories of the past. "Bittersweet" is a good word to describe this. You can feel the sweetness of the holiday but also the bitterness of your loved one's absence. Together they can give you a full, rich feeling, marked with love for those present and those gone whom you will never forget.

Plan ahead for your shopping tasks. Make a list ahead of time. Then, if you have a good day, capitalize on it and do the shopping you can. Try to consolidate the stores you want to visit. If you have trouble with shopping right now, do your shopping by catalog or mail order, or ask friends to help you out.

Tears and sadness do not have to ruin the entire holiday for you or for others. Let yourself have the cry you need and you will be surprised that you can go on again until the next time you need to release the tears. Facing family holidays in your loved one's absence are normal mourning experiences and part of the healing process. Let your tears and sadness come and go throughout the whole day if necessary. The tears and emotions you do not express will be the ones which are destructive to you.

Ask for what you want or need from others during the holidays. One bereaved mother said that, as appropriate, she wanted to hear her dead daughter mentioned. She knew everyone was thinking of her daughter and wanted them to share their thoughts.

You may find yourself reminiscing about other holidays you shared with your deceased loved one. This is normal. Let the memories come. Talk about them. This is part of mourning and doesn't stop just because it is a holiday. In fact, the holidays usually intensify it.

Having some fun at the holidays does not mean you don't miss your loved one. It is not a betrayal. You must give yourself permission to have joy when you can, just like you must give yourself permission to mourn when you have the need.

You may have to let your limits be known to concerned others who are determined not to let you be sad or alone. Let others know what you need and how they can best help you. Don't be forced into doing things you don't want to do or don't feel up to solely to keep others happy. Determine what and how much you need, and then inform others.

Discuss holiday tasks and responsibilities that must be attended to—for example, preparing the meals, doing the shopping, decorating the house.

Consider whether they should be continued, reassigned, shared, or eliminated. Break down your goals into small, manageable pieces that you can accomplish one at a time. Don't overwhelm or overcommit yourself. The holidays are stressful times for everyone, not just the bereaved, so you will need to take it slow and easy.

Look at your plans and ask what they indicate. Are you doing what you want or are you placating others? Are you isolating yourself from support or are you tapping into your resources? Are you doing things that are meaningful or are you just doing things?

Do something for someone else. Although you may feel deprived because of the loss of your loved one, reaching out to another can bring you some measure of fulfillment. For example, give a donation in your loved one's name. Invite a guest to share your festivities. Give food to a needy family for Thanksgiving dinner.

Physically and Practically Living with Your Loss

"What do I do with my husband's clothes that are still hanging in our closet five months after his death?"

"What should I do with my daughter's room and all her possessions?"

"Am I wrong to keep photos of my dead brother in our house?"

"Is it inappropriate for me to display some of the mementos I have from our relationship?"

These and other questions pertain to what to do with your deceased loved one's personal effects and with other possessions and symbols of that person. Unfortunately, too often society pushes grievers to get rid of these things prematurely, or else interprets the desire to retain them as unhealthy. However, this is not necessarily the case. As noted in chapter 14, it will be how you integrate these things into your ongoing life that will determine whether or not your keeping them is healthy—not solely the fact that you keep them.

There is no "right" answer about what to do with the personal effects of someone you love who has died. This must be individually tailored to the type of person you are, the grief you are experiencing, and all of the factors which have influenced this loss for you. For instance, for some grievers it is important to give or pack away the clothing of the deceased within a few months after the death, while others will need to undergo a gradual process in which the clothes are moved from the closet in the bedroom to a closet which holds out-of-season clothes, and then finally moved to a box in the attic.

The key issue here is not whether your loved one's clothes are retained but whether they interfere with your ongoing life. If they hold you back from resolving your grief, or interfere with your healthy functioning, then there is a problem. However, you must be realistic and recognize that decisions about what to do with the effects of your loved one, and actually carrying these decisions out, will take time. For many, it will be a gradual process and not occur all at once.

It is important for you not to strip yourself of the effects of your loved one too early. Indeed, looking at the clothing or personal effects of your loved one and recognizing that she is not there to use them can assist you in confronting your loss and recognizing its implications. By the same token, just the presence of these articles can make you feel a little less distant from the person you loved and can assist you to make the transition gradually from that person not being physically present in your life to being a memory symbolized by these articles.

Some people believe that the best way to deal with a death is to clean out of the house all of the deceased's possessions and remembrances. However, these grievers are then left with a bare (in terms of the effects of the deceased) environment which can make their loss more difficult to endure during the early times after the death. This is especially true in cases of sudden death.

Unfortunately, it is quite true that some people end up using the personal effects to cling to the deceased in an unhealthy way and to prevent their lives from going on. One family turned the bedroom of the deceased child into a shrine. No other children were allowed to go in it. The problem was that the room which had been occupied at night by the child actually was the family living room, and it was necessary to walk through it in order to get to other areas of the house. This meant that a major pathway through the house was blocked—family members had to go out of their way to reach another point in the house if they were not going to walk through the room the deceased child had occupied. This is a case where not only did the unresolved mourning interfere with the emotional recovery of the family, but it interfered with the social and practical recovery as well.

You may not want to change things after your loved one has died. This is very understandable. You already have lost this person and may resist changing those things which would illustrate to you further that the person is gone from you. Yet, acting as if the person were still alive and could use her effects is not healthy. There is a difference between not wanting to change things, but then eventually doing so gradually, and turning a room into a shrine that is dysfunctional for others as well as for yourself.

All of this must be differentiated from situations in which, for the period of time between the death and the time you are able to make changes in your loved one's room, you use the room as a place where you can go, think about your loved one, and perhaps cry or do some of your grief work. It would not be uncommon, for example, for a woman to go into her husband's den, sit in his chair, and think about the times they had together and all that she has lost. Indeed, this is part of her grief work. However, if this were to continue for several years, and if the widow did not get on with her life but retreated to her husband's room and failed to relate appropriately to new people and pursuits in her new world, then this would be an indication of unresolved grief.

Many times bereaved parents are reluctant to change the room of their deceased child. And this is not exclusive to bereaved parents. The most dramatic and famous example of this was Queen Victoria who, after the death of her husband, Prince Albert, had his clothes laid out daily and acted in other ways as if he were going to return. She carried this on for many years.

If you are a bereaved parent, it may be particularly difficult for you to see toys that had belonged to your deceased child being used by your other children. This can go beyond being bittersweet and become conflicted. Parents may give other children the toys of the deceased and then take them away or become angry when the children actually use them. It is important for you not to share these toys with your other children until your feelings about them have been resolved to the extent where they do not have to be acted out with the children. It is not fair to them.

Many times people erroneously interpret having photographs or mementos of the deceased as being unhealthy. However, there really is nothing wrong with this as long as you are continuing to resolve your grief and go on in your life. We have pictures and images of deceased famous national personalities in all areas of our society—from the dollar bill to museums to postage stamps. Why would it be any less appropriate to have pictures of people that you have loved and lost on your desk or on your walls? Again, the key issue is how these are integrated into your ongoing life and whether or not they interfere with your functioning and resolution of grief. You need to recognize what is appropriate with regard to remembering your loved one and keeping her "alive," and how this interfaces with what is necessary to recover from grief. As long as you recognize that the person truly is dead, then it is acceptable to have various memorabilia and personal possessions. If you are successfully resolving your grief by completing the processes discussed in chapter 14, then you don't have to worry if you choose to retain photographs, memorabilia, and clothing of your deceased loved one.

Communicating about the Loss

"What do I do when I meet someone in the grocery store and she asks how my husband is, being unaware that he died two months ago?"

"How do I inform others of the death of my mother?"

"Now that my son is dead, how do I respond to the question of how many children I have?"

These and other questions reveal concerns about how you will communicate about your loss to other individuals. Depending upon the nature of your loss, how it happened, and where you are in your grief, this can be a more or less difficult task.

There are several things to remember in communicating about the loss of your loved one:

For a long time, do not think that there is anything wrong if you become upset, cry, or in any other way are unable to communicate information about your loss without some measure of grief. Depending upon the nature of your loss and your point in grief, it will take quite a while for you to be able to do this without distress.

Do not feel that you must go into all the details of the death unless you are comfortable in doing so. For example, there are some people to whom you would want to tell the entire story of your loved one's death, whereas there are others to whom you would only want to deliver the basic facts. You alone are the one who can make this decision.

Recognize that for a while, or at least for the first few times, when you communicate about the death to others or have to check off the box marked "widowed" as opposed to "married," this is a confrontation with the death. As such, you can expect that you may have a brief upsurge of grief on these occasions.

In some situations you may be uncomfortable about sharing the cause of death, for example, suicide or homicide. You may be concerned about how it reflects on you and your deceased loved one. There are no easy answers as to how you should approach this, but there is one important thing to keep in mind: No matter what your loved one died from, you are entitled to your grief. And, unless you were the one who actually caused your loved one's death directly, you are not responsible for that death. (Please see chapter 7 for sections on suicide and homicide to address some of these issues.) You must not fall victim to your embarrassment or uncomfortable feelings about this type of death such that you do not let others know your loved one has died and what you need in your grief, and thereby not receive necessary support.

If you are a bereaved parent, you know that the question "How many children do you have?" is one that you fear. Again, as in most of these other situations, there is no correct answer. You need to do what is right for you. However, most bereaved parents are concerned about not in-validating the fact that they had a child who now is dead. As a result, some feel comfortable saying: "I have three children. Two are alive and living at home and one died two years ago." Many times you may wonder whether you should let others know that you had a child who died. The way many handle this is to disclose the information when it is truly important in order for the other individual to know them as a person. If this is the case, since the death of your child is a significant part of you, you might want to reveal this information. In other circumstances, where the relationship is more superficial, you may choose not to reveal it. On the other hand, you may want to inform everyone that you had a child who died and you may not discriminate among whom you tell.

This brings up the more general issue of when and to whom to confide in about your loss. You may be the type of person who wants others to know what you have undergone, or you merely may want to make it known so that someone will not ask you a question suddenly when you are unprepared. In contrast, you could prefer not to talk about the more private aspects of your life and will not reveal this information unless specifically asked, if then. In any case, you should decide what the purpose is in giving information about your loved one's death and then decide if and how you would be comfortable doing this.

Some individuals must contend with informing others by mail about the death of their loved ones. If you are in this situation, you may choose to send a preprinted announcement (many use the funeral acknowledgment or "Thank You" cards for this purpose) or may write a personal note specifically informing them of the death of your loved one. Some include the information in a Christmas card. You should recognize that others may be somewhat shocked by your candid revelation of the death. One bereaved mother felt that it was very important to inform her friends of the death of her child and she included this in a Christmas card along with a photograph of her son. Some of her friends were appalled and quite shocked. However, there were others who saw that this was an important way in which this mother could acknowledge her loss, do something ritualistic at the holidays that would ensure that her child was not forgotten, and also inform her extended social network.

Resumption of Dating and Sex in Today's World

"I have not dated for thirty years. How do I begin?"

"What do I have to know in today's day and age in order to be safe as an unmarried woman?"

If you had been married or in a monogamous relationship for some time, you may be quite uncomfortable with the notion of dating or the idea of having sex with someone besides your deceased partner. It may be helpful for you to look at this issue in several contexts. First, it is a grief-related issue. You will need to have reached the point in your grief work where you either will have no guilt about resuming social relations with the opposite sex or you will be able to deal with the guilt that you do have. Any relationship with another person must not be on a "replacement" basis, since such a relationship is doomed to failure. Ideally, you will have resolved your grief work to the extent that you will see the commencement of social and sexual relations with new partners as a part of your continuing to live on in the new world without forgetting that once you were married or committed to another. (See chapter 14 for a further discussion of this.)

The question of when to commence dating is often a major one. Ask yourself why you are interested in starting dating now. Are you being pushed by friends or relatives? Do you feel you need to do this to "prove" you have dealt with your grief? Does it feel "right" to you now? It may help if you clarify your own thoughts on when you think a person is ready to date, what the specific indications could be which reveal that one is ready, and what your own needs, goals, and hopes are with regard to forming new relationships. Be frank with yourself. This will be a good way to get in touch with your thoughts, feelings, and dreams, along with your fears and conflicts, about what dating will mean for you.

The other issues to be addressed when considering dating again concern the content and process of dating and sex in today's society. It will be important for you to have accurate information about sexually related concerns such as AIDS, what must be done to practice "safe sex," and other knowledge necessary to be an informed, sexually active adult who understands the social climate of today. The process of dating and sex may be much different at this time than when you originally dated. You will need an accurate perception of what it is like. This usually is more of a practical issue for women than for men, although emotionally and socially it pertains to both. You may have to exercise more caution in certain areas and may experience more liberation in others. For instance, it is not uncommon now for women to ask men for dates. Yet, by the same token, it is quite important for women to protect themselves. If you now are single again, you may find it beneficial to speak with other widows, divorcees, or single women who have practice in starting off a dating relationship in the safest way possible. For example, this may mean giving your work phone number but not your home phone number, or it may mean meeting your date at a public place until you get to know him, rather than having him pick you up at your home. This is not to say that you have to be overly paranoid; you just need to be aware of the social realities.

If you are widowed, it will be important for you to recognize that your children may be quite conflicted about your dating someone else. This is a very common, but nevertheless stressful, problem that widows and widowers encounter. Frequently, children can feel threatened not only emotionally and physically but financially as well. This is especially true if they think your new partner is interested in you exclusively for financial gain. However, you and they should recognize that dating does not necessarily mean you are planning to remarry, although sometimes this is the case. You can have a relationship with a partner in which you enjoy each other's companionship for emotional, social, physical, or financial reasons, but do not wish to marry.

With younger children, it is very important that they be made to feel comfortable and secure with you. If they feel they are losing you to another person, this will only compound the loss they already have experienced with the death of their other parent. Be careful about allowing your new relationship to interfere with the relationship you have with your children. While certainly your children will have to accept that you may have other interests in life, it is important that you prepare them and make sure that they are getting what they legitimately can expect from you in the role of parent. This is also important for adult children.

There may be times when you will have to set limits on your children and be assertive in stating your need to resume dating. However, this always should be done in appropriate ways and after sufficient time has passed, to allow all parties involved to deal with the loss to whatever extent is possible at that point. While your children ultimately will have to give you the liberty to run your own life, do not expect that they will like how you are doing it. Many will perceive the resumption of dating as a betrayal to their deceased parent. For this reason, it is important that you exercise sensitivity in this matter and try to strike a balance between taking care of your own needs and recognizing the difficulty your children may have in accommodating to this new change. (See chapter 13 for more on achieving this balance.) If you have open and trusting relationships with your children, this usually is a transition that you and they can make gradually and with respect for one another. Nevertheless, it frequently is not without considerable heartache for some period of time.

Male and Female Role Switches
after the Death of a Spouse

The death of your spouse may require that you undertake roles and responsibilities which traditionally had been reserved for your spouse. It will be helpful for you to solicit input from individuals who are experienced in these areas and to plan consciously for meeting these responsibilities. Books, high school adult education courses, YMCA programs, and so forth can often help you in these areas. Some of these areas are briefly discussed below.

Especially if you are a woman who has been out of the labor market for a long time, resuming employment, or even determining whether, when, how, or in what area to find a job is a major issue. It will affect not only you but also the rest of your family, who will have to readjust to your working. This can bring up many concerns on everyone's part. You will need to address these carefully with those who can help you sort out the cost and benefits, not only financially but psychologically, socially, and physically as well. You may require career testing and guidance. Often it will be helpful to contact women's centers, career and counseling centers, state employment offices, widowed programs, the American Association of Retired Persons in Washington, D.C., and the Displaced Homemakers Network whose national office is in Washington, D.C., for further information, referral, and guidance.

For traditionally trained women, the practical problems of home and auto maintenance will need immediate attention. This means, for example, that you will need to become familiar with home security. You will need to plan for continual expenses and chores, such as auto repair, as well as time-limited expenses and chores such as snow shoveling. You will need to become familiar with the necessary upkeep in your home, such as oil burner cleaning. It may be helpful for you to keep a diary and note when these activities take place and what the charges are, in order that you can be better prepared in subsequent years. Ideally, you can ask for the assistance of someone who can predict these events for you. This can be done, for example, by having someone tell you for the first year whenever he or she gets their oil burner cleaned, reminding you to see if you need the same thing. If you are included as your friend undergoes his or her normal routines, this can be a way of keeping up with necessary responsibilities. You also may be able to determine some of these yourself by looking at your household checkbook and other receipts which indicate where payments previously have gone.

You may find that your children are more or less interested in assisting you in these chores. Remember not to give them responsibilities that are inappropriate to their ages or other role responsibilities. The ten-year-old boy who feels that he has to be the man around the house and burdens himself with all of these responsibilities is given an unfair role which will only hurt him in the long run.

If your wife has died, you will find that you may benefit from female input about home management and child rearing. Home management involves such things as food buying, clothing for children, arranging school and social activities, and household upkeep. It may be important for you to sit down and make a list of what practical responsibilities you now will have to assume for yourself and your children. You may need to develop new perspectives on matters in which you formerly were not involved.

For instance, you may be quite surprised at how rapidly children grow and require new clothing and astonished at the number of their social activities. If you do not have a friend or family member who can assist you in understanding this, contact your children's teacher, school nurse, or guidance counselor. One of those people may be able to provide you with appropriate advice or identify someone who can. (See the Parents Without Partners support group reference in chapter 20.)

For both widows and widowers, the basic premise is that you will need to become aware of what roles and functions your deceased spouse performed and then, if you determine that these are essential, make a plan to see that these are fulfilled. Sometimes this will happen with role reassignment in the family, as when an older teenager can take over the responsibility for preparing meals. However, in other situations, because of the ages of your children, you will be called upon to assume most of the responsibilities. It is important for you to approach this task in as methodical a way as possible. Usually, it takes some time after a death in order for the routine to settle down. Consequently, you must not expect too much of yourself too soon. As noted in chapter 13, you must be realistic about what you can expect of yourself with regard to surviving children when you yourself are bereaved. However, the main issue is that you recognize the practical necessities that must continue to be addressed and get assistance in identifying them, input in how they should be carried out, and support in implementing them.

Concerns about Survival Issues and Finances, Insurance, Supplementary Income, and Legal Matters

You may have serious concerns about housing, employment, child care, transportation, and medical assistance. These are critically important to you and your family's physical, as well as psychosocial, survival. It is beyond the scope of this book to provide complete information about these important areas and those briefly mentioned below. You are advised to contact the various organizations and types of people mentioned in this chapter and in chapters 19 (on professional assistance) and 20 (providing resource listings) for specific input and assistance with these issues.

Especially with regard to finances, unless you are qualified in these matters, it is important for you to secure professional advice. The advice should be on both a short- and long-term basis. For example, you may need direction as to how to deal with money that you have right now or is disbursed to you from insurance benefits, and you also will need to do budgeting and financial planning for the future. If finances are a concern, and you cannot afford financial advice, you can get assistance from your bank, from local school courses, from the American Association of Retired Persons, or from appropriate local community organizations. You can get referrals from the United Way, from various hot lines and information services, and under the appropriate listings in the telephone book.

You would be well advised to seek social and community practical support if you are having difficulty providing food, heat, light, and, depending upon the circumstances, telephone service. Immediately after the death, and for a short time thereafter, your funeral director can be of assistance to you with regard to some of the financial, insurance, and legal questions you encounter. This is part of his or her advisor role. If your questions are outside of your funeral director's domain, ask that person to refer you to the appropriate individual who can answer them for you. Such groups as Parents Without Partners and other support groups may be helpful in giving you tips on how to secure necessary resources for you and your dependent children. It may benefit you to check local community action agencies for other sources of advice and practical assistance.

This concludes the section devoted to resolving your grief and coping with its practical problems. The next section examines how to determine if you need additional help and how to go about getting it.

PART
V

Getting Additional Help

19

Finding Effective Professional and Self-Help Group Assistance

Y ou may find yourself wondering whether you could benefit from organized assistance in your mourning. This could involve seeing a mental health professional or attending a self-help group. We will look first at professional mental health clinicians by discussing when and how to get help and what to expect when you get it. Then we will look at the use of self-help groups in your bereavement.

Professional Mental Health Assistance

In seeking professional assistance there are three concerns to keep in mind: (1) when to go for help, (2) how to find a qualified mental health clinician who fits with you, and (3) what to expect in your treatment.

When to Go for Help

There are a number of diverse signs which can signal that different people need professional help in their bereavement. This is always dependent upon the unique characteristics of the particular griever, the specific death and what it means to the griever, and the social and physical factors influencing the mourner's grief. However, there are some general indicators to keep in mind. You should go for professional help whenever:

Compared to normal grief, your grief, or important reactions in it, is absent, delayed, excessive, distorted, or overly prolonged (for example, symptoms appropriate in acute grief persist too long without changing).

You talk about your deceased loved one in the present tense or in other ways inappropriately act as if she still were alive.

You think that you need it. If you feel that you could benefit from professional help, then go seek it out, especially if you feel you are falling apart or are no longer in control.

You feel "stuck" in your mourning and are not able to make any forward progress in it for a period of time. Or after a sufficient amount of time you still feel closed to the prospect of living a full life.

A number of others tell you that they think you need professional assistance. Certainly, not everything that your family and friends say is valid. This especially may be the case with regard to their expectations about you in your mourning. However, if you find that others consistently make this suggestion to you, then you would do well to follow up on it.

Other professionals refer you to a mental health professional. For example, if your minister or your physician feels that you need the assistance of a mental health professional, you should consider that he or she usually is trained in spotting bereaved individuals who require additional professional assistance, and you should at least go for an evaluation.

You have a history of severe emotional disturbance.

You are having active suicidal thoughts, if you have a suicide plan, or if you are finding yourself engaged in self-punishing or self-destructive actions.

Your addictive behaviors increase (for example, smoking, drug-taking, alcohol consumption, increased eating, or gambling).

You repeatedly behave in ways that bring about unnecessary situations of loss, such as setting yourself up to be rejected by others or acting in ways that ensure your being fired from your job.

Sufficient time has elapsed, but you continue to feel no interest or joy in other people, things, your job, or your life. And you deeply resent those who do.

Your behaviors change markedly and in ways that are not good for you. Many times you will not have symptoms of grief as such, but you may be acting out your feelings inappropriately (for example, having accidents, getting into foolish social and economic situations, entering bad relationships, altering your good relationships or radically changing your lifestyle, or starting affairs).

Any of the symptoms of normal mourning become dangerous to your functioning or well-being (for example, bleeding ulcers, depression that causes you to lose your job, anxiety that prevents you from leaving the house, or overidentification with your deceased loved one).

You are isolated and have no one else to turn to.

It is difficult to pinpoint specific indications for any particular griever unless all of the circumstances of that particular death and the factors influencing the grief response are known. When there is a question, it is better to err in the side of going for professional help and then finding out that what you are undergoing is normal. Nothing is written in stone; if you do not feel you need professional help, you do not have to continue to go for it.

The Proper Perspective

It is critical for you to put your going for professional assistance into the proper perspective. If you had been physically assaulted, you would most probably not be reluctant to go to a physician for treatment. If your leg had been broken, you would most likely be willing to go for physical therapy. The same thing applies here. Loss, grief, and mourning all assault the mind, the spirit, the heart, and the body. They attack you in the personal, social, and work worlds. Going for professional assistance in grief does not mean that you are "crazy." It means that you are seeking what you need in order to resolve your grief and recover optimally from your loss.

There are two levels on which you can receive assistance. Some mourners go for counseling in order that their grief can be facilitated. In this situation their grief is uncomplicated and they seek someone who will support their natural experience of mourning. The clinician will not attempt to change the bereaved person, only to encourage, promote, and ease the natural mourning responses. The goal is to foster and assist natural healing, and the intervention is on the surface level of the psyche. It is noninvasive. The helper must be a good, nonjudgmental listener and have appropriate information about grief.

In contrast, other mourners seek therapy where the intervention is on a deeper level. This calls for a change in the bereaved person and her functioning on a deeper level of consciousness. It requires that the therapist actively intervene to identify and help the person resolve the conflicts interfering with the successful completion of mourning. In addition to knowledge about mourning, this demands an in-depth knowledge of personality functioning and psychodynamics, as well as of therapy skills. Any concerned person can facilitate a mourner's grief; only specially trained therapists, however, should attempt to intervene in a concerted way in deeper levels of the personality.

Once you decide you are interested in securing professional assistance, you will need to find out who is the best person for you to see.

How to Find a Qualified Mental Health Clinician Who Fits with You

If you are fortunate enough to know people who have had successful experiences in treatment in the past, a personal referral is always the best to have. If you lack this personal knowledge, you would be well advised to look to the professional organizations of psychologists, psychiatrists, social workers, psychiatric nurses, and counselors, and to religious bodies for clergy who offer mental health services. You can ask for the names of professionals in these respective areas who have the proper training and interest in serving the bereaved.

Family service agencies, hospitals, community service programs, mental health clinics, and college or university counseling centers are among other resources you could turn to for the names of professionals servicing this area. Also, ask groups specifically related to terminal illnesses and death, such as a hospital oncology department, your local hospice, the local chapter of the American Cancer Society, and so forth. Having experience in dying and bereavement, these people may know which clinicians could be most helpful to you.

Frequently you will find that local funeral directors and self-help bereavement groups have lists of preferred experts to whom they could refer you. At least in this way you would be assured of seeing someone who knew something about bereavement. You can even look in the telephone directory and go through the professional advertisements there. Some individuals will identify themselves as having a special interest in bereavement.

Be well aware of the fact that a person can be professionally trained in a mental health field and have little or no experience or understanding about bereavement. Also, while a clinician may understand bereavement in general, he or she may not have sufficient knowledge or experience about your particular bereavement. For example, he or she may know something about widowhood after a cancer death but nothing about bereavement following the loss of a child or bereavement following suicide. This is why it is very important for you to talk with the clinician to determine whether he or she has the type of knowledge and experience you need. These questions are legitimate for you to ask:

What are your credentials?

Where have you been trained?

What is your theoretical orientation and approach in therapy?

What types of experiences have you had with bereaved individuals such as myself?

How do you approach treatment with a bereaved individual?

The mental health professional who will not consider at least talking with a potential patient or client on the telephone about his or her interests, training, therapeutic approach, and so forth is probably not the type of person you should see. This does not mean that you would be free to take up an inordinate amount of time with this person, since of course their time is money. It means that several minutes over the telephone is not too much to ask. You need to be a smart consumer. You are purchasing the professional services of someone in whom you will need to place your trust. Recognize that you are entitled to certain professional information about this person, and do not be afraid to ask for it.

When you do find someone, make sure that that person is covered by your insurance. Some third-party insurers limit the types of professionals they will reimburse for mental health treatment. Also, review your policy to determine if your coverage is limited in sessions. Your clinician will need to know this in order to make appropriate treatment plans or to refer you elsewhere if he or she is uncomfortable with the amount of time you could afford to be in treatment.

Sometimes, once they start to see a clinician, people are concerned that they will not be able to evaluate whether or not they are seeing a good one. It is difficult to set objective standards for this, since what appeals to you may not appeal to another. However, there are a few standard questions you should be able to answer positively for yourself:

How do you "feel" with this person?

Are you comfortable, despite the normal anxiety about seeing a mental health professional?

Does the person look and act competent to you?

Does the person treat you with respect?

If you are seeing this person for several sessions, does it feel like you are going somewhere and as if there is a purpose?

Does the person act in appropriate ways and conduct himself/herself in a professional manner?

One of the problems is that at times it is difficult for you to understand precisely what the purpose of certain discussions are or the reasons why the clinician does something. For this reason, it is important not to disengage prematurely. Unless there is a strong feeling on your part that this person is not right for you, at least go for a couple of sessions. Sometimes your initial anxiety and unfamiliarity with the therapeutic process may make you wonder whether you are getting anywhere, or getting anywhere fast enough. Remember that the clinician is not a magician. He or she will not take away your pain but can only help you to gradually work through your grief.

If you feel that things are not progressing in your treatment as you believe they should, bring this up with your clinician. He or she may explain the situation in a way that will make it meaningful to you, or perhaps will agree with you that it does not seem that the two of you are able to work together effectively.

What to Expect from Professional Assistance

Although you may be going to a mental health professional to speak specifically about the death of your loved one, you must recognize that this person has to get a sense of you as a person and will need to have an understanding of your past experience as well as of the current situation. Among other things, the clinician most probably will need to have information from you about your family of origin, your growing up, your previous relationships, and how you have coped with crises in the past. This information will provide important data with which to understand you in this distinct loss situation.

If you have any questions about what your mental health clinician is doing or saying, it is most important for you to address them specifically. Remember, you are one-half of the couple that is working to help you successfully resolve your grief. While there may or may not be certain pieces of information your clinician will choose to share with you, you *always* have the right to ask the questions.

It will be important for you to recognize that counseling and therapy take time. Although you want an immediate cure, this rarely, if ever, happens. Recognize, too, that mental health treatment is hard and slow work. The types of "quick fix" therapy situations portrayed on television or in the movies are usually quite exaggerated.

Much of the work of your grieving will be done outside of the therapy session. This is where you will have to work on and put into effect what you have discussed with your clinician. If you fail to do the work outside of the session, you probably will see little resolution of your grief.

Self-Help Bereavement Groups

Self-help groups can be wonderfully therapeutic in assisting you with your mourning. They do not replace in-depth professional assistance if it is warranted, but they are uniquely supportive. They give encouragement, provide important information and accurate norms, and transmit advice, concrete guidance, and practical suggestions for dealing with bereavement. This can be quite helpful, since there are few sources of information in our society about how to be a mourner. Other mourners can serve as models for you. You can learn what to do and what not to do from the stories of others. Additionally, you can gain hope from seeing others who have overcome their problems.

Self-help groups can offer you the added benefits of opportunities to assist others. The experience can bring you an enhanced sense of interpersonal confidence, increased self-worth, and purpose and meaning through being of help to others. This allows you to break out of the passive victim role of bereavement. Some self-help groups move in the direction of public and political involvement. For example, Mothers Against Drunk Driving has promoted legislative changes concerning drunk driving. They have gained social and political benefit and along the way have enhanced their members' self-esteem and assertiveness.

Depending upon the particular type of death your loved one had, you may find that a self-help group is the only place where you can receive the support and nurturance you need. Frequently, those who lose children or whose loved ones die from suicide or homicide find that other people tend to shy away from them. These groups can fill the gap. As a member, you can get the unconditional acceptance and feelings of belonging that other members of society may withhold from you. Such groups also can be of great benefit to individuals while family members are dying. For example, support groups for families and members with terminal and chronic illnesses can be quite effective.

In considering a self-help group, look at its printed materials and see if their objectives meet your own. Most times you can sit in on the group and do not have to participate if you don't wish to. Also, it may be helpful to meet the chapter or group leader ahead of time. Most of these people are committed individuals who have started these support groups because of their own losses. It is true that some individuals stay involved in support groups for an over-extended period of time and use it as an inappropriate way of hanging on to their deceased loved one. However, in the greater majority of cases this is not true, and the support groups are used quite therapeutically by those who attend them.

Whatever you do or wherever you turn for additional support and assistance in your mourning process, remember that this is not an indictment against you. It merely means that you are wise enough to recognize that you require assistance in the very complex, complicated, and painful processes of grief, which must be completed successfully for you to go on and live a fulfilling life. It is to your credit that you have seen what you need and are going after it. The next chapter will look at specific groups, books, and other resources that may help you in your grief work.

20

Resource Listing

This chapter lists various organizations and publications which may be helpful to you in your grief. The listings are by no means exhaustive, but they will give you a good start in finding resources to assist you in your grief. A number of organizations have local and/or regional chapters across the country. As no list can be totally comprehensive or up-to-date, check with your local mental health professionals, social service agencies, community information centers, clergy, funeral directors, and senior citizens agencies for local resources in your community.

Organizations and Support Groups

General Information

Concern for Dying
250 West 57th Street
New York, New York 10107
(212) 246–6962

This organization provides information and resources on issues related to health care and dying. It promotes the Living Will and the Durable Power of Attorney, and provides free copies of these documents in response to inquiry.

Association for Death Education and Counseling
638 Prospect Avenue
Hartford, Connecticut 06105-4298
(203) 232–4825

This organization is devoted to promoting effective death education and death-related counseling. It prepares and distributes educational materials, provides educational programs and conferences for the dissemination of information and research in death education and death-related counseling, and offers opportunities for professional networking and resource referral.

The Elisabeth Kübler-Ross Center
South Route 616
Head Waters, Virginia 24442
(703) 396–3441

Dr. Kübler-Ross, a noted expert in dying and death, has established a nonprofit organization dedicated to the promotion of the concept of unconditional love as an attainable ideal and the enrichment of life with the values all people inherently cherish. The center provides advocacy, clinical and educational services, and audio-visual materials.

Chronic and Terminal Illness*

National Hospice Organization
1901 North Moore Street, Suite 901
Arlington, Virginia 22209
(703) 243–5900

Although NHO does not provide direct patient services, it can give you the names of hospices and related service organizations in your area.

Make Today Count
P.O. Box 222
Osage Beach, Missouri 65065
(314) 346–6644

This is a national support group for persons with life-threatening diseases and their families.

---

*Look under specific illness organizations for further information e.g., the American Cancer Society or the American Heart Association. Also, look under organizations and services for the aged such as the National Institute on Aging.

Exceptional Cancer Patients (ECaP)
1302 Chapel Street
New Haven, Connecticut 06511
(203) 865–8392

This nonprofit organization was founded by Bernie Siegel, M.D. It provides clinical services for people and their loved ones who face cancer, AIDS, and other catastrophic or chronic illnesses, emphasizing the healing powers within the individual and the philosophy of living to the fullest. ECaP also provides: educational programs, training, and consulting services; information and referral services; and relevant books, audiocassettes, and videotapes.

Center for Attitudinal Healing
19 Main Street
Tiburon, California 94920
(415) 435–5022

This organization, providing support and educational services, is devoted to the alleviation of stress and illness through the power of love and positive thinking.

National Association for People with AIDS
2025 I Street, NW, Suite 1101
Washington, D.C. 20006
(202) 429–2856

NAPA is a nonprofit organization providing information on self-empowerment education and technical assistance to local PWA (People with AIDS) groups. It works to insure that the individual and collective needs of people living with HIV infection are being met on every level.

National AIDS Hotline
American Social Health Association
P.O. Box 13827
Research Triangle Park, North Carolina 27709
1–800–342–AIDS

This organization provides recorded information, 24 hours a day, along with referrals to medical and test centers and free literature.

Suicide

American Association of Suicidology
2459 South Ash Street
Denver, Colorado 80222
(303) 692–0985

AAS is an information clearinghouse which can supply information about local resources for survivors of suicide and literature about suicide and its aftermath.

*Murder**

National Organization for Victim Assistance
717 D Street, NW
Washington, D.C. 20004
(202) 232–8560
24-hour hot line (202) 393–6682

NOVA is a private, nonprofit organization dedicated to providing national advocacy for victims' rights, help for crime victims, service to local programs, and membership support. It can help you locate your local victim assistance resources. NOVA also provides 24-hour telephone crisis counseling for all types of victims.

National Victim Center
307 West 7th Street, Suite 1001
Fort Worth, Texas 76102
(817) 877–3355

This is a nonprofit organization founded to assist victims of violent crimes and to serve the victims' rights movement. It provides services and information to individuals and organizations concerned with victimization, and functions as a national data bank of information about victims' rights and criminal justice issues.

*Also see listing for Parents of Murdered Children under "Death of a Child."

Concerns of Police Survivors, Inc. (COPS)
16921 Croom Road
Brandywine, Maryland 20613
(301) 888–2264

This nonprofit organization is dedicated to offering support, education, and advocacy for survivors of slain police officers.

Widowhood

Widowed Persons Service
American Association of Retired Persons
1909 K Street, NW
Washington, D.C. 20049
(202) 872–4700

WPS offers nationwide programs to the newly widowed, along with numerous publications, bibliographies, and other audio-visual resources concerned with widowhood.

THEOS (They Help Each Other Spiritually)
1301 Clark Building
717 Liberty Avenue
Pittsburgh, Pennsylvania 15222
(412) 471–7779

THEOS is a national group devoted to the support and education of the widowed and their families.

Parents Without Partners, Inc.
8807 Colesville Road
Silver Spring, Maryland 20910
(301) 588–9354

PWP offers services nationally which are devoted to the welfare of single parents and their children through crisis intervention, education, social programs, and publications.

Death of a Child*

The Compassionate Friends
P.O. Box 3696
Oak Brook, Illinois 60522–3696
(708) 990–0010

This is an international self-help group devoted to supporting parents whose children have died. They have local chapters throughout the country and extensive publications devoted to parental and sibling bereavement.

The Candlelighters Childhood Cancer Foundation
1901 Pennsylvania Avenue, NW, Suite 1001
Washington, D.C. 20006
(202) 659–5136

This is an international peer-support network of parents of children who have or have had cancer. They have over 200 parent groups and contacts throughout the world, disseminate extensive publications, and run community outreach programs.

Mothers Against Drunk Driving (MADD)
669 Airport Freeway, Suite 310
Hurst, Texas 76053
(817) 268–6233
Victim Line 1–800–438–MADD

MADD is a national organization devoted to supporting victims, families, and friends in the aftermath of a drunk driving offense and to creating changes in public awareness and social and political policy to reflect the seriousness of drunk driving. Numerous publications on the topic are available from the organization. Chapter support groups are found nationwide.

*Many of these organizations also offer services for surviving siblings. Also, see listings under "Suicide" and "Murder."

Parents of Murdered Children
100 East Eighth Street, Room B41
Cincinnati, Ohio 45202
1–800–327–2499 Ext. 4288
Emergencies (513) 721–5683

This national self-help organization works to provide support and resources to families whose children have been murdered. The group has local chapters across the country.

National Sudden Infant Death Syndrome (SIDS) Foundation
8200 Professional Place, Suite 104
Landover, Maryland 20785
(301) 459–3388 (Maryland residents)
1–800–221–SIDS (outside Maryland)

This group offers services to families who have lost a child to SIDS, provides education to bereaved parents and professionals, and promotes research in the field. It disseminates many publications about SIDS.

National SIDS Clearinghouse
8201 Greensboro Drive, Suite 600
McLean, Virginia 22102
(703) 821–8955

This organization responds to all who seek information about SIDS and its many related issues. It provides publications and referrals to national and local support groups.

Resolve Through Sharing
Lutheran Hospital–La Crosse
1910 South Avenue
LaCrosse, Wisconsin 54601
(608) 791–4747

Resolve Through Sharing is an international support program developed for parents who lose a baby during pregnancy or shortly after birth. Through one-to-one counseling and follow-up support groups, counselors offer assistance to parents at the time of loss and afterwards. Educational and training programs, certification courses for counselors, and support materials are offered for bereaved families and professionals who wish to assist them.

The Pregnancy and Infant Loss Center
1421 E. Wayzata Boulevard
Wayzata, Minnesota 55391
(612) 473–9372

This organization offers literature, national support group information, parent outreach programs, and professional training on miscarriage, stillbirth, and infant death.

SHARE (Source of Help in Airing and Resolving Experiences)
St. Elizabeth's Hospital
211 South Third Street
Belleville, Illinois 62222
(618) 234–2415

This is a national self-help group devoted to parents grieving a miscarriage, stillbirth, ectopic pregnancy, or early infant death. The group has numerous publications pertinent to bereaved parents and to health care providers.

Funeral Associations and Memorial Societies

National Funeral Directors Association
11121 West Oklahoma Avenue
Milwaukee, Wisconsin 53227
(414) 541–2500

NFDA can provide you with specific resources explaining all aspects of bereavement, funerals, and the various types of body disposition.

Continental Association of Funeral and Memorial Societies
20001 S Street, NW, Suite 630
Washington, D.C. 20009
(202) 462–8888

This organization can provide you with the information necessary to arrange simple, inexpensive funerals.

Death of a Pet

Holistic Animal Consulting Centre
29 Lyman Avenue
Staten Island, New York 10305
(718) 720–5548

This center provides consultation, education, and intervention in relation to the human-animal bond during life and after death.

Finding Other Support Groups

National Self-Help Clearinghouse
Room 620N
Graduate School and University Center
City University of New York
33 West 42nd Street
New York, New York 10036
(212) 840–1259

This clearinghouse provides information on peer support groups of all kinds.

***The Encyclopedia of Associations*, 1986 edition**
Katherine Gruber, ed.
Gale Research Company

This encyclopedia lists hundreds of smaller groups that may suit your needs.

Canadian Resources

Death of a Child

The Compassionate Friends of Canada
685 William Avenue
Winnipeg, Manitoba
R3E 0Z2
(204) 787–2460

This is an international self-help group devoted to supporting parents whose children have died. They have local chapters throughout the country and extensive publications devoted to parental and sibling bereavement.

The Canadian Foundation for the Study of Infant Deaths (SIDS)
Box 190, Station R
Toronto, Ontario
M4G 3Z9
(416) 488–3260

This is a nonprofit organization dedicated to responding to the needs of families experiencing a sudden and unexpected infant death, finding the cause of SIDS, educating the public, and emotionally supporting SIDS families.

General Bereavement

These organizations service and/or make referrals for all types of bereavements.

Canadian Mental Health Association
2160 Yonge Street
Third Floor
Toronto, Ontario
M4S 2Z3
(416) 484–7750

Bereaved Families of Ontario
Ottawa-Carleton
Box 9384 Ottawa Terminal
Ottawa, Ontario
K1G 3V1
(613) 738–7171

Books*

The following books have been particularly helpful to many people, although the list is not exhaustive by any means.

The books are classified "P" when written for professional audiences, "L" when written for laypersons, and "P/L" when suitable for both.

*Check with specific organizations and support groups for their literature. Much of it is excellent and is free or at very low cost.

Grief in General

Bowlby, J. *Attachment and Loss: Loss, Sadness and Depression*, (Vol. III). New York: Basic Books, 1980. (P)

Colgrove, M., H. Bloomfield, and P. McWilliams. *How to Survive the Loss of a Love: 58 Things to Do When There Is Nothing to Be Done*. New York: Lion Press, 1976. (L)

Doka, K., ed., *Disfranchised Grief: Recognizing Hidden Sorrow*. Lexington, MA: Lexington Books, 1989. (P/L)

Donnelly, K. *Recovering from the Loss of a Sibling*. (For children and adults of all ages) New York: Dodd, Mead & Company, 1988. (L)

Grollman, E. *Living When a Love One Has Died*. Boston: Beacon Press, 1977. (L)

Jackson, E. N. *Understanding Grief: Its Roots, Dynamics, and Treatment*. Nashville: Abingdon Press, 1957. (P/L)

Jackson, E. N. *You and Your Grief*. New York: Hawthorn Books, Inc., 1962. (L)

LaGrand, L. *Coping with Separation and Loss as a Young Adult*. Springfield, IL: Charles C. Thomas, Publisher, 1986. (P/L)

Lewis, C. S. *A Grief Observed*. Greenwich, CT: Seabury Press, 1963. (L)

Manning, D. *Don't Take My Grief Away From Me*. Hereford, TX: Insight Books, Inc., 1979. (L)

Osterweis, M., F. Solomon, and M. Green, eds., *Bereavement: Reactions, Consequences, and Care*. Washington, D.C.: National Academy Press, 1984. (P)

Parkes, C. *Bereavement: Studies of Grief in Adult Life*. 2nd American edition. Maddison, CT: International Universities Press, Inc., 1987. (P/L)

Parkes, C. M., and R. S. Weiss. *Recovery from Bereavement*. New York: Basic Books, 1983. (P/L)

Rando, T. A. *Grief, Dying and Death: Clinical Interventions for Caregivers*. Champaign, IL: Research Press, 1984. (P/L)

Rando, T. A. *Treatment of Complicated Mourning*. Champaign, IL: Research Press, 1991. (P)

Raphael, B. *The anatomy of bereavement*. New York: Basic Books, 1983. (P/L)

Sanders, C. *Grief: The Mourning After*. New York: John Wiley & Sons, 1989. (P/L)

Schoeneck, T. (compiled materials) *Hope for Bereaved: Understanding, Coping and Growing through Grief*. Rev. Ed. Hope for Bereaved, 1342 Lancaster Avenue, Syracuse, New York 13210, 1982, 1986. (L)

Simos, B. *A Time to Grieve*. New York: Family Service Association of America, 1979. (P/L)

Tatelbaum, J. *The Courage to Grieve: Creative Living, Recovery, and Growth through Grief*. New York: Harper & Row Publishers, 1980. (P/L)

Worden, J. W. *Grief Counseling and Grief Therapy: A Handbook for the Mental Health Practitioner*. New York: Springer, 1982, 1991. (P/L)

Widowhood

Caine, L. *Widow*. New York: Bantam Books, 1975. (L)

Campbell, S., and P. Silverman. *Widower: What Happens When Men Are Left Alone*. New York: Prentice-Hall, 1987. (P/L)

Loewinsohn, R. *Survival Handbook for Widows*. Washington, D. C.: an AARP book published by Scott, Foresman and Company, Glenview, IL, 1984. (P/L)

Silverman, P. *Widow-to-Widow*. New York: Springer, 1986. (P/L)

Suicide

Alvarez, A. *The Savage God: A Study of Suicide*. New York: Bantam Books, 1973. (P/L)

Bolton, I., and C. Mitchell. *My Son . . . My Son . . . A Guide to Healing After a Suicide in the Family*. (Available from Bolton Press, 1325 Belmore Way NE, Atlanta, GA 30338). (L)

Clarke, J. *Life After Grief: A Soul Journey After Suicide*. Marietta, GA: Personal Pathways Press, 1989. (L)

Hewett, J. *After Suicide*. Philadelphia, PA: The Westminster Press, 1980. (L)

Lukas, C. *Silent Grief: Living in the Wake of Suicide*. New York: Bantam Books, 1990. (P/L)

Murder

Lord, J. *Beyond Sympathy: What to Say and Do for Someone Suffering an Injury, Illness, or Loss*. Ventura, CA: Pathfinder Publishing, 1988. (P/L)

Lord, J. *No Time for Goodbyes: Coping with Sorrow, Anger and Injustice After a Tragic Death*. Ventura, CA: Pathfinder Publishing, 1987. (L)

Redmond, L. *Surviving: When Someone You Love Was Murdered*. Psychological Consultation and Education Services, Inc., P. O. Box 61111, Clearwater, FL 34618–6111, 1989. (P/L)

Adult Loss of a Parent

Angel, M. D. *The Orphaned Adult*. New York: Human Sciences Press, 1987. (P/L)

Donnelly, K. *Recovering from the Loss of a Parent*. New York: Dodd, Mead & Company, 1987. (P/L)

Myers, E. *When Parents Die: A Guide for Adults*. New York: Viking, 1986. (L)

Loss of a Child

Borg, S., and J. Lasker. *When Pregnancy Fails: Families Coping with Miscarriage, Stillbirth, and Infant Death*. Boston: Beacon Press, 1981. (P/L)

DeFrain, J. D., J. Taylor, and L. Ernst. *Coping with Sudden Infant Death*. Lexington, MA: Lexington Books, 1982. (P/L)

DeFrain, J. D., L. Martens, J. Stork, and W. Stork. *Stillborn: The Invisible Death*. Lexington, MA: Lexington Books, 1986. (P/L)

Donnelly, K. *Recovering from the Loss of a Child*. New York: Macmillan, 1982. (L)

Knapp, R. *Beyond Endurance: When a Child Dies*. New York: Schocken Books, 1986. (P/L)

Limbo, R., and S. Wheeler. *When a Baby Dies: A Handbook for Healing and Helping*. La Crosse, WI: Resolve Through Sharing, La Crosse Lutheran Hospital/Gundersen Clinic, Ltd., 1986. (P/L)

Rando, T. A., ed., *Parental Loss of a Child*. Champaign, IL: Research Press, 1986. (P/L)

Schiff, H. *The Bereaved Parent*. New York: Crown Publishers, 1977. (L)

Chronic and Terminal Illness

Adams, D., and E. Deveau. *Coping with Childhood Cancer: Where Do We Go from Here?* Ontario: Kinbridge Publications, 1984, 1988. (P/L)

Buckman, R. *I Don't Know What to Say. How to Help and Support Someone Who Is Dying*. Toronto: Key Porter Books, 1988. (P/L)

Cousins, N. *Anatomy of an Illness as Perceived by the Patient*. New York: Bantam Books, 1979, 1981. (P/L)

Jevne, R., and A. Levitan. *No Time for Nonsense: Self-help for the Seriously Ill*. San Diego: CA: LuraMedia, 1989. (P/L)

Kübler-Ross, E. *On Death and Dying*. New York: Macmillan, 1969. (P/L)

Pitzelle, S. *We Are Not Alone: Learning to Live with Chronic Illness*. New York: Workman Publishing, 1986. (P/L)

Rando, T. A. *Grief, Dying, and Death: Clinical Interventions for Caregivers.* Champaign, IL: Research Press, 1984. (P/L)

Rando, T. A., ed., *Loss and Anticipatory Grief.* Lexington, MA: Lexington Books, 1986. (P/L)

Siegel, B. *Love, Medicine and Miracles.* New York: Harper & Row Publishers, 1986. (P/L)

van Bommel, H. *Choices: For People Who Have a Terminal Illness, Their Families and Their Caregivers.* Toronto: NC Press, 1986, 1987. (P/L).

Pet Loss

Cusak, O. *Pets and the Elderly.* New York: Haworth Press, 1983. (P/L)

Kay, W. J., et al. *Pet Loss and Human Bereavement.* Ames, IA: Iowa State University Press, 1984. (P/L)

Nieberg, H. A., and A. Fischer. *Pet Loss.* New York: Harper & Row, 1982. (P/L)

Sussman, M., ed., *Pets and the Family.* New York: Haworth Press, 1985. (P/L)

Other

Conley, B. *Handling the Holidays: C. O. P. E.* Booklet information available from Human Services Press, P. O. Box 2423, Springfield, IL 62705. (217–528–1756) 1979, 1986. (P/L)

Grollman, E. *Time Remembered: A Journal for Survivors.* Boston: Beacon Press, 1987. (L)

Kastenbaum, R., and B. Kastenbaum, eds., *Encyclopedia of Death.* Phoenix, AZ: Oryx Press, 1989. (P/L)

LaGrand, L. *Changing Patterns of Human Existence: Assumptions, Beliefs, and Coping with the Stress of Change.* Springfield, IL: Charles C. Thomas, Publisher, 1988. (P/L)

Morgan, E. *A Manual of Death Education and Simple Burial*, 10th edition. Burnsville, NC: Celo Press, 1984. (P/L)

Pine, V. R., et al., eds., *Acute Grief and the Funeral.* Springfield, IL: Charles C. Thomas, Publisher, 1976. (P/L)

Segal, J. *Winning Life's Toughest Battles: Roots of Human Resilience.* New York: Ivy Books, 1986/Ballantine Books, 1987. (P/L)

Simpson, M. *The Facts of Death.* Englewood Cliffs, NJ: Prentice-Hall, 1979. (P/L)

Slaikeu, K., and S. Lawhead. *The Phoenix Factor: Surviving and Growing Through Personal Crisis.* Boston: Houghton Mifflin, 1985. (L)

Stearns, A. *Living Through Personal Crisis*. New York: Ballantine Books, 1985. (L)

Tatelbaum, J. *You Don't Have to Suffer: A Handbook for Moving Beyond Life's Crises*. New York: Harper & Row Publishers, 1989. (P/L)

Children and Grief

Bernstein, J. E. *Loss and How to Cope with It*. New York: Seabury, 1977. (L)

Bernstein, J. E. *Books to Help Children Cope with Separation and Loss*, 2nd edition. New York and London: R. R. Bowker Company, 1983. (P/L)

Coburn, J. *Anne and the Sand Dobbies*. New York: Seabury, 1967. (L)

Corr, C., and J. McNeil, eds., *Adolescence and Death*. New York: Springer Publishing Company, 1986. (P)

Fassler, J. *My Grandpa Died Today*. New York: Human Sciences Press, 1971. (L)

Grollman, E. *Talking About Death: A Dialogue Between Parent and Child*, 3rd edition. Boston: Beacon Press, 1970, 1976, 1990. (P/L)

Jackson, E. *Telling a Child About Death*. New York: Hawthorn Books, 1965. (L)

Juneau, B. *Sad But O. K. My Daddy Died Today: A Child's View of Death*. Grass Valley, CA: Blue Dolphin Publishing, 1988. (L)

Klagsbrun, F. *Too Young to Die: Youth and Suicide*. Boston: Houghton Mifflin, 1976; New York: Pocket Books, 1977. (P/L)

Krementz, J. *How it Feels When a Parent Dies*. New York: Knopf, 1982. (L)

LeShan, E. *When a Parent Is Very Sick*. Boston: Joy Street Books Division of Little, Brown and Company, 1986. (L)

LeShan, E. *Learning to Say Good-by: When a Parent Dies*. New York: Macmillan, 1976. (L)

Levy, E. L. *Children Are Not Paper Dolls: A Visit with Bereaved Siblings*. Greeley, CO: Counseling Consultants, 1982. (L)

Miles, M. *Annie and the Old One*. Boston: Little, Brown and Company, 1971. (L)

Rosen, H. *Unspoken Grief: Coping with Childhood Sibling Loss*. Lexington, MA: Lexington Books, 1986. (P/L)

Schaefer, D., and C. Lyons. *How Do We Tell the Children?* New York: Newmarket Press, 1986. (L)

Stein, S. B. *About Dying.* New York: Walker, 1974. (L)

Viorst, J. *The Tenth Good Thing About Barney.* New York: Atheneum, 1971. (L)

Wass, H., and C. Corr, eds., *Childhood and Death.* Washington, D.C.: Hemisphere, 1984. (P)

Wass, H., and C. Corr, eds., *Helping Children Cope with Death: Guidelines and Resources.* Washington, D. C.: Hemisphere, 1982, 1984. (P/L)

White, E. B. *Charlotte's Web.* New York: Harper, 1952. (L)

Wolfelt, A. *Helping Children Cope with Grief.* Muncie, IN: Accelerated Development, Inc., 1983. (P/L)

References

Attig, T. 1986. Grief, Love and Separation. Paper presented at the Eighth Annual Conference of the Forum for Death Education and Counseling, Atlanta, Georgia.

Averill, J.R. 1968. "Grief: Its Nature and Significance." *Psychological Bulletin* 70:721–748.

Bowlby, J. 1980. *Attachment and Loss: Loss, Sadness and Depression* (Vol. III). New York: Basic Books.

Caplan, G. 1974. Foreword to *The First Year of Bereavement*, by I.O. Glick, R.S. Weiss, and C.M. Parkes. New York: Wiley.

Futterman, E.H., and I. Hoffman. 1973. "Crisis and Adaptation in the Families of Fatally Ill Children." In E.J. Anthony and C. Koupernik, eds., *The Child in His Family: The Impact of Disease and Death* (Vol. 2), 127–143. New York: Wiley.

Grollman, E. 1974. "Children and Death." In E. Grollman, ed., *Concerning Death: A Practical Guide for the Living*. Boston: Beacon Press.

Kohlberg, L., and O.Z. Ullman. 1974. "Stages in the Development of Psychosexual Concepts and Attitudes." In R.C. Friedman, R.M. Richart, and R.L. Vande Wiele, eds., *Sex Differences in Behavior*, 209–222. New York: Wiley.

Lazare, A. 1979. "Unresolved Grief." In A. Lazare, ed., *Outpatient Psychiatry: Diagnosis and Treatment*, 498–512. Baltimore: Williams & Wilkins.

Lindemann, E. 1944. "Symptomatology and Management of Acute Grief." *American Journal of Psychiatry* 101:141–148.

Parkes, C.M., and R.S. Weiss. 1983. *Recovery from Bereavement*. New York: Basic Books.

Rando, T.A. 1984. *Grief, Dying, and Death: Clinical Interventions for Caregivers*. Champaign, Ill.: Research Press.

Rando, T.A., ed. 1986. *Loss and Anticipatory Grief*. Lexington, Mass.: Lexington Books.

Rando, T.A., ed. 1986. *Parental Loss of a Child*. Champaign, Ill.: Research Press.

Raphael, B. 1983. *The Anatomy of Bereavement*. New York: Basic Books.

Siggins, L. 1966. "Mourning: A Critical Survey of the Literature." *International Journal of Psycho-Analysis* 47:14–25.

Steinem, G. 1986. *Marilyn*. Toledo: East Toledo Productions.

Index

About the Author

T HERESE A. RANDO, Ph.D., is a clinical psychologist in private practice in Warwick, Rhode Island. She is the clinical director of Therese A. Rando Associates, Ltd., a multidisciplinary team providing psychotherapy, training, and consultation in the area of mental health, specializing in loss and grief, traumatic stress, and the psychosocial care of the chronically and terminally ill. She is the founder and executive director of the Institute for the Study and Treatment of Loss in Warwick, R.I. Dr. Rando has consulted, conducted research, provided therapy, written, and lectured internationally in areas related to grief and death since 1970.

Dr. Rando holds a doctoral degree in clinical psychology from the University of Rhode Island and has received advanced training in psychotherapy and in medical consultation–liaison psychiatry at Case Western Reserve University Medical School and University Hospitals of Cleveland. A former consultant to the U.S. Department of Health and Human Services' Hospice Education Program for Nurses, she developed their program for training hospice nurses to cope with loss, grief, and terminal illness. Her research interests focus on the operations and course of mourning, the experience of bereaved parents, and the emotional reactions of rescue workers. Currently, Dr. Rando is the Principal Investigator in The National Bereavement Study, a longitudinal, multidisciplinary research project investigating the processes and effects of grief. She has written over forty articles and chapters pertaining to the clinical aspects of thanatology, and is the author of *Grief, Dying, and Death: Clinical Interventions for Caregivers* (Research Press, 1984) and *Treatment of Complicated Mourning* (Research Press, 1991), and the editor of *Loss and Anticipatory Grief* (Lexington Books, 1986) and *Parental Loss of a Child* (Research Press, 1986). Dr. Rando is the recipient of the Association for Death Education and Counseling's 1987 award for "Outstanding Contribution to the Study of Death, Dying, and Bereavement" and a grantee of its lifetime certification as "Certified Death Educator."